An Oklahoma Law Review Book

AMERICAN PIPE LINES

AMERICAN
PIPE LINES

Their Industrial Structure
Economic Status
and Legal Implications

By GEORGE S. WOLBERT, *Jr.*

UNIVERSITY OF OKLAHOMA PRESS
NORMAN

The text of this volume was first published serially under the title of "The Pipe Line Story" in the four issues of Volume 4 of the *Oklahoma Law Review* during 1951, and it is here reproduced by kind permission of the editors of the *Oklahoma Law Review* and of the College of Law of the University of Oklahoma.

PREFACE

Despite the richness of the literature available on the oil industry in general, the specific subject of pipe lines has remained virtually unexplored. This situation is rendered even more unfortunate by the aura of controversy which has surrounded pipe lines during the past two decades. Protagonists on both sides of the great debate have hurled accusations and counteraccusations at their opponents, too often, however, with ardor unencumbered by sure knowledge of the facts. It is into these troubled matters that the present book ventures. Many of the conclusions set forth are personal judgments of the author. It is obvious that, even though they are based upon careful research evidence, they are open to challenge. Hence the citation of authorities in this book is more complete than is usual in books of its type. I have felt that if the source materials were indicated to the reader, the real grounds for the judgments and conclusions I have reached would be clear and unmistakable.

This book, then, contains a discussion of the issues raised by vertical integration of pipe lines and the present concentration of ownership in the hands of the so-called "major" companies. Quite frankly, no panacea is offered. In fact, more questions are raised than are answered. I believe, however, that the framing of the issues alone, stripped of spurious contentions, will be of material assistance to the solution of pipe-line problems. Moreover, in certain areas the evidence adduced permitted definite conclusions to be drawn.

I acknowledge a lasting obligation to the innumerable persons in the petroleum industry and in government service who gave unstintingly of their time and advice. Especially deserving of mention is Professor Russell A. Smith of Ann Arbor, Michigan, who rendered many services, including reading the manuscript. I acknowledge also the kindness of the *Oklahoma Law Review* in permitting republication of material which originally appeared in Volume 4 under the title "The Pipe Line Story." Finally, it must be said of my wife, Winifred E. Wolbert, that without her aid this book never could have been written.

G. S. W.

Fort Leonard Wood, Mo.
14 December 1951

CONTENTS

SECTION ONE

FACETS OF CONTROVERSY

INTRODUCTION

In recent years, demands for vertical disintegration of the oil industry have swelled, roared, and sullenly subsided, only to rise again like the crest of an angry sea.[1] The apex of the attack has been directed at divorcement of pipe lines from major[2] integrated[3] oil companies.[4] The fact of integra-

[1] *E.g.,* H.R. 7800 and companion bill S. 2879, 75th Cong., 1 Sess. (1937) (divorce marketing); S. 3752 and companion bill H.R. 10089, 75th Cong., 3d Sess. (1938) (divorce marketing); S. 448 and companion bill H.R. 2318, 76th Cong., 1st Sess. (1939) (divorce marketing); *Hearings before Temporary National Economic Committee, pursuant to Pub. Res. 113* (75th Cong.), 76th Cong., 2d & 3d Sess., Parts 14–17A (hereinafter cited *TNEC Hearings*) 7376, 7588, 7652 (1939–41) (divorce all four branches); *Id.* at 8852, 8867, 9167 (divorce marketing & transportation); *Id.* at 8898, 8927, 9181, 9210 (divorce marketing); H.R. 2318, 76th Cong., 3d Sess. (1940) (divorce marketing); S. 3718, 76th Cong., 3d Sess. (1940) (divorce tankers and barges); S. 170 and companion bill H.R. 1402, 77th Cong., 1st Sess. (1941) (divorce marketing); S. 171 and companion bill H.R. 1401, 77th Cong., 1st Sess. (1941) (divorce tankers and barges); Rostow, A National Policy for the Oil Industry 118–120, 123–124, 139–140 (1948) (complete disintegration); S. 572, 81st Cong., 1st Sess. (1949) (divorce marketing); S. 573, 81st Cong., 1st Sess. (1949) (divorce tankers and barges). The Department of Justice recently has sought divorcement of marketing facilities of the west coast majors. Complaint, pp. 51–52, United States v. Standard Oil Company of California, Civil No. 11584-C, S.D. Cal., May 12, 1950.

[2] A distinction first was drawn between the Standard Oil Group and the "independents," *TNEC Hearings* 9932, then between those who had interstate pipe line facilities and those who did not. Laidler, Concentration of Control in American Industry 27 n.13 (1931). The "major" classification was asserted by Mr. Berquist of the Department of Justice to consist of twenty integrated companies ". . . that represent more or less arbitrarily, and yet commonly accepted grouping within the industry." *TNEC Hearings* 7111. These companies, listed in order of their assets as of December 31, 1938, are: (1) Standard Oil Co.(N.J.); (2) Socony-Vacuum Oil Co.; (3) Standard Oil Co.(Ind.); (4) The Texas Corp.; (5) Standard Oil Co. of California; (6) Gulf Oil Corp.; (7) Cities Service Co. (Holding company of Arkansas Fuel Co., Cities Service Oil Co., and Empire Gas and Fuel Co.); (8) Shell Union Oil Corp., (9) Consolidated Oil Corp. (formerly Sinclair Consolidated); (10) Phillips Petroleum Co.; (11) Tide Water Associated Oil Corp.; (12) Atlantic Refining Co.; (13) The Pure Oil Co.; (14) Union Oil Co. of California; (15) Sun Oil Co.; (16) Ohio Oil Co.; (17) Continental Oil Co.; (18) Standard Oil Co. (Ohio); (19) Mid-Continent Petroleum Corp.; and (20) The Skelly Oil Co. *TNEC Hearings* 7110–7111. The common denominator of these organizations appears to be assets in excess of $25,000,000. *TNEC Hearings* 7111. Two other companies, Barnsdall Oil Co. and Standard Oil Co. (Ky.), were given "major" rank in the complaint in United States v. American Petroleum Institute, Civil No. 8524, D. D.C., Sept. 30, 1940. *Quaere,* what status does Sunray have now that it has taken over Barnsdall?

[3] Integration has been defined as vertical combination, uniting in one corporate structure

3

tion has been viewed by some as an original sin,[5] with pipe lines the serpent,

the various operations through which the raw material passes in its transformation into refined products ready for the market. *TNEC Hearings* 7180; see *Id*. at 9748, 9940. In the oil industry, an integrated company substantially controls its own crude supply, transportation system, refineries, and marketing facilities. *TNEC Hearings* 7111, 8373, 8518, 8676. Disintegration or divorcement is the separation of one or more of these branches from the others. It is interesting to note that many of the "independent" (non major) companies are as fully integrated as the majors, *TNEC Hearings* 8631–8632, and many others have combined two or more operations. *TNEC Hearings* 7173, 8332, 8677, 8491, 9662.

[4] *E.g.*, The original efforts to extend the Commodities Clause of the Hepburn Act of 1906, 34 STAT. 585 (1906), 49 U.S.C. § 1(8) (1946), to pipe lines. 40 CONG. REC. 9340 (1906) (House); 40 CONG. REC. 6361 (1906) (Senate). The proposed Senate amendment is said to have been in response to the special message of the President transmitting the Bureau of Corporations' report on transportation and freight rates in the oil industry. In the Matter of Pipe Lines, 24 I.C.C. 1, 4 (1912).

From 1931 to the present, bills to divorce pipe lines from other branches of the industry have been introduced in every Congress except the 80th. The earlier bills sought to extend the Commodities Clause to pipe lines: *e.g.*, H.R. 16,695, 71st Cong., 3d. Sess. (1931); H.R. 172, 72d Cong., 1st Sess. (1931); H.R. 420, 72d Cong., 1st Sess. (1931); S. 1579, 73d Cong., 1st Sess. (1933); H.R. 4681, 73d Cong., 1st Sess. (1933); H.R. 5530, 73d Cong., 1st Sess. (1933); H.R. 8572, 73d Cong., 2d Sess. (1934); S. 2995, 73d Cong., 2d Sess. (1934); S. 573, 74th Cong., 1st Sess. (1935); H.R. 6794, 75th Cong., 1st Sess. (1937); S. 1398, 75th Cong., 1st ess. (1937); H.R. 4862, 76th Cong., 1st Sess. (1939); and S. 2009, 76th Cong., 1st Sess. § 12 (1939). The later bills have attempted to prevent pipe lines from transporting any crude or products owned or controlled directly or indirectly by the pipe line or any person or company to whose control the pipe line is subject. Examples of this type are: S. 2181 and companion bill H.R. 7136, 76th Cong., 1st Sess. (1939); S. 172 and companion bill H.R. 1393, 77th Cong., 1st Sess. (1941); H.R. 2503, 77th Cong., 1st Sess. (1941); H.R. 1516, 78th Cong., 1st Sess. (1943); H.R. 55, 79th Cong., 1st Sess. (1945); and S. 571, 81st Cong., 1st Sess. (1949).

On April 3, 1933, President Franklin D. Roosevelt unqualifiedly recommended emergency legislation divorcing interstate oil pipe lines from other branches of the industry. FRANCIS, DIVORCEMENT OF PIPE LINES 4 (1935) (paper presented before the Mineral Law Section, American Bar Ass'n on July 16, 1935).

The provisions of the N.I.R.A. authorized the President to institute proceedings to divorce from any holding company any pipe line company controlled by it, which pipe line company by unfair practices or exorbitant rates in the transportation of petroleum or its products tended to create a monopoly. 48 STAT. 200 (1933). However, before any action was taken under this section, the Act was declared unconstitutional as a delegation of legislative power. Schechter Poultry Corp. v. United States, 295 U.S. 495, 55 Sup.Ct. 837, 79 L.Ed. 1570, 97 A.L.R. 947 (1935); *cf.* Panama Refining Co. v. Ryan, 293 U.S. 388, 55 Sup.Ct. 241, 79 L.Ed. 446 (1935).

The *TNEC Hearings* furnished an arena for divorcement proposals, see note 1 *supra*.

The Department of Justice announced its intention to utilize the antitrust laws to seek pipe line divorcement in 1940. N.Y. Times, July 30, 1940, p. 27, col. 5.

Two writers recently have advocated divorcement of pipe lines: Black, *Oil Pipe Line Divorcement by Litigation and Legislation*, 25 CORN. L. Q. 510 (1940) and ROSTOW, A NATIONAL POLICY FOR THE OIL INDUSTRY (1948).

Finally, divorcement of both crude and products pipe lines was recommended in SEN. REP. No. 25, 81st Cong., 1st Sess. 21, 23 (1949), otherwise known as the "Wherry" report.

[5] See MacLachlan, Book Review, 13 LAW & CONTEMP. PROB. 715 (1948), and Marshall, Book Review, 57 YALE L. J. 1323, 1326 (1948) for that interpretation of Professor Rostow's views. See also Boulding, *In Defense of Monopoly*, 59 Q. J. ECON. 524 (1945).

and "monopolistic profits" the apple.[6] But common experience tells us that the world is not all black and white, nor can an industry clearly be placed either in the category of competition or of monopoly.[7] Into the warp and woof of the oil industry, spun by demands of the consumers it serves, are woven the remembrances of things past,[8] the competitive thrusts of the present,[9] and the hopes of the future. With this in mind, a re-examination of the development of pipe lines against the backdrop of the present anatomy, behavior and performance of the oil industry is necessary in order to understand the peculiarities of their structure and intelligently to evaluate their social performance.

As Max Ball has stated graphically: "Oil in the field tanks is like a fat steer on the range; it needs to be taken thence and made into something useful."[10] This need to realize the profits from investment in exploration and production has been the controlling theme in pipe line evolution. When the first oil field was undergoing a frenzied development initiated by the pioneer discovery well "brought in" by Colonel Drake on August 27, 1859, the problem of transportation had few alternative solutions. Since the railroads were twenty to twenty-five miles away,[11] and the drilling program at that time, resting on a principle of "creekology,"[12] had caused wells to be adjacent to streams tributary to the Allegheny River, the natural course of events led to water transportation down these tributary streams to the Allegheny, thence to Pittsburgh. But as the limits of the producing fields

[6] Rostow, A National Policy for the Oil Industry 117 (1948).

[7] Eastern Wine Corp. v. Winslow-Warren, Ltd., 137 F.2d 955, 959 n.7 (2d Cir. 1943); Picard v. United Aircraft Corp., 128 F.2d 632, 643 n.19 (2d Cir. 1942); Loevinger, The Law of Free Enterprise 23 (1949); Hamilton, The Pattern of Competition 25 (1940); Wilcox, Competition and Monopoly in American Industry 308, 314–315 (*TNEC* Monograph 21, 1940); see Edwards, Maintaining Competition 1–3 (1949); Chamberlin, The Theory of Monopolistic Competition 4 (6th ed. 1948); Hamilton *et al*, Price and Price Policies 2–10 (1938); Watkins, Oil: Stabilization or Conservation? x (1937); Adelman, *Effective Competition and the Antitrust Laws*, 61 Harv. L. Rev. 1289, 1298 (1948).

[8] Hamilton *et al*, Price and Price Policies 6–11 (1938).

[9] Rostow, A National Policy for the Oil Industry 53 (1948); Arnold, The Bottlenecks of Business 92 (1940).

[10] Ball, This Fascinating Oil Business 173 (1940). Permission to quote granted by the publisher and copyright holder, The Bobbs-Merrill Company.

[11] *TNEC Hearings* 8584; Giddens, The Birth of the Oil Industry 101 (1938).

[12] The first wells were discovered along Oil Creek and the prevailing view was that the source of the oil was an underground stream which roughly paralleled the surface waters. See maps of the early developments of the first field in Giddens, The Birth of the Oil Industry 69, 79 (1938); see also map in Funk v. Halderman, 53 Pa. 229, 231 (1867). This concept gave way to the magic "doodlebug" and forked witch-hazel divining rod; later came the concepts of geological "structure" and stratigraphic traps, the former found by plotting dip and strike of surface outcrops or by instruments such as torsion balances, magnetometers, refraction and reflection seismographs, and the latter by random drilling such as "Dad" Joiner's discovery of the great East Texas Field in October, 1930.

were extended, it became necessary to employ horse-and-wagon teams to haul the oil to shipping points. The charges for this service varied with the distance, road condition and season of the year, ranging from one to five dollars per barrel, with an average of two dollars and a half.[13] The producers first sought relief from this excessive expense by building flat boats which were floated down Oil Creek on naturally high water levels or by means of "pond freshets," a device adapted from the lumbermen whereby synchronized flood gate operation would loose a stage of water sufficient to carry the boats downstream to deeper water.[14] However, the expense and hazard of this method of operation precluded its employment as a permanent solution.

The challenge thus presented became the stimulus of pipe line invention. As early as November, 1860, Colonel S. D. Karnes had envisioned a pipe line project.[15] In 1862 a small diameter pipe line was laid from a producing well over a hill to a refinery, oil being siphoned approximately 1000 feet from this point.[16] Shortly thereafter, a two inch line spanned the three mile haul from the fiield to a railroad terminal,[17] but numerous leaks rendered operation unsatisfactory.[18] It remained for Samuel Van Syckel to complete the first successful pipe line on October 7, 1865, a two inch wrought-iron line carrying eighty-one barrels an hour over the five mile journey from Pithole City to Miller's Farm, Pennsylvania.[19] The teamsters reacted violently, cutting the line and tearing up portions of it, necessitating armed guards for protection. Resistance was futile. The pipe line was a mechanical success and the first transportation bottleneck was broken.[20]

At this time, the railroads favored pipe line development as it fed increased quantities to the loading racks along the right-of-way, whence the oil was loaded into tank cars[21] and shipped to refineries on the Eastern

[13] *TNEC Hearings* 8584–8585; LEVEN, DONE IN OIL 512 (1941); GIDDENS, THE BIRTH OF THE OIL INDUSTRY 103 (1938).

[14] *Ibid*. A very interesting portrait of this process is the painting "Oil Transport—Before Steel" by Orison MacPherson.

[15] LEVEN, DONE IN OIL 513 (1941); FINNEY, *Oil Pipe-Line Transportation* in ELEMENTS OF THE PETROLEUM INDUSTRY 310 (1940).

[16] GIDDENS, THE BIRTH OF THE OIL INDUSTRY 142 (1938); THE HUMBLE WAY 8 (Nov.-Dec. 1949).

[17] LEVEN, DONE IN OIL 48 (1941); THE HUMBLE WAY 8 (Nov.-Dec. 1949).

[18] See note 16 *supra*.

[19] LEVEN, DONE IN OIL 513 (1941); FINNEY, *supra* note 15, at 310. GIDDENS, THE BIRTH OF THE OIL INDUSTRY 143 (1938) gives the date as October 9, 1865.

[20] *Ibid*.

[21] The invention of the first tank car generally is credited to Amos Densmore. In the summer of 1865 he constructed two wooden tanks on an ordinary railroad flat-car, mounting one tank filled with forty-two to forty-five barrels of oil on each end of the flat-car over the

Seaboard. However, the railroads merely created another transportation problem by establishing a monopoly of their own, dictating prices to producers and driving shippers from the field.[22] The oil pioneers promptly met this new threat by building trunk pipe lines[23] directly from the fields to the refineries. By 1874 a four inch line was laid from the producing fields to Pittsburgh.[24] This turn of events quickly changed the tolerant attitude of the railroads into one of determined resistance. Pipe lines were refused access across railroad rights-of-way, and numerous physical and legal clashes occurred as a result of the violent competition which ensued. But again economics tipped the scales in favor of the lines, which established themselves as the favored means of oil transportation. In 1878 a line was started which eventually traversed the Allegheny mountains and moved oil to the Atlantic Seaboard cheaply, swiftly, and in enormous quantities.[25]

trucks. *TNEC Hearings* 8586; GIDDENS, THE BIRTH OF THE OIL INDUSTRY 151 (1938). For a picture of this type of tank-car, see THE HUMBLE WAY 12 (Nov.-Dec. 1949). The Empire Transportation Company introduced the iron boiler tank car in February, 1869, and the modern tank car has developed from that innovation. AMERICAN PETROLEUM INSTITUTE (hereinafter cited as A.P.I.), PETROLEUM: THE STORY OF AN AMERICAN INDUSTRY 59 (1949); GIDDENS, THE BIRTH OF TNE OIL INDUSTRY 152 (1938). Despite the obvious adaptability of the tank car to the growing petroleum traffic, the railroads steadfastly have asserted that box cars are satisfactory and have refused to furnish tank cars, labelling them "special equipment." An order of the Interstate Commerce Commission requiring railroads to furnish tank cars, Pennsylvania Paraffine Works v. Pennsylvania R.R., 34 I.C.C. 179 (1915), was appealed to the United States Supreme Court, where the railroads obtained a ruling in their favor. United States v. Pennsylvania R.R., 242 U.S. 208, 37 Sup.Ct. 95, 61 L.Ed. 251 (1916) (I.C.C. exceeded its authority). This ruling remains law today and explains the great percentage of tank cars owned or leased by the integrated oil companies. See Chicago, R.I. & Pac. Ry. v. Lawton Refining Co., 253 Fed. 705 (8th Cir. 1918); St. Louis & S. F. Ry. v. State, 76 Okla. 60, 184 Pac. 442 (1919); In the matter of Private Cars, 50 I.C.C. 652 (1918).

22 GIDDENS, THE BIRTH OF THE OIL INDUSTRY 152 (1938).

23 Pipe lines are generally divided into three categories: gathering lines, crude trunk lines, and gasoline or products trunk lines. The gathering lines are the smaller (generally two to four inch) lines which "gather" the oil from the various lease tanks which have received the production from the wells on the lease through "lead" lines (from a pumping well) or "flow" lines (from a flowing well). The lines which funnel the oil into the trunk lines are known as "feeder" lines, and are generally considered part of the gathering system. See FTC, REPORT ON PIPE-LINE TRANSPORTATION OF PETROLEUM 60 (1916) for map of a gathering system. The "trunk" lines are the "main lines" of a pipe line system and normally range from six to sixteen inches in diameter. During World War II, a crude trunk line of twenty-four inches diameter was constructed from Longview, Texas, to Phoenixville, Pennsylvania, and a products line of twenty inches diameter was laid from Beaumont, Texas, to Linden, New Jersey. The lines built from the producing fields to the railroads in the 1860's properly would be considered gathering lines.

24 Built by Captain Vandergrift and George W. Foreman, this line was sixty miles long and had a capacity of 7,500 barrels a day. A.P.I., PETROLEUM: THE STORY OF AN AMERICAN INDUSTRY 16 (1949); LEVEN, DONE IN OIL 48 (1941); THE HUMBLE WAY (Nov.-Dec. 1949).

25 *Ibid.*

By 1880, over 1200 miles of pipe lines served the Appalachian producing fields.[26] The year 1900 found about 18,000 miles of pipe lines operating in the United States.[27] Four years later, pipe lines were built from the Mid-Continent Area to join the eastern carriers, and the rough framework of our existing system was sketched out.[28] Since that time, extensions to new fields, "looping" of lines along existing routes to increase capacity, and the advent of gasoline or products lines have greatly increased pipe line mileage.[29]

The role played by the "Big Inch" and "Little Big Inch" lines in solving the transportation problem during World War II is well known.[30] A less publicized but equally important contribution was made by military pipe lines on the battlefront.[31] In addition, the industry may point with pride to the tremendous improvement in construction methods and operational techniques which have increased the capacity of the lines and contributed to flexibility and efficiency of operation. These have made possible large reductions in pipe line rates.[32] These reductions, together with the increasing rail tariffs, have created such a differential in shipping costs[33]

---

[26] A.P.I., PETROLEUM FACTS AND FIGURES 138 (1947); THE HUMBLE WAY 9 (Nov.-Dec. 1949).

[27] *Ibid.;* THE PETROLEUM ENGINEER, THE PETROLEUM DATA BOOK H-13 (1947).

[28] LEVEN, DONE IN OIL 49 (1941); A.P.I., A SURVEY OF THE PRESENT POSITION OF THE PETROLEUM INDUSTRY AND ITS OUTLOOK TOWARD THE FUTURE (hereinafter cited as SURVEY) 51 (1935).

[29] The following figures, taken from THE PETROLEUM ENGINEER, THE PETROLEUM DATA BOOK H-13 (1947), give a rough approximation of the growth: 1910, 40,090 miles; 1920, 64,367 miles; 1930, 110,650 miles; 1940, 125,950 miles; 1945, 145,001 miles; 1946, 149,700 miles. The average length of hauls in 1946 for gathering lines was 18 miles, for crude trunk lines, 325 miles, for products lines, 382 miles. Spal, *Oil Pipe Lines,* 15 ICC PRACT. J. 563, 565 (1948).

[30] See Reed, *Some Operating Features of WEP Big-Inch Lines,* THE OIL & GAS JOURNAL, March 16, 1944, p. 78; Hyde, *Electrical Sinews for WEP Products Line,* THE PETROLEUM ENGINEER, March, 1944, p. 200; Finney & Adoue, *The Big Inch Pipe Line,* THE PETROLEUM ENGINEER, Jan., 1944, p. 185; For an interesting overall account, see the brochure published by War Emergency Pipe Lines, Inc., entitled "Big Inch" and "Little Big Inch" (1946).

[31] See King, *Military Pipe Line Systems: A World War II Development,* THE PETROLEUM ENGINEER, March, 1946, p. 150; *Ingenuity Used to Lay India-China Pipe Line,* THE PETROLEUM ENGINEER, Oct. 1945, p. 102; Thompson, *Oil Wins in Europe,* THE OIL WEEKLY, June 18, 1945, p. 64; Love, *Invasion-Type Military Pipe Lines,* THE PETROLEUM ENGINEER, April, 1945, p. 164; *Oil-Field Methods Aid Army,* THE OIL WEEKLY, Aug. 21, 1944, p. 38.

[32] It is estimated that a barrel of oil could be moved 1500 miles by pipe line in 1949 for about half as much (45 cents) as it costs to move it five miles through the first pipe line ($1.00). THE HUMBLE WAY 11 (Nov.-Dec.) 1949. Rates will be discussed more thoroughly in the section devoted to that topic *infra.*

[33] Railroad—8.3 mills per ton mile vs. Pipe Lines—3.2 mills per ton-mile. 1 BAIN, THE ECONOMICS OF THE PACIFIC COAST PETROLEUM INDUSTRY 76 (1944); COOK, CONTROL OF THE PETROLEUM INDUSTRY BY MAJOR OIL COMPANIES 19 (*TNEC* Monograph 39, 1941); SHUMAN,

that the railroads have lost steadily to the pipe lines the carriage of crude oil.[34] Moreover, it was inevitable that the transportation of gasoline and other refined products should follow the same trend.[35] Tankers are even cheaper than pipe line rates,[36] but their utility is limited to coastal and inland water movement. Recently, barges have taken an increasing share of petroleum shipments. Long-distance trucking is beginning to assert itself as a competitive force. Still, today, pipe lines are the dominant medium of overland petroleum transportation.

Concomitant with the growth of pipe lines has been a marked tendency toward concentration of ownership. At the *TNEC Hearings,* testimony was adduced to the effect that twenty integrated majors[37] owned or controlled 57.4 percent of the crude oil gathering pipe line mileage, 89 percent of the crude oil trunk mileage and 96.1 percent of the gasoline line mileage.[38] It would seem that the trend toward increased concentration has not abated since the date of the hearings.[39] This situation has caused alarm in some sectors and provoked violent attack on the major oil companies. Insofar as the concentration of pipe line ownership is concerned, the explanation is relatively simple. The construction of long-distance pipe lines in-

THE PETROLEUM INDUSTRY 100 (1940); Pogue, *Economics of the Petroleum Industry* in ELEMENTS OF THE PETROLEUM INDUSTRY 453, 479 (1940).

[34] Spal, *Oil Pipe Lines,* 15 ICC PRACT. J. 563, 569 (1948); see ASS'N OF AMERICAN RAILROADS, REPORT BY SUBCOMMITTEE ON PIPE LINE TRANSPORT 23 (1944). In 1946, receipts at refineries were 78% by pipe line, 20% by tanker, 2% by tank-car or truck. A.P.I., PETROLEUM FACTS & FIGURES 135 (1947) (calculated).

[35] *Hearings before Subcommittee of Committee on Interstate Commerce on S. 3753,* 76th Cong., 3d Sess. 12, 13, 18 (1940). *Compare* A.P.I., PETROLEUM FACTS & FIGURES 137 (1947) *with Id.* at 152.

[36] Pogue, *supra* note 33, at 479 gives a figure of 1.25 miles per ton-mile; approved by COOK, *op. cit. supra* note 33, at 19 and BAIN, *op. cit. supra* note 33, at 76.

[37] Listed in note 2 *supra.*

[38] *TNEC Hearings* 7103–7104; COOK, *op. cit. supra* note 33, at 5. Industry's spokesman, Mr. William S. Farish, President, Standard Oil Company (N.J.), while reserving the accuracy of the quoted figures, admitted that a substantial portion of the industry's business was being conducted by the large concerns, saying: "These facts have long been well known." *TNEC Hearings* 9931.

[39] *Hearings before Subcommittee on Study of Monopoly Power of the Committee on the Judiciar,* 81st Cong., 1st Sess., Part 1, 71–72, 87, 91, 213–218, 229 (1949); SEN. DOC. No. 17, 80th Cong., 1st Sess. 21 (1947); SEN. DOC. No. 206, 79th Cong., 2d Sess., 169–171 (1946); ROSTOW, A NATIONAL POLICY FOR THE OIL INDUSTRY 10–11 (1948); Spal, *Oil Pipe Lines,* 15 ICC PRACT. J. 563, 566 (1948); Houghton, *The Growth of Big Business,* 38 AM. ECON. REV. 72 (Supp., May, 1948) *passim; but see* Lintner & Butters, *Effect of Mergers on Industrial Concentration,* 1940–1947, 32 REV. ECON. STATISTICS 46 (No. 1, 1950); Adelman, *Effective Competition and the Antitrust Laws,* 61 HARV. L. REV. 1289, 1293 (1948). Modern concentration problems first were publicized in BERLE & MEANS, THE MODERN CORPORATION AND PRIVATE PROPERTY (1932).

volves a tremendous initial outlay of capital,[40] and few small producers or independent firms are able to provide such a facility.[41]

A second explanation of this concentration is the great hazard or risk of capital inherent in pipe line operation. Once laid, a line is committed to the chance that the "runs" from the producing district to which it is connected will amortize its cost. Provision usually is made for this by initially high tariff rates, but even this expedient has not prevented failure where the decline of the producing field is unexpectedly rapid. An instance of this is the extension by the Prairie Pipe Line Company of its line to the Ranger Field in Texas.[42] Another hazard is that a new field, closer to the refineries served, may be discovered. To the extent of its production, the new field will displace the oil previously transported by the pipe line. A graphic example of this contingency is the Illinois boom in 1937 and 1938

[40] The following chart shows the estimated construction cost *per mile*, including pumping stations for both gasoline and crude lines. Daily capacities shown are based on a 100 per cent load factor. Basis of calculation was 15 psi drop per mile, 900 psi discharge pressure at stations. The data was taken from Ass'n of American Railroads, Report by Subcommittee on Pipeline Transport 14 (1944). A graphical presentation of the source data may be found in Hill, *Engineering Economics of Long Petroleum Pipe Lines in* Petroleum Development & Technology 231, 233–234 (1942).

Nominal	Cost per mile—Dollars		Approximate Daily Capacity—Barrels	
Diameter—Inches	Gasoline	Crude	Gasoline	Crude
6	10,000	9,000	12,000	8,000
8	13,000	12,000	22,000	18,000
10	18,000	17,000	40,000	35,000
12	22,000	21,000	70,000	50,000
14	26,000	24,000	85,000	65,000
16	30,000	28,000	125,000	95,000
18	35,000	33,000	170,000	135,000
20	45,000	42,000	230,000	180,000
22	52,000	48,000	290,000	230,000
24	65,000	60,000	370,000	295,000

Data from War Emergency Pipe Lines, Inc., "Big Inch" and "Little Big Inch" 16 (1946) indicate a construction cost of $78,500,000 for 1478 miles of 24-inch and $60,000,000 for 1714 miles of 20-inch line, which give roughly $53,000 per mile for 24-inch crude line and $35,000 per mile of 20-inch products line, somewhat less than the estimate above.

[41] Prairie Oil & Gas Co. v. United States, 204 Fed. 798, 801 (Comm.Ct. 1913); *TNEC Hearings* 9708, 9936; FTC, Report on Pipe-Line Transportation of Petroleum XXXI, 25 (1916); Cook, *op. cit. supra* note 33, at 20; Whitesel, *Recent Federal Regulation of the Petroleum Pipe Line as a Common Carrier*, 32 Corn. L. Q. 337, 350 (1947).

[42] Brundred Brothers v. Prairie Pipe Line Co., 68 I.C.C. 458, 461 (1922); see *TNEC Hearings* 8302; *but cf.* FTC, Report on Pipe-Line Transportation of Petroleum XXVII, 4, 10 (1916) which concludes that pipe line investment is not so hazardous because although particular wells or pools decline rapidly, new pools are constantly being discovered and the overall amount declines very slowly.

which caused traffic through the Ajax Pipe Line, carrying midcontinent oil to eastern refineries, to plunge from 99 percent of its capacity in 1936 to 25 percent of capacity in 1938.[43] These risks necessitate pipe line ownership by large corporations whose assets can survive these occasional mishaps.

A third factor tending to concentrate pipe line ownership consists in the interdependence of large-scale refineries and pipe lines. The large-scale refiner must maintain a high percentage of throughput capacity in order to avail himself of large-scale operational economies.[44] In addition, he must also reach a workable compromise between the need to locate his plant convenient to consuming territory and the requirement of access to many sources of supply.[45] The most satisfactory resultant of these multidirectional forces is the acquisition of pipe lines by the refining group. This solution is reflected by testimony at the *TNEC Hearings* that 80 to 90 percent of American refiners own some pipe line facilities,[46] and it would seem to follow that the larger refiners would naturally control the larger (and longer) pipe lines.

On the pipe line side of the picture, the economies of operation are keyed to the percentage of line capacity utilized.[47] It is obvious that the maintenance of a throughput volume as close to capacity as possible is a criterion of successful operation. Translated into practicalities, the pipe line operator must be assured of a constant high-level demand for the product transported. In the case of crude lines, this demand is furnished by the refiner's need for input stock with which to charge his refinery. Thus, the argument goes, pipe lines and refineries are economically bound like the head and tail of a coin. This interdependence has been challenged by the opponents of integration as being more fancied than real. Such a charge goes more to the question of whether the present concentration and integration are socially desirable than to the explanation for the present con-

---

[43] Reduced Pipe Line Rates and Gathering Charges, 243 I.C.C. 115, 123, 126 (1940); *TNEC Hearings* 9731, 9761. The flush Illinois field also drastically affected Sun Oil's line from Philadelphia to Cleveland. *TNEC Hearings* 7184, 7253.

[44] A.P.I., SURVEY, 53–54 (1935). See LEARNED, INTEGRATION IN AMERICAN INDUSTRY 3 (1949) (paper presented before American Petroleum Institute on Nov. 9, 1949).

[45] Reduced Pipe Line Rates and Gathering Charges, 243 I.C.C. 115, 118 (1940); A.P.I., SURVEY 53–54 (1935).

[46] *TNEC Hearings* 8332.

[47] *TNEC Hearings* 7203, 8302, 9936; FTC, REPORT ON PIPE-LINE TRANSPORTATION OF PETROLEUM 14, 436 (1916); SHUMAN, THE PETROLEUM INDUSTRY 95 (1940); STOCKING, THE OIL INDUSTRY AND THE COMPETITIVE SYSTEM 218–219 (1925); Emerson, *Salient Characteristics of Petroleum Line Transportation*, 26 LAND ECON. 27, 32 (No. 1, 1950). The "break-even" figure is 70–75 percent. *TNEC Hearings* 7203; Hill, *supra* note 40, at 243.

centration,[48] for, real or fancied, the interdependence tenet unquestionably has played a significant part in the formation of the present structure.[49]

A fourth force responsible for concentration is the wide-open competition formerly engaged in by the oil industry. The machinations and intrigues of John D. Rockefeller's Standard Oil Company are well known, having been publicized by newspapers, books, and even the courts. But almost unnoticed was the employment by other companies such as Texas, Shell, Gulf, Pure, and Sun of the only effective means of counter-attack, namely, integration of their own pipe line and production facilities with their refineries. After the dissolution of the Standard Oil Trust in 1911 in response to the Supreme Court's order in *Standard Oil Company of New Jersey v. United States,*[50] the dissolved companies, dealing largely with only one phase of the industry, found they could not compete effectively with the new integrated companies. They, too, undertook to combine the various operations from well-head to service station pump.[51] The result has been that integration of all phases of the industry has become a competitive necessity for large scale operators.[52] Today the structure of the industry is composed of many fully integrated companies,[53] more partially integrated companies,[54] and a "competitive fringe" of independents in each phase, the numbers of which vary according to the phase and the situs of operation.[55]

No matter how satisfactory may be the explanation of concentration and integration, explanation is not synonymous with justification, and

---

[48] This question will be examined in the discussion of divorcement, *infra.*

[49] *TNEC Hearings* 8593; MILLS, THE PIPE LINE'S PLACE IN THE OIL INDUSTRY 19–21 (1935); Whitesel, *Recent Federal Regulation of the Petroleum Pipe Line as a Common Carrier,* 32 CORN. L. Q. 337, 338 (1947).

[50] 221 U.S. 1, 31 Sup.Ct. 502, 55 L.Ed. 619 (1911).

[51] *TNEC Hearings* 7168; COOK, *op. cit. supra* note 33, at 5–6; MacLachlan, Book Review, 13 LAW & CONTEMP. PROB. 715, 716 (1948).

[52] *Cf.* United States v. Standard Oil Co. (N.J.), 47 F.2d 288, 299–300, 309 (E.D.Mo. 1931); *TNEC Hearings* 7231; COOK, *op. cit. supra* note 33, at 1, 19; WATKINS, OIL: STABILIZATION OR CONSERVATION? 23–24 (1937); MILLS, *op. cit. supra* note 49, at 18; BURNS, THE DECLINE OF COMPETITION 423, 428–429 (1936); MacLachlan, Book Review, 13 LAW & CONTEMP. PROB. 715, 716 (1948).

[53] All four branches, *i.e.,* production, transportation, refining, and marketing, are owned or controlled by one company. Few integrated companies are in balance at all stages, they have to buy or sell products made at one stage and not required at another. This is due to technical as well as financial reasons. EDWARDS, MAINTAINING COMPETITION 130 (1949); LEARNED, INTEGRATION IN AMERICAN INDUSTRY 2 (1949); COOK, *op. cit. supra* note 33, at 1.

[54] Two or more phases are combined. It was estimated in 1939 that there were 200 or more wholly or partially integrated oil companies. *TNEC Hearings* 9662–9663.

[55] LEARNED, *op. cit. supra* note 53, at 2; WATKINS, OIL: STABILIZATION OR CONSERVATION? 27–29 (1937).

there remains the examination of results fostered by the present concentration. Complaints against pipe line ownership by the major companies have taken three general heads: (1) alleged denial of independent company access to pipe lines; (2) inequalities of competition engendered by major company pipe line ownership; and (3) alleged creation of monopoly in the oil industry through the instrumentality of pipe line control. These charges deserve detailed treatment and it is the purpose of this book to evaluate their substance.

COMPLAINTS

I. ALLEGED DENIAL OF INDEPENDENT COMPANY ACCESS TO PIPE LINES

For convenience of discussion, this heading will be subdivided into the following aspects: rates, service requirements, ratable taking, and shippers' use of pipe lines.

A. Rates

The independent's position on the rate question is summarized by the allegation that crude pipe line rates are set low enough to prevent effective competition by other methods of long distance petroleum transportation and high enough to "squeeze" independent refiners by forcing them to operate at so low a margin of profit that they cannot locate their refineries convenient to heavily populated consuming areas. The charge against products pipe lines is the establishment of rates high enough to prevent independent refiners from reaching the populous consuming areas and profitably marketing their products. The net result is asserted to be an economic restriction of independent-refiner marketing to the area immediately contiguous to producing fields.[56]

These complaints essentially are two-fold: (1) rates are excessive, and (2) repressive tactics are being employed. The latter aspect will be treated in a later section of this book.

One item of evidence adduced in support of the charge of excessive rates is the unusually high profits formerly earned by pipe line companies. The favorite figure quoted in this connection is the dividend of 21,500 per-

---

[56] *E.g.*, Complaint, p. 38, United States v. American Petroleum Institute, Civil No. 8524, D. D.C., Sept. 30, 1940; *TNEC Hearings* 8168–8169; Sen. Rep. No. 25, 81st Cong., 1st Sess. 10 (1949); Rostow, A National Policy for the Oil Industry 62 (1948); Hamilton *et al.*, Price & Price Policies 151 (1938); Prewitt, *The Operation and Regulation of Crude Oil and Gasoline Pipe Lines*, 56 Q. J. Econ. 177, 190–193 (1942); 9 U. of Chi. L. Rev. 503, 504–505 (1942); Comments, 51 Yale L. J. 608, 622 (1942); 51 Yale L. J. 1338, 1339, 1341 (1942).

cent paid by the Ajax Pipe Line Company in 1933.[57] Those who seek to explain this phenomenal figure cite the gross undercapitalization of pipe lines[58] due to the practice of building and equipping lines largely with funds advanced by the parent organization in lieu of issuing capital stock sufficient to cover expenditures.[59] It has been suggested that if pipe lines were financed by stocks and bonds, as are many other common carriers, the reported dividends would assume more modest proportions. For example, a common carrier pipe line paid a divided of 343.51 percent in 1933 on a capitalization of $1,000,000. However, the actual investment aggregated $12,431,458.00 which, if used for a base, would drop the return to about 27.5 percent.[60] In addition, dividends frequently are declared from surplus funds, and therefore do not necessarily reflect the true status of rates. For example, more than half of the 1941 dividends paid by pipe line companies came from surplus.[61] Granting that these figures are out of proportion, the rates were still too high. The *TNEC* staff, compiling statistics from reports made to the Interstate Commerce Commission, reported an overall average rate of return on all pipe lines in 1938 of 25.4 percent on investment less depreciation, a 26.0 percent rate of return on major company crude line investment less depreciation, and 29.7 percent on major company gasoline lines, as compared to 9.4 percent return on independent company crude line investment (excluding depreciation).[62] Faced with these statistics, the Presidents of both Sun Oil Company and Standard Oil Company (N.J.) admitted that pipe line rates had been rather high in the past.[63] However, they suggested that rates had been reduced consistently and were not exhorbitant in the light of conditions at the time of their testimony. They took vigorous exception to the method of computing returns on the basis of net investment in the pipe line department alone, asserting that pipe line success is dependent entirely on the maintenance of active producing and marketing divisions, and that, therefore, costs of these departments should be included in calculations of rate

[57] *Hearings before Subcommittee of Committee on Interstate Commerce on S. 3753,* 76th Cong., 3d Sess. 36 (1940). Phillips Pipe Line Co. paid a dividend of 16,700 percent in 1934, *Ibid.,* and 11,100 percent in 1937. Beard, Regulation of Pipe Lines as Common Carriers 77 (1941).

[58] Reduced Pipe Line Rates and Gathering Charges, 243 I.C.C. 115, 130 (1940); H.R. Rep. No. 2192, 72d Cong., 2 Sess. LXXIII (1933); FTC, Report on Pipe-Line Transportation of Petroleum XXVII (1916) (fixed investment on books approximates actual construction cost); Beard, *op. cit. supra* note 57, at 79; Mills, The Pipe Line's Place in the Oil Industry 51, 53 (1935).

[59] Beard, *op. cit. supra* note 57, at 79; Mills, *op. cit. supra* note 58, at 51, 53.

[60] *Ibid.*

[61] 56 ICC Ann. Rep. 14 (1942).

[62] *TNEC Hearings* 7797.

[63] *TNEC Hearings* 7253 (Sun), 9760 (Standard).

returns.[64] In addition, Mr. Farish of Standard Oil pointed out that using "net investment" as a base ignored current assets and other capital items.[65] It should be noted also that the above-shown returns are not based on original investment but on original investment *less depreciation,* which has a substantial effect on the percentage return.[66] Deduction of depreciation is debatable; it could be considered to represent sums expended for renewals and replacements, or it could be argued that it is a reserve which would be a return of capital, and properly deductible. A compromise position is that of the Interstate Commerce Commission valuation which takes into account original cost, replacements, depreciation, additions, and a number of other factors commonly used in valuation.[67] However, for our present purpose of determining whether profits (*ergo* rates) were too high, the argument over the base to be used is somewhat academic, inasmuch as capital investments on the lines under consideration have long since been returned in the form of dividends.[68] Suffice it to say that nominal profits derived from transportation, reflected by dividends paid, were generally enormous prior to 1940.[69] Since 1940, pipe line rates and profits have

[64] *TNEC Hearings* 9709, 9760. This is another facet of the interdependence or "plant facility" theory. See *Dry Bones,* THE OIL & GAS JOURNAL, Feb. 17, 1949, p. 69. This argument was rejected in Reduced Pipe Line Rates and Gathering Charges, 243 I.C.C. 115, 141 (1940).

[65] *TNEC Hearings* 9759, 9942. This includes such items as operating oil stock, warehouse materials and supplies, and working cash balance. See MILLS, *op. cit. supra* note 58, at 48.

[66] The corresponding rates based on original investment are: rate of return on all lines, 11.8%; major company crude lines, 11.7%; major company gasoline lines, 20.7%; independent company crude lines, 3.5.% *TNEC Hearings* 7797.

[67] *TNEC Hearings* 8263, 9942. See Atlantic Pipe Line Co., 47 Val.Rep. 541, 584 (1937) for statement of I.C.C. method.

[68] Reduced Pipe Line Rates and Gathering Charges, 243 I.C.C. 115, 131, 132 (1940). The argument over the accounting base will reappear conspicuously in the discussion of the consent decree in *United States v. Atlantic Refining Company,* Civil No. 14060, D. D.C., Dec. 23, 1941.

[69] Texas-Empire Pipe Line Co. v. Com'r of Internal Revenue, 127 F.2d 220, 225 (10th Cir. 1942); Reduced Pipe Line Rates and Gathering Charges, 243 I.C.C. 115, 140 (1940). Perhaps a more quantitative picture of this situation may be obtained from the following chart showing, for typical pipe lines owned by large oil companies and one independent carrier (Buckeye Pipe Line Co.), the investment, depreciation and dividends paid during the period January 1, 1929, to June 30, 1938. *Id.* at 131:

Carrier	Investment	Accrued Depreciation	Dividends
Atlantic Pipe Line Co.	$ 19,273,44.26	$12,841,666.14	$ 30,925,000
Buckeye Pipe Line Co.	19,926,868.55	12,681,032.43	6,950,000
Humble Pipe Line Co.	101,274,008.05	46,391,277.97	138,250,000
Illinois Pipe Line Co.	38,711,114.08	26,029,570.44	38,600,000
Shell Pipe Line Corp.	55,806,806.48	27,593,517.43	101,450,000
Stanolind Pipe Line Co.	90,767,740.06	54,234,275.35	111,041,632

Note that not only have dividends returned the investment in the major pipe lines listed, but the accrued depreciations have almost matched the investments for a second "pay-out." See Comment, 51 YALE L. J. 1338, 1343 (1942).

shown a marked decline.[70] The forces responsible for the reduction seem to be changes in the tax laws,[71] the recent Interstate Commerce Commission decisions,[72] and the modern development of competing forms of bulk petroleum transportation.[73]

A second item advanced in support of the contention that excessive pipe line rates are employed to deny access to independent shippers is the disparity between pipe line rates and costs.[74] Testimony before the *TNEC* furnished illustrations of this situation. In one instance the rate averaged 20 cents a barrel, while the cost was only 10 cents per barrel.[75] In another instance, the rate was seventeen and one-half cents per barrel as opposed to a cost of five cents per barrel.[76] Again, the four crude lines connecting the midcontinent area to Chicago[77] maintained a rate of 46 cents per barrel prior to June 21, 1934,[78] although the average cost per barrel-mile of these lines in 1933 was only $0.0002797.[79] Calculating on the basis of the above cost and rate figures and an average distance of 700 miles, the difference would be approximately $0.00066 per barrel-mile.[80] Even using the 38.5

[70] Comment, 51 YALE L. J. 1338, 1342 (1942). *Compare* Petroleum Rail Shippers' Ass'n v. Alton & Southern R.R., 243 I.C.C. 589, 616 (1941) *with Id*. at 665.

[71] Reduced Pipe Line Rates and Gathering Charges, 243 I.C.C. 115, 127, 139 (1940); ROSTOW, A NATIONAL POLICY FOR THE OIL INDUSTRY 59, 60 (1948); HAMILTON *et al.*, PRICE & PRICE POLICIES 152 (1938); MILLS, THE PIPE LINE'S PLACE IN THE OIL INDUSTRY 53 (1935); 9 U. OF CHI. L. REV. 503, 504 n. 15 (1942).

[72] Reduced Pipe Line Rates and Gathering Charges, 272 I.C.C. 375 (1948) (confirmed earlier ruling, *infra*); Minnelusa Oil Corp. v. Continental Pipe Line Co., 258 I.C.C. 41 (1944) (reduction in crude line rates ordered); Petroleum Rail Shippers' Ass'n v. Alton & Southern R.R., 243 I.C.C. 589 (1941) (gasoline line rates reduced); Reduced Pipe Line Rates and Gathering Charges, 243 I.C.C. 115 (1940) (crude line revenues ordered reduced). These decisions will be discussed in part two of this book.

[73] Water transportation, especially river barge movement has provided cheaper rates on long hauls. In addition, tank-truck operation has developed into a very important competitor of pipe lines, particularly in the Nebraska and Iowa area. Petroleum Rail Shippers' Ass'n v. Alton & Southern R.R., 243 I.C.C. 589, 656, 661–662 (1941); *TNEC Hearings* 8275–8277, 8590–8592, 9943; ASS'N OF AMERICAN RAILROADS, REPORT BY SUBCOMMITTEE ON PIPE LINE TRANSPORT 10 (1944).

[74] The material here is drawn largely from Prewitt, *The Operation and Regulation of Crude Oil and Gasoline Pipe Lines*, 56 Q. J. ECON. 177, 189–193 (1942) and Comments, 51 YALE L. J. 1338, 1341–1343 (1942).

[75] *TNEC Hearings* 7338.

[76] *TNEC Hearings* 7582.

[77] Shell Pipe Line Corp., Sinclair Refining Co., Stanolind Pipe Line Co., and Texas-Empire Pipe Line Co.

[78] Reduced Pipe Line Rates and Gathering Charges, 243 I.C.C. 115, 125 (1940).

[79] Prewitt, *supra* note 74, at 189.

[80] See note 78 *supra*.

cent rate which became effective in 1934 and remained in force during the hearing before the Interstate Commerce Commission in *Reduced Pipe Line Rates and Gathering Charges*,[81] the ratio between earnings from the rate charged and the cost of transportation approached 2 to 1.[82] Nor are gasoline lines "as white as paper." Despite the admitted operating cost differential between gasoline lines and railroads,[83] the earlier rates charged by the gasoline pipe lines tended to match the existing rail rates.[84] For example, the rate quoted by the Great Lakes Pipe Line Company from Tulsa to Omaha was $0.94 per barrel or 33.9 cents per 100 pounds, which is rather close to the rail rate of 33.0 cents.[85] Phillips Pipe Line Company posted a rate of $0.705 per barrel for shipment from Borger, Texas, to Wichita, Kansas, which exactly matches the 25.5 cents per 100 pounds rail rate.[86] Moreover, when an additional one percent emergency charge was made available to the railroads, the Great Lakes Pipe Line advanced its rate an equivalent amount.[87]

In view of foregoing discussion of large capital investment and pay-out risk,[88] one might wonder if the early rates were not justifiably high in order to recover the heavy investment by charging a rate comparable to existing competitive forms of transportation. This argument loses weight when one realizes that although the pipe lines were paid out fully by 1941[89] the rates

[81] 243 I.C.C. 115 (1940).

[82] See note 79 *supra*.

[83] For 1937, railroad cost was $0.01640 per ton-mile, while the gasoline pipe line cost was $0.00527 per ton-mile *TNEC Hearings* 7178 (Pew of Sun Oil Co.).

[84] H.R. REP. No. 2192, 72d Cong., 2d Sess. (1933). "In conclusion it may be stated that an analysis of the pipe-lines rates of these trunk pipe lines moving gasoline from the Southwest to northern and eastern points indicated the tendency to use the existing rail rates as the basis for th pipe-line rates and charges." *Id.* at 493. *Accord, Hearings before Subcommittee of Committee on Interstate Commerce on S. 3753*, 76th Cong., 3d Sess. 21 (1940).

[85] H. R. REP. No. 2193, 72d Cong., 2d Sess. 491 (1933).

[86] *Id.* at 492. Phillips' present tariff is twenty-nine cents per barrel. Phillips Petroleum Company, I.C.C. Tariff No. 88, Dec. 1, 1949, Item No. 95.

[87] See note 85 *supra*.

[88] See notes 40–42 *supra*.

[89] Great Lakes Pipe Line Company: investment as of Dec. 31, 1931, $15,578,160.89; dividends paid as of Dec. 31, 1939, $34,877,138.50. H.R. REP. No. 2192, 72d Cong., 2d Sess. 79 (1933) (investment); Complaint, p. 9, United States v. Great Lakes Pipe Line Co., Civil No. 183, D. Del., Sept. 30, 1940 (dividends), Phillips Pipe Line Company: investment as of Dec. 31, 1931, $12,202,111.89; dividends paid as of Dec. 31, 1939, $18,920,000.00 H.R. REP. No. 2192, 72d Cong., 2d Sess. 128 (1933) (investment); Complaint, p. 6, United States v. Phillips Petroleum Co. and Phillips Pipe Line Co., Civil No. 182, D. Del., Sept. 30, 1940 (dividends). Great Lakes Pipe Line Company investment as of Dec. 31, 1939, is given as $23,975,667 in Petroleum Rail Shippers' Ass'n v. Alton & Southern R.R., 243 I.C.C. 589, 662 (1941), but still this is less than the dividend returned, so the validity of the pay-out statement remains unaltered.

still were well above cost plus 6 percent on investment.[90] Moreover, the complaints concerning the virtual use of Tulsa as a basing point[91] and the collection of "quasi-phantom freight"[92] are numerous.[93] The prevalence

[90] The following chart, taken from Petroleum Rail Shippers' Ass'n v. Alton & Southern R.R., 243 I.C.C. 589, 616 (1941), gives some idea of the discrepancy:

Group 3 (Okla.) to—	Rate (cents per 100 lbs.)	Cost + 6%
Kansas City, Mo.	28	6.95
St. Louis, Mo.	33	11.76
Indianapolis, Ind.	48	18.18
Chicago, Ill.	40	18.72
St. Paul, Minn.	46	19.25
South Bend, Ind.	53	19.78
Marquette, Mich.	63	27.28

[91] For discussions of basing points in general, see OPPENHEIM, CASES ON FEDERAL ANTI-TRUST LAWS 432–437 (1948); FTC, THE BASING POINT PROBLEM (TNEC Monograph 42, 1941); BURNS, THE DECLINE OF COMPETITION cc. VI, VII (1936); FETTER, THE MASQUERADE OF MONOPOLY (1931); Clark, *The Law and Economics of Basing Points: Appraisal and Proposals*, 39 AM. ECON. REV. 430 (1949); Clark, *Machlup on the Basing-Point System*, 63 Q. J. ECON. 315 (1949); Kaysen, *Basing Point Pricing and Public Policy*, 63 Q. J. ECON. 289 (1949); Smithies, *Economic Consequences of the Basing Point Decisions*, 63 HARV. L. REV. 308 (1949); Head, *The Basing Point Cases*, 26 HARV. BUS. REV. 641 (1948); and see cases cited in note 92 *infra*. For use of basing points in the oil industry, see *TNEC Hearings* 8124–8145, and discussions in COOK, CONTROL OF THE PETROLEUM INDUSTRY BY MAJOR OIL COMPANIES 43–44 (TNEC Monograph 39, 1941) and FARISH & PEW, REVIEW ON BEHALF OF STANDARD OIL CO. (N.J. AND SUN OIL CO. OF MONOGRAPH No. 39 WITH REJOINDER BY MONOGRAPH AUTHOR 49–51, 91–93 (TNEC Monograph 39-A, 1941). See also Gill, *Gill Sees No Threat in FTC Move Against Collusive Price System*, THE OIL & GAS JOURNAL, Dec. 30, 1948, p. 135; Rodman, *Basing-Point Pricing Essential to Oil Industry, Rodman Insists*, THE OIL & GAS JOURNAL, Dec. 30, 1948, p. 134; *Basing-Point Rule is Ruinous, Oil Men Say*, THE OIL & GAS JOURNAL, Dec. 9, 1948, p. 45; *Basing-Point Confusion*, THE OIL & GAS JOURNAL, July 22, 1948, p. 43.

[92] Under a basing point system, any time a purchaser pays an allowance for freight which is greater than the actual cost of freight delivery, he is said to be paying "phantom freight." LOEVINGER, THE LAW OF FREE ENTERPRISE 156 (1949). This can take either of two forms, sales by non-basing point refineries or shipments made by a medium of transportation other than that which is used in calculating the delivered price. FTC, THE BASING POINT PROBLEM 63 (TNEC Monograph 42, 1941). (1) To illustrate the first method:

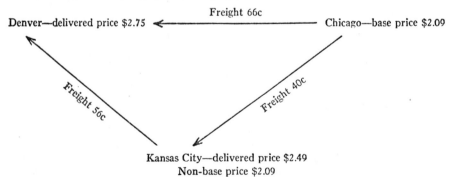

Quoting the Chicago base price of $2.09 plus freight, the delivered price to Denver is $2.75 (2.09 + .66). By shipping from Kansas City to Denver at an actual cost of $2.65 (2.09 + .56), a phantom freight of $0.10 (2.75 — 2.65) is collected. The extreme example is a sale to a Kansas City merchant at the "Chicago plus" delivered price of $2.49, which represents $0.40 phantom freight. On these facts, this practice was held to constitute illegal price discrimination under Section 2a of the Clayton Act by the Supreme Court in Corn Products Refining Co. v. Federal Trade Commission, 324 U.S. 726, 65 Sup.Ct. 961, 89 L.Ed. 1320 (1945), distinguishing Maple Flooring Manufacturers Ass'n v. United States, 268 U.S. 563, 45 Sup.Ct. 578, 69 L.Ed. 1093 (1925) and Cement Manufacturers Protective Ass'n v. United States, 268 U.S. 588, 45 Sup.Ct. 586, 69 L.Ed. 1104 (1925) on the ground that the latter were suits to restrain violations of the Sherman Act, and did not involve the prohibition of the Clayton Act against discriminations in price. For subsequent litigation on this question, see Federal Trade Commission v. A. E. Staley Manufacturing Co., 324 U.S. 746, 65 Sup.Ct. 971, 89 L.Ed. 1338 (1945) ; Federal Trade Commission v. Cement Institute, 333 U.S. 683, 68 Sup.Ct. 793, 92 L.Ed. 1010 (1948) ; and Triangle Conduit & Cable Co. v. Federal Trade Commission, 168 F.2d 175 (7th Cir. 1948), *aff'd by equally divided court sub nom.*, Clayton Mark & Co. v. Federal Trade Commission, 336 U.S. 956, 69 Sup.Ct. 888, 93 L.Ed. 1110 (1949). S. 1008, 81st Cong., 1st Sess. (1949), designed to amend the Federal Trade Commission and Clayton Acts so as to declare it not an unfair method of competition for a seller, acting independently, to quote or sell at delivered prices or to "absorb freight" was vetoed by President Truman on June 16, 1950. N.Y. Times, June 17, 1950, p. 18, col. 1. See text of Mr. Truman's message to Congress accompanying his veto. CCH Trade Reg. Rep. ¶ 61,274. (2) The second method is similar:

```
            Freight (water) $2                         Freight (rail) $3
Basing Point A ──────────────> Consuming Point X <────────────── Basing Point B
base price $40                    delivered price                   base price $40
   mill net $41                        $43                            mill net $40
```

Shipping by water, the shipper at Basing Point A sells at a delivered price of $43 and realizes a phantom freight of $1 (43 — 40 — 2). FTC, The Basing Point Problem 35 (TNEC Monograph 42, 1941). (3) The quasi-phantom freight is as follows:

```
            Pipe Line                          Rail & Pipe Line
Tulsa ────────── Cost ──────────> Des Moines <────────── Rate ────────── Tulsa
              $12.83                                       36c
```

The rail rate and pipe line rate are 36 cents per 100 pounds. The pipe line cost, including six per cent return on investment, is 12.83 cents per 100 pounds. Therefore the quasi-phantom freight is 23.17 cents per 100 pounds. The figures were taken from Petroleum Rail Shippers' Ass'n v. Alton & Southern R.R., 243 I.C.C. 589, 616 (1941). See Sen. Rep. No. 25, 81st Cong., 1st Sess. 22 (1949).

[93] *E.g.*, United States v. Socony-Vacuum Oil Co., 310 U.S. 151, 192, 60 Sup.Ct. 811, 830, 84 L.Ed. 1129, 1152 (1940) ; Petroleum Rail Shippers' Ass'n v. Alton & Southern R.R., 243 I.C.C. 589, 627 (1941) ; Complaint, pp. 38, 46, United States v. American Petroleum Institute, Civil No. 8524, D. D.C., Sept. 30, 1940; *Hearings before Subcommittee of Committee on Interstate and Foreign Commerce on H.R. 290*, 76th Cong., and H.R. 15 & H.R. 118, 77th Cong., 1st Sess. 192–192 (1941) ; *Hearings before Subcommittee of Committee on Interstate Commerce on S. 3753*, 76th Cong., 3d Sess. 23–24, 40–43, 56, 192 (1940) ; Cook, *op. cit. supra* note 91, at 43–44; Comment, 51 Yale L. J. 1338, 1341–1343 (1942). For a discussion of proportionate rate abuses, see *TNEC Hearings* 9335 and Prewitt, *The Operation and Regulation of Crude Oil and Gasoline Pipe Lines*, 56 Q. J. Econ. 177, 191–193 (1942). Evidence adduced in the *Petroleum Rail Shippers Ass'n* case tended to show that pipe line companies refused to permit jobbers to carry gasoline from the pipe line terminals in common-carrier trucks to their own bulk plants at destination, requiring movement from the terminals by pipe line company trucks or railroad tank cars in order to permit the proportional rates to effect an overall cost equivalent to the through rail rate. 243 I.C.C. at 631–632. See Tables A & B, Appendix L, H.R. Rep. No. 2192, 72d Cong., 2d Sess. 494–498 (1933).

of these abuses led Commissioner Aitchison to say: "It is evident that the rates charged by the respondents are not made with any relation to the cost of service, but rather are measured by the benefits to be derived therefrom by the owners, in the ultimate, rather than by the benefits directly derived from common-carrier operations."[94] Perhaps the most recent example of charging purchasers the price of gasoline at the refinery plus an amount roughly equal to the through rail freight is that considered by the Supreme Court in *Champlin Refining Company v. United States.*[95] Champlin, through its wholly owned subsidiary, Cimarron Valley Pipe Line Company, constructed a six inch products line from Enid, Oklahoma, to Superior, Nebraska, in 1935; later extending the line to Rock Rapids, Iowa, in 1941. The prices quoted to purchasers at Champlin's three terminals in Kansas, Nebraska, and Iowa were refinery price at Enid plus a differential roughly equal to the through rail rate, modified in some cases due to competition.[96]

Because pipe line ownership mainly lies in the hands of the major oil companies,[97] the high rate charged to themselves as shipper-owners represent a mere bookkeeping transaction[98] insofar as *their* costs are concerned but they create a considerable competitive disadvantage to the independent shipper attempting to utilize the lines as common carriers. This aspect of the situation will be treated in the section devoted to inequalities of competition engendered by major pipe line ownership.

In summary, it would seem that, formerly, pipe line owners charged initial rates as stiff as the traffic would bear, the amount being determined largely by comparable through rail rates. After the lines had paid themselves out, in the absence of regulation or adverse effects of tax laws, rates were maintained at an unreasonably high level, since the charging of rates to shipper-owners was only a bookkeeping transaction, a figurative shifting of money from one corporate pocket to another, and the higher rates dis-

[94] Reduced Pipe Line Rates and Gathering Charges, 243 I.C.C. 115, 139 (1940).

[95] 329 U.S. 29, 67 Sup.Ct. 1, 91 L.Ed., 22 (1946); 35 Geo. L. J. 404 (1947); 20 Temp. L. Q. 592 (1947); 33 Va. L. Rev. 212 (1947).

[96] Champlin Refining Co. v. United States, 59 F.Supp. 978, 980 (W.D.Okla. 1945), finding approved by Supreme Court in Champlin Refining Co. v. United States, 329 U.S. 29, 34, 67 Sup.Ct. 1, 3, 91 L.Ed. 22, 26 (1946).

[97] See note 38 *supra*, and textual material related thereto.

[98] Reduced Pipe Line Rates and Gathering Charges, 243 I.C.C. 115, 140 (1940); Kaul Lumber Co. v. Central of Georgia Ry., 20 I.C.C. 450, 453 (1911); *TNEC Hearings* 7475, 9716, 9757; H.R. Rep. No. 2192, 72d Cong., 2d Sess. LXXII (1933); Rostow, A National Policy for the Oil Industry 65 (1948); Black, *Oil Pipe Line Divorcement by Litigation and Legislation,* 25 Corn. L. Q. 510, 513 (1940); Pogue, *Economics of the Petroleum Industry* in Elements of the Petroleum Industry 453, 478 (1940); Comment, 51 Yale L. J. 1338, 1341 (1942).

couraged use of the lines by independents. In recent years, the **tax laws** have changed considerably and not only are the large profits shown by the pipe line companies mulcted by a large surtax but double taxation to the extent of 15 percent occurs when dividends are declared to the parent company. In addition to this factor, the consent decree in *United States v. Atlantic Refining Company*[99] limits dividends by pipe line companies to shipper-owners to 7 percent of the pipe line valuation, and the Interstate Commerce Commission has prescribed rates which would result in earnings not exceeding 8 percent of pipe line property valuation for crude lines[100] and 10 percent for gasoline lines.[101] As a result, pipe line rates have dropped considerably, and today they constitute a reasonable transportation expense to shippers and a reasonable return for the pipe line proprietors.[102]

[99] Civil No. 14060, D. D.C., Dec. 23, 1941.

[100] Reduced Pipe Line Rates and Gathering Charges, 243 I.C.C. 115 (1940).

[101] Petroleum Rail Shippers' Ass'n v. Alton & Southern R.R., 243 I.C.C. 589, 663 (1941).

[102] Figures taken from the INTERSTATE COMMERCE COMMISSION, BUREAU OF TRANSPORT ECONOMICS & STATISTICS, STATEMENT No. 4944, October, 1949, Tables 1 & 8, and rates of return calculated therefrom are as follows:

Year	Investment	Investment Less depreciation	Operating Income	Rate w/dep.	Rate w/o dep.
1948	$1,381,402,464	$707,754,859	$58,805,645	4.26%	8.32%

It is said that the real rate of return should be based on the "latest final value" and net income. No final value figures for *all* reporting pipe lines have been issued by the Interstate Commerce Commission since December 31, 1934. However, the latest final value closely approaches 75 per cent of the recorded investment, so approximate figures for 1948 would be:

Year	Investment	Estimated Final Value	Net Income	Rate of Return
1948	$1,381,402,464	$1,036,051,848	$56,679,058	5.48%

In the calculation of rates, a forecast is made of the anticipated line traffic for the prospective period, frequently one year. Past experience furnishes the planning group with an estimate of the volume, origin and destination of movements in general through the company's lines. This prediction for crude lines must take into account the loss of old connections, the acquisition of new connections, the effect of competing lines, and production trends of the fields from which the gathering systems draw their oil. The products lines must consider the capacities of the refineries served, the seasonal variations affecting products requirements and the varying market demands. Based on these estimates, the operating or out-of-pocket costs can be calculated. These include the usual operating expenses plus certain taxes such as ad valorem, payroll, federal transportation, and income taxes. The second main item is the depreciation allowance prescribed by the Interstate Commerce Commission's Bureau of Accounts. Finally, a profit figure is obtained by taking a percentage of the valuation of company property established by the Commission's Bureau of Valuation. This percentage is seven percent in the case of pipe lines "living" under the *Atlantic Refining Company* consent decree. The allowance set by the *Reduced Pipe Line Rate* case for other crude lines is eight percent; whereas ten percent was prescribed for other products lines by the *Petroleum Rail Shippers' Ass'n* decision. The overall revenue for the estimated movement is obtained by adding the operating costs, the depreciation allowance, and the profit figure. Then this sum must be allocated to the individual movements. There are many methods of allocations, *e.g.,* (1) proration on the basis of barrel-miles—this is the simplest insofar as the calculation is concerned, however it does not allow for local variations; (2) section of line method—under this method each section of line is consid-

However, it is important to note that such results did not come about naturally, but were the result of governmental intervention, and the record of major companies in the absence of any regulation is not calculated to reassure the worried independent operator.

B. Service Requirements

1. MINIMUM TENDERS. (*a*) *The Formal Record.* Any discussion of minimum tenders necessarily must begin with the early days of the oil industry. The figure of John D. Rockefeller, like Hamlet's ghost, constantly casts its shadow on discussion of this subject. It is common knowledge that at one time the Standard Oil Trust had control of every important pipe line east of California. Even after the enactment of the Hepburn Amendment[103] to the Interstate Commerce Act,[104] impressing common carrier status on interstate pipe lines, the large Standard pipe line companies refused to consider themselves common carriers since they did not hold themselves out as transporters of independent oil, but only pumped crude belonging to members of the Trust or that which had been purchased from independent producers at the well-head.[105] This state of affairs was changed by the Supreme Court's decision in *The Pipe Line Cases*[106] which held that the

---

ered by itself and the three elements are calculated for it; (3) combination of the first two methods, using section of line method to compute operating cost and depreciation, and the proration method to allocate the profit figure.

The resultant allocation is the tentative rate for the individual movements. But sometimes modifications are made. One modification is due to a historical custom of zoning. For example, crude from Kansas, Oklahoma and North Texas going to Chicago or Detroit will generally be in a different zone than East Texas crude and perhaps the rate on the latter will be as much as 5 cents per barrel more. This is really little more than a field expedient based on the barrel-mile allocation but modified to give a working field figure. Another modification must be made when the allocated rate is not competitive with that of another pipe line serving the field. In such a case, the lower rate must be met and the burden shifted to another part of the system which will stand it. A third situation requiring alteration of the allocated rate is that of the stripper-well areas. If these were made to pay their own way, the gathering charges would have to be raised continually, but the responsible large pipe line companies stay in there and take the loss without raising rates in order to run the oil. The loss is passed on to another section of the line.

The problem of division or joint rates generally is settled by the so-called "10-90 rule." Under this rule, the first ten percent of the rate is divided equally between the initial and final carriers in order to defray the cost of gauging, testing and other terminal services. The remaining ninety percent is allocated on a mileage basis. Again, there are modifications of this rule, but they are beyond the scope of this book.

[103] 34 STAT. 584 (1906), as amended, 49 U.S.C. § 1 (1946).

[104] 24 STAT. 379 (1887), as amended, 49 U.S.C. §§ 1–27 (1946).

[105] The Pipe Line Cases, 234 U.S. 548, 559, 34 Sup.Ct. 956, 958, 58 L.Ed. 1459, 1470 (1914); Prairie Oil & Gas Co. v. United States, 204 Fed. 798, 801 (Comm.Ct. 1913); In the Matter of Pipe Lines, 24 I.C.C. 1, 3 (1912); 26 HARV. L. REV. 631, 633 (1913).

[106] 234 U.S. 548, 34 Sup.Ct. 956, 58 L.Ed. 1459 (1914).

practice of running oil purchased from many independent producers constituted common carriage in fact and therefore the law could make those engaged in this practice common carriers in form.[107] Thereafter, the large pipe line companies evaded the import of this decision by onerous shipping requirements.[108] As an example, beginning in 1914, the Standard Lines from the midcontinent fields to the East required a minimum tender of 100,000 barrels for a single shipment.[109] Although it was possible for individuals to pool their shipments in order to make up the minimum tender, practical considerations such as the difficulty in finding enough oil destined for the same location[110] rendered the large minimum tender requirement a device through which pipe line owners were able to withdraw their line from outside use.[111] This situation received the attention of the Federal Trade Commission in 1916. Observing that the pipe line companies did not prescribe minimum tenders for their own shipping accounts,[112] the Commission felt that requiring high tenders acted to prevent small producers or refiners from shipping by pipe line,[113] and that the burden of proving technical or commercial justification for high tenders should be on the pipe line companies.[114] The Commission concluded that it was ". . . evident that the prosperity and perhaps even the existence of many small concerns depend on lower pipe-line rates and reasonable minimum shipments."[115] In 1922 a complaint was filed with the Interstate Commerce Commission against the Prairie Pipe Line Company and its connecting carriers[116] seeking reduction of the 100,000 barrel tender required for crude oil shipment from wells in Kansas, Oklahoma, and Texas to Franklin and Lacy Station, Pennsylvania. The Commission found the 100,000-

---

[107] *Id.* at 561, 34 Sup.Ct. at 958, 58 L.Ed. at 1470.

[108] *TNEC Hearings* 8157; SEN. DOC. NO. 61, 70th Cong., 1st Sess. 33, 40 (1928); see COOK, CONTROL OF THE PETROLEUM INDUSTRY BY MAJOR OIL COMPANIES 24 (*TNEC* Monograph 39, 1941); BEARD, REGULATION OF PIPE LINES AS COMMON CARRIERS 94 (1941); KEMNITZER, REBIRTH OF MONOPOLY 82, 86 (1938); 9 U. OF CHI L. REV. 503, 504 (1942). The main regulations relate to: (1) minimum tenders; (2) identity of product shipped; (3) quality of product accepted; (4) loss in transit; and (5) terminal facilities. FTC, REPORT ON PIPE-LINE TRANSPORTATION OF PETROLEUM 21, 448 (1916); Prewitt, *The Operation and Regulation of Crude Oil and Gasoline Pipe Lines,* 56 Q. J. ECON. 177, 184 (1942).

[109] *Ibid.*

[110] Brundred Brothers v. Prairie Pipe Line Co., 68 I.C.C. 458, 463 (1922); BEARD, *op. cit.* supra note 108, at 93.

[111] SEN. DOC. NO. 61, 70th Cong., 1st Sess. 73 (1928); Prewitt, *supra* note 108, at 184.

[112] FTC, REPORT ON PIPE-LINE TRANSPORTATION OF PETROLEUM 21 (1916).

[113] *Id.* at 20.

[114] *Id.* at 21.

[115] *Id.* at XXXII.

[116] Indiana Pipe Line Co., Buckeye Pipe Line Co., Northern Pipe Line Co., and National Transit Co.

barrel tender to be unreasonable and ordered it reduced to 10,000 barrels,[117] but the reduction was limited to the delivery points involved in the complaint.[118] Later this reduced minimum tender became applicable for shipments to a number of other points in Western Pennsylvania,[119] and as shipments to Standard refineries on the Atlantic seaboard had fallen off, the eastern independent refiners began to make use of these pipe lines in ever increasing amounts.[120] Notwithstanding this trend, the situation in 1933 led Dr. Walter M. W. Splawn to report that the most common requirement for interstate shipment was 100,000 barrels.[121] He concluded that this fact discouraged independent-refiner shipping over the pipe lines[122] and contributed to the high degree of concentration which characterized the oil business at that time.[123] The *TNEC Hearings* in 1938–1940 disclosed that tender requirements of interstate pipe lines varied from zero to 100,000 barrels[124] with a typical tender of 50,000 barrels.[125] About this time, the Interstate Commerce Commission also had the question of minimum tenders under consideration and found the same variance in tender requirements.[126] After referring to its earlier decision in *Brundred Brothers v. Prairie Pipe Line Company*,[127] which had found tenders required by the Prairie in excess of 10,000 barrels to be unreasonable, the Commission directed the numerous respondents to show cause why the 10,000 barrel crude line minimum tender should not apply to them, and provided that, in the absence of such a showing, an order would be entered on the record im-

---

[117] Brundered Brothers v. Prairie Pipe Line Co., 68 I.C.C. 458 (1922).

[118] SEN. DOC. No. 61, 70th Cong., 1st Sess. 33 (1928) ; Prewitt, *supra* note 108, at 206.

[119] Oil City, Titusville, and Tiona.

[120] SEN. DOC. No. 61, 70th Cong., 1st Sess. 41 (1928).

[121] H.R. REP. No. 2192, 72d Cong., 2d Sess. LXVI (1933) ; See Appendix D, part I, p. 451 of this report for table of minimum tenders.

[122] *Id.* at LXXVII; see BEARD, REGULATION OF PIPE LINES AS COMMON CARRIERS 94 (1941).

[123] *Id.* at LXVI; see also Prewitt, *The Operation and Regulation of Crude Oil and Gasoline Pipe Lines*, 56 Q. J. ECON. 177, 185 (1942).

[124] FARISH & PEW, REVIEW AND CRITICISM ON BEHALF OF STANDARD OIL CO. (N.J.) AND SUN OIL CO. OF MONOGRAPH No. 39 WITH REJOINDER BY MONOGRAPH AUTHOR 32 (TNEC Monograph 39-A, 1941).

[125] *TNEC Hearings*, 7202–7203, 8299–8300, 8344–8345, 9704–9705; COOK, CONTROL OF THE PETROLEUM INDUSTRY BY MAJOR OIL COMPANIES 24 (TNEC Monograph 39, 1941) ; Comment, 51 YALE L. J. 1338, 1343 (1942). In the reply, FARISH & PEW, *op. cit. supra* note 124, at 32, an analysis of tenders by number of companies was offered to show that the common requirement was 10,000 barrels. In the rejoinder, FARISH & PEW, *op. cit. supra* note 124, at 87, Mr. Cook explains his basis of using a weighted average, *i.e.*, using the ratio of pipe line mileage to determine the typical tender. It would seem that Mr. Cook's figure is more reliable.

[126] Reduced Pipe Lines Rates and Gathering Charges, 243 I.C.C. 115, 134 (1940) (500—100,000 barrels).

[127] 68 L.C.C. 458 (1922).

posing the 10,000 barrel limit.[128] The next year a 25,000 barrel minimum tender was approved for gasoline lines.[129] By 1948 the specified minimum tenders generally were being observed,[130] and in another hearing of *Reduced Pipe Line Rates and Gathering Charges*,[131] the Commission ordered seven recalcitrant respondents to conform to the 10,000 barrel minimum tender.

(b) *Practical Operations.* Although there is little question that minimum tenders of 50,000 barrels and larger can be, and have been, used to keep independent shippers from using the line,[132] the establishment of minimum tenders may be justified by the requirements of physical operation.[133] First, some erroneous ideas about tenders should be dispelled. The view seems prevalent among persons who are uninformed that a tender is a *formal* act performed by a shipper who has a tank battery full of crude waiting to be transported. Strangely enough, the legal and economic literature on the subject of pipe line regulation practically is devoid of reference to actual field practice in handling tenders.[134] This fact may be responsible for some of the present misconceptions on the subject.

What, then, is a tender? The answer varies with the pipe line company involved: some consider tenders strictly accounting records against which the daily receipts and deliveries are charged; other companies consider an accepted tender to be a contract; still other companies treat the tender as a device to permit scheduling of traffic through the line. Perhaps the simplest method of explaining tenders is to trace the physical procedure of tendering oil to a pipe line for shipment. Let us consider the case of a producer, or purchaser, of new production who desires to ship his crude to a distant refiner-consignee. He contacts the pipe line company whose line is nearest to his particular location and informs the appropriate official of the quantity and quality of the crude. He specifies the origin and destination of the desired shipment. At the same time, he will make out a form generally called a "request to connect," giving the pipe line company sufficient information upon which to predicate a business judgment of commercial

---

[128] Reduced Pipe Lines Rates and Gathering Charges, 243 I.C.C. 115, 136–137 (1940).

[129] Petroleum Rail Shippers' Ass'n v. Alton & Southern R.R., 243 I.C.C. 589, 665 (1941).

[130] *Cf.* Minnelusa Oil Corp. v. Continental Pipe Line Co., 258 I.C.C. 41, 43 (1944).

[131] 272 I.C.C. 375, 383 (1948).

[132] For instance, the investment in oil alone at $2.65 a barrel would be $132,500, not to mention the transportation and gathering charges.

[133] Dow, THE ISSUE OF PIPE LINE DIVORCEMENT 12 (1930) (mimeographed); A.P.I., SURVEY 59 (1935); MILLS, THE PIPE LINE'S PLACE IN THE OIL INDUSTRY 38–40 (1935).

[134] Perhaps the most "extensive" discussion of the nature of tenders is found in Eureka Pipe Line Co. v. Hallanan, 257 U.S. 265, 271, 274, 42 Sup.Ct. 101, 103–104, 66 L.Ed. 227, 231–233 (1921).

feasibility.[135] After deciding to make the connection, the pipe line company notifies the prospective shipper and aids him in filling out the tender form[136] in the amount called for by the applicable tariff.[137] After this has been accomplished, the shipper submits the tender to the pipe line company which schedules the movement and "accepts" the tender by signing the tender form and returning a copy to the shipper. The pipe line com-

[135] "The determining factor seems to be whether the prospects of production in the new territory are sufficient reasonably to justify the expectation that an extension of the lines will result in profit to the company." Brundered Brothers v. Prairie Pipe Line Co., 68 I.C.C. 458, 463 (1922). This is discretionary with the pipe line company as there is no obligation upon a common carrier to extend its facilities to areas which it has not undertaken to serve. Hollywood Chamber of Commerce v. Railroad Comm., 192 Cal. 307, 219 Pac. 983, 30 A.L.R. 68 (1923); Atchison, Topeka & Santa Fe Ry. v. Railroad Comm., 173 Cal. 577, 160 Pac. 828, 2 A.L.R. 975 (1916), *error dismissed,* 245 U.S. 638, 38 Sup.Ct. 191, 62 L.Ed. 525 (1918); *cf.* Fidelity Title & Trust Co. v. Kansas Natural Gas Co., 219 Fed. 614 (D.Kan. 1913). It probably cannot be compelled to do so, and definitely not before full hearings have been held before some duly authorized tribunal and all opportunities to obtain review of an adverse decision have been exhausted. Interstate Commerce Commission v. Oregon-Washington R.R. & Nav. Co., 288 U.S. 14, 53 Sup.Ct. 266, 77 L.Ed. 588 (1933); *cf.* Atlantic Coast Line R.R. v. Public Service Comm., 77 F.Supp. 675, 684 (E.D.S.C. 1948); Dow, The Issue of Pipe Line Divorcement 18 (1938).

[136] When completed, generally these forms contain the following information: date, shipper's name; carrier's name; origin and destination points; consignee's name; volume of tender in barrels; the routing to be used where connecting carriers are involved; the applicable tariff numbers; and if the tariff permits, and the service is desired, instructions for storage in transit. Frequently, tender forms will contain a warranty that the shipper is the legal owner of the oil tendered and will save the pipe line company harmless from all claims to the contrary. The tender rules published in the tariffs frequently provide that a tender for shipment shall be deemed a warranty of title by the party making the tender.

The shipper signs the forms and sends them to the carrier who "accepts" the tender and returns a signed copy to the shipper. Procedures vary, but the two methods of handling tender forms most commonly used are as follows: (1) duplicate copies—here the duplicate is retained by the shipper and the original is sent to the pipe line company; (2) multiple copies—four copies are executed by the shipper, who retains one copy, sending in the original and two copies. The acceptance then is made by the pipe line company's signing the original and returning it to the shipper. One of the other copies is used as a shipping order and the remaining copy is utilized as a receipt copy which is signed by the pipe line company and sent to the shipper when shipments against the tender have been completed.

[137] Tariffs consist of two parts, the tender rules and the rates. Some companies publish both together, others separately. Interstate crude shipments usually have a 10,000 barrel minimum tender, interstate products lines usually have a 25,000 barrel minimum tender. Intrastate crude tenders vary due to local laws. Texas, for example, has a 500 barrel or one tank-car-load minimum. Rule 7 of Oil and Gas Circular No. 10, promulgated by the Railroad Commission of Texas, reproduced in the Texas tariffs. Oklahoma is considerably higher, judging from the 50,000 barrel minimum tender specified in Phillips Pipe Line Company, Oklahoma Tariff No. 2, Aug. 15, 1949, Item No. 30. On the other hand, Tex. Civ. Stat. Ann., art. 6045 (Vern. 1949) provides that pipe lines shall not be required to accept more than 3,000 barrels per day from any single shipper. See Rule 1 on all Texas Tariffs. Some companies have carried this provision over to their interstate tariffs. See Humble Pipe Line Company, I.C.C. Tariff No. 448, Sept. 16, 1947, Item No. 1.

pany then "straps"[138] the shipper's tanks and completes the connections to the pipe line. When the shipper has a tank ready to run, the pipe line company sends out a guager who samples the crude with a "thief,"[139] and takes a steel-tape measurement of the oil level in the tank.[140] He tests the crude for temperature,[141] BS&W,[142] and gravity.[143] Having recorded this

[138] The process of determining accurately the volume that each tank contains at a given level is called strapping. Measurements of the circumference of the tanks are taken at several heights. The thickness of tank walls and the displacement of internal bracing members is ascertained. From these data computations are made which result in tank tables showing volumes (to 1/100 barrel) corresponding to each ¼-inch increment in height for small tanks and each ⅛-inch for large tanks. This procedure is standardized by A.P.I. Code 25.

[139] A thief is a cylindrically shaped instrument with a spring-closed bottom plate which enables the gauger to obtain a sample from any depth in the tank. The usual practice is to take a sample from the oil just below the surface and one from the oil adjacent to the pipe line outlet. The reason for this is that the BS&W (see note 142 *infra*) tends to be greater at the latter point than at one higher in the tank due to the gravitational settling action. If either sample "grinds out" (see note 142 *infra*) over one percent BS&W, the tank is turned down. Otherwise, the two readings are averaged. It is customary also to require the level of BS&W in tank bottoms to be a specified minimum clearance (usually four inches) below the height of the pipe line connection. This is checked by the gauger who makes a "bottom thief," which is recorded on the run ticket.

[140] This is known as the first or "opening" gauge.

[141] Because all crude oils and products expand with rising temperature and contract with falling temperature, it is necessary to select an arbitrary base temperature, so that volumes at different temperatures may be correlated. The temperature selected as a standard is 60° F. For this reason, it is important that the gauger obtain the temperature of the oil about to be run. The pipe line company makes a volume correction by applying expansion coefficients to the measured volume. These coefficients or multiplying factors are obtained from the National Bureau of Standards' April 20, 1937, Supplement to Circular C-410, entitled "Abridged Volume Correction Tables for Petroleum Oils." Example, where the true gravity is 32° A.P.I. and the temperature 50° F, the volume shown in the tank table corresponding to the tape measurement is multiplied by 1.0040 to obtain the corrected volume. It is standard practice to correct both opening and closing gauge volumes for their own temperatures. Because lease tanks usually are small (210–1000 barrels) and the closing gauge represents such a small volume, some companies use the temperature of the opening gauge to correct both volumes in order to save the cost of making a second temperature reading and the additional computations on the run ticket.

[142] Officially, this is basic sediment and water. This is considered euphemistic in the "oil patch." No matter what you call it, the volume of this undesirable material is deducted from the temperature-corrected volume to obtain net barrels. It is measured by means of a portable, hand-operated centrifuge equipped with two graduated glass test tubes. Rapid revolution creates a centrifugal force which deposits the heavier BS&W on the bottom of the test tubes. In order to secure a sharper reading, it is customary to dilute the crude sample with an equal volume of gasoline or other solvent. This provides a greater weight differential and improved solvent action. The percentage of BS&W then is obtained from the sum of the percentages shown by the two test tubes.

[143] The gravity is obtained by floating a graduated hydrometer in the sample secured by the thief. It is measured in units known as "A.P.I. degrees," which bear the following relation to specific gravity: $\text{S.G.} = \dfrac{141.5}{131.5 + \text{A.P.I.}}$. Thus a specific gravity of 0.8448 is equal to 36° A.P.I. The observed gravity measured by the hydrometer is corrected to "true" gravity at

information on a "run ticket,"[144] he "turns the tank on the line" by opening the valve to the pipe-line connection and sealing all other outlets. After the oil has run from the tank, the gauger closes and seals the line valve. At that time he takes a second measurement, known as the "closing gauge," which also is recorded on the run ticket.[145]

The run tickets are sent into the central office where they are calculated and entered on a shipping order record which was established for the tender under which the run is made. On the other side of the ledger are the deliveries made to the consignee or connecting carrier specified in the tender.[146] The shipper is sent a monthly statement of the runs and deliveries, together with the current status of the tender. He is billed for the gathering charges on the oil gathered during the month, and usually he receives an invoice for transportation charges and the deduction of "allowance oil"[147] based on the month's deliveries.[148]

60°F. For example, a 39° A.P.I. hydrometer reading at 73°F. would be corrected to 38° A.P.I. at 60°F. The gravity is important to the producer because higher A.P.I. gravity crude brings a better price (usually two cents per degree A.P.I.). It is important also in that it determines the proper coefficient of expansion to be used in correcting the volume for temperature, mentioned in footnote 141.

[144] A run ticket is a form used by the gauger to record the information referred to previously, *i.e.*, oil level measurements, observed gravity, temperature, BS&W in suspension, BS&W in the tank bottom, and height of pipe line connection. The run ticket also shows who furnished the power to pump the oil into the line. If someone other than the pipe line furnished the power, he is due reimbursement from the carrier. The ticket is signed by the gauger and a representative of the operator, usually the pumper. Four copies are made, the gauger retaining the original, the operator's representative is given the duplicate, and two copies are sent to the central office. As a matter of control over run tickets, the ticket must contain the number of the seal removed from the pipe line valve when the tank was "turned on" and the number of the seal used to lock the valve after the run was made. The closing seal reported on the last run must be the same as the one removed to make the present run. Sometimes tickets are prenumbered or are numbered in sequence by gauger's districts. Account must be rendered for missing numbers.

[145] In the usual case, where the shipper is an oil purchaser rather than a producer, the entry of oil into the pipe line has a dual aspect. The oil is committed to the pipe line for transportation, and at the same time, title passes from the producer to the purchaser. BALL, THIS FASCINATING OIL BUSINESS 175 (1940). Consequently, run tickets can be considered to be drafts on the purchaser in amounts equal to the value of the oil run at the agreed or posted price. Information compiled from run tickets forms the basis for payment of producers and royalty interests. MILLS, THE PIPE LINE'S PLACE IN THE OIL INDUSTRY 38 (1935).

[146] Tickets known as Delivery or Transit Receipts, record deliveries. The process virtually is the reverse process of runs.

[147] A deduction is made for losses inherent in the transportation of crude petroleum by pipe line. This covers such items as evaporation and shrinkage from mixtures. The amount of deduction varies with the carrier, the product being transported, and the distance traveled. Crude allowances run from $\frac{1}{4}$ to one percent, the latter being the most common. In the old days, it ran as high as three percent. FTC, REPORT ON PIPE-LINE TRANSPORTATION OF PETROLEUM 22, 455, 456 (1916). When natural gasoline and butane is mixed with crude, the allowance goes up to 2-5 percent.

In the event that connections already are made to the pipe line, such as where a purchaser has acquired a prior shipper's interest, virtually the same tender process takes place, except that the "request to connect" and the tank strapping phases are eliminated. The pipe line simply receives shipments for the account of the new shipper, instead of the old.

Deliveries lag behind receipts in point of time due to the period required for transportation. Consequently, where there is a continuous shipper-carrier relation, it is common practice for the pipe line company, on its own initiative, to fill out a new tender form and send it to the shipper for signature when "runs" have equaled the previous tender, even though deliveries have not been completed. In fact, although it is not considered good practice, instances exist where "runs" have been made in the field and tenders covering them have been executed thereafter.

Such is the present procedure of tendering oil. It is highly informal and extremely flexible. It is very important to note that the shipper is not required to deliver the amount of the tender at one time, but delivers his daily shipping requirements against the tender until the total quantity has been delivered.[149]

(c) *Commingling or Contamination.* Another problem encountered in the analysis of tenders is the commingling or intermixing of two fluids in the region of contact as they are pumped through a pipe line. This intermixing has been termed "contamination" by an expert, who referred to the quantity of commingled material extending from pure product to the leading fluid to pure product of the following fluid as "spread of contamination."[150] We might ask if the strict use of the word "contamination" is not governed by the basis of our interest; that is to say, if we were concerned with the lower grade product, would we say that it had been "contaminated" by the infiltration of the higher grade product? However, this appears to be merely a matter of definition. So long as we know what we are discussing, we may adopt the existing definition as useful and convenient. Accordingly, hereafter the terms "contamination" and "spread of contamination" will be employed as defined above.

The contamination problems occurring in crude lines and products

[148] Some carriers render this invoice only upon the completed delivery of the tender.

[149] Brundred Brothers v. Prairie Pipe Line Co., 68 I.C.C. 458, 462 (1921); *Hearings before Special Committee to Study Problems of American Small Business Pursuant to S. 20,* 80th Cong., 1st Sess., Part 10, 1237 (1947); *TNEC Hearings* 8298, 8299, 9705; FARISH & PEW, REVIEW AND CRITICISM ON BEHALF OF STANDARD OIL CO. (N.J.) AND SUN OIL CO. OF MONOGRAPH NO. 39 WITH REJOINDER BY MONOGRAPH AUTHOR 32 (TNEC Monograph 39-A, 1941). See Atlantic Pipe Line Company, I.C.C. Tariff No. 84, Aug. 1, 1949, Item No. 45.

[150] Birge, *Contamination Control in Products Pipe Lines,* THE OIL & GAS JOURNAL, Sept. 20, 1947, p. 176.

lines differ considerably. For the most part, crude lines only agree to deliver specified quantities of "common-stream" crude. If this arrangement is in effect, there is no contamination problem and the question of minimum shipments would seem to be limited only by the operational problems involved in making small deliveries. Although legally not required to prevent contamination, and forbidden to render a special service causing discrimination between shippers, crude lines sometimes are faced with the problem of separating shipments. For example, suppose shipper A has 10,000 barrels of 38° A.P.I. crude and shipper B has a like amount of 34° crude. If these shipments are not segregated, A would suffer a 2 cents per-barrel-per-degree loss in gravity. Naturally, he will seek to prevent this. There are only two ways to accomplish this: either have one shipper purchase all the oil at the shipping point and sell at the destination, both transactions on the basis of gravity, or have the pipe line segregate the shipments. Another example is the desire of a shipper of sweet crude to avoid contamination by a sour crude such as that from West Texas. In this example, segregation would be the only answer. If segregation is desired, essentially the same problems are encountered by the crude lines as are met by the products lines. Therefore, a brief general discussion of contamination problems and their influence on minimum shipments seems appropriate.

Sources of contamination may be classified into artificial and "normal" sources. The artificial sources may be subdivided into factors inherent in line design and those accountable to faulty operational technique. The design factors include such items as line loops,[151] station bypasses and equipment,[152] and tanks "floating" on the line.[153] Most of these "dead

[151] *Id.* at 177, 179, 273. Where there are loops in lines of different diameters, different velocities of flow will ensue unless regulated. Thus, where a 6-inch line and a 10-inch line are looped or paralleled, the uncontrolled velocity through the 6-inch line will be only 78 percent of that through the 10-inch line. To illustrate the contamination effect, assume the length of the loops to be ten miles. A contact face between two products going through the 10-inch line would reach the point where the lines joined at a time when that going through the 6-inch line lacked 2.2 miles of reaching the injunction. The result would be that the 6-inch line would feed the first product into the second product until the 2.2 miles had been flushed out. The amount of the second product thus contaminated would be $2.2 \times 100/78$ or 2.8 miles (of 10-inch). The contamination from this loop alone would be 1478 barrels. *Id.* at 179, 273. One would think that if both lines were the same internal diameter and the same length, the velocity would be the same, and this problem would be eliminated. However, field experience does not bear this out. Some divergence is due to different "C" factors (Hazen & Williams formula), but field opinion is that even two identical lines would "hunt" unless regulated. Consequently, many products lines employ regulatory devices to equalize the flow. Roach, *Factors Influencing Commingling in a Products Pipe Line,* WORLD OIL, Jan., 1948, pp. 172–174; *but cf.* Neptune, *Operation of Partial Loops,* THE OIL & GAS JOURNAL, Sept. 23, 1944, pp. 204–207.

[152] Roach, *supra* note 151, at 172, 174; Birge, *supra* note 150, at 178, 273. This includes such items as station bypasses, scraper traps, hay tanks, sump pits, and pumps not operating.

fluid" pockets are the result of design work completed prior to 1937 when the importance of eliminating sources of dead fluid was not given full consideration.[154] However, most modern lines, particularly products lines, are designed to eliminate features which would add to the mixing effect.[155]

The operational techniques which affect contamination include methods of sampling;[156] "flying switches";[157] blocking off and draining sediment traps and station bypasses, pumping their contents from the sump into the leading products stream before the interface arrives; flushing out the remaining dead pockets such as scraper traps or shut-down pumps;[158] operating the sump pump continuously through the change from one prod-

[153] Birge, *supra* note 150, at 177, 178, 273. This is the distinction between "open" and "closed" systems. Most older crude lines operated with each station discharging into a tank at the downstream station. The downstream station took suction from the tank and in turn pumped into a tank at the next station. This permitted different pumping rates along various sections of the line as the tanks would receive the excess or supply the deficit, thus "floating" on the line. This was deemed necessary because of the different viscosities of the "batches" being pumped through the line. The modern tendency, particularly in products lines, is toward a closed system, with one station discharging directly into the suction of the other. Automatic controls are installed to protect equipment against excess pressures and unfavorable line conditions. SMITH & SCHULZE, INTERFACIAL MIXING CHARACTERISTICS OF PRODUCTS IN PRODUCTS PIPE LINES 48 (paper presented before the American Petroleum Institute on Nov. 10, 1947); Anderson, *Recent Developments in Pipe-Line Technology*, THE OIL & GAS JOURNAL, Nov. 16, 1946, p. 241. For an account of a modern crude line which changed from an open system to a closed system mainly because of excessive contamination created by the "over-and-short" tanks, see Batchelder & Rockwell, *Automatic Control on Portland-Montreal Pipe Line*, THE OIL & GAS JOURNAL, Sept. 27, 1947, pp. 74–75.

[154] Roach, *supra* note 151, at 172.

[155] Lundberg, *Magnolia Pipeline's Hebert Terminal designed and planned to provide for Minimum Interruption and Product Commingling*, THE OIL & GAS JOURNAL, Oct. 6, 1949, pp. 208, 211, 213; see SMITH & SCHULZE, *op. cit. supra* note 153, at 71.

[156] The older method was to secure samples at 1 minute intervals to be tested by an ordinary field hydrometer, but this method is being replaced by continuously recording gravimeters and special sight glass installations. Lundberg, *supra* note 155, at 211, 213, 214; see SMITH & SCHULZE, *op. cit. supra* note 153, at 62.

[157] One of the most troublesome contamination factors is the inability to make sharp cuts on the interfaces. The so-called "flying switches" made across a finite time interval, often introduce an appreciable admixing of the products. Petroleum Rail Shippers' Ass'n v. Alton & Southern R.R., 243 I.C.C. 589, 657 (1941); SMITH & SCHULZE, *op. cit. supra* note 153, at 68. Modern design is bent on solving this problem.

[158] This is accomplished by directing the incoming stream, or a portion thereof, through these items.

[159] Because the spread of contamination is much more rapid at the beginning and diminishes with the distance traveled, it is advisable to avoid making intermediate deliveries from the ends of the batch and suffering the greater contamination all over again. The best way is to allow the two contaminated ends to proceed undisturbed to their last terminal, and to take intermediate deliveries out of the pure product in the "heart" of the batch. Hence the name. Birge, *Contamination Control in Products Pipe Lines*, THE OIL & GAS JOURNAL, Sept. 20, 1947, p. 276.

uct to another in order to prevent pumping the sump into a dissimilar product; and making "heart-cut" intermediate deliveries.[159]

The source of normal contamination appears to be an undetermined function of velocity, density differential between the two products, viscosity, the pipe friction factor and other factors not yet identified.[160] All the writers agree that the velocity must be sufficient to maintain turbulent flow in order to prevent excessive contamination.[161] Turbulent flow commences when the Reynolds number[162] is between 2,000 and 2,500.[163] The early writers believed that once turbulent flow had been achieved, a further increase in Reynolds number caused a decrease in contamination.[164] This gave rise to a rule-of-thumb that pipe line flow must not fall below two and one-half feet per second to avoid excessive contamination. However, recent experiments tend to disprove this. For example, kerosene-gasoline and kerosene-diesel fuel contacts have been handled in a commercial line at velocities as low as 0.5 feet per second (Reynolds number 20,000) without appreciable abnormal spread of contamination.[165] This would seem to indicate that so long as the flow remained above a Reynolds number of 20,000, the velocity does not affect appreciably the spread of contamination.[166]

[160] Birge, *supra* note 159, at 278.

[161] *Id.* at 178; Williams, *Pumping Various Products Through The Same Pipe-Line System,* THE OIL & GAS JOURNAL, Sept. 22, 1945, p. 197; Fowler & Brown, *Contamination by Successive Flow in Pipe Lines,* THE PETROLEUM ENGINEER, August, 1944, p. 121. Roach, *supra* note 151, and SMITH & SCHULZE, *op. cit. supra* note 153, accept this without comment.

[162] The number derives its name from Professor Osborn Reynolds who performed the pioneer experiments in the field. Reynolds introduced colored liquids into streams of water flowing through pipes and observed that under given conditions, the flow assumed a streamline or viscous character at certain velocities and became turbulent at others. He determined that the character of the flow was a function of the relation $DV\delta/\mu$, where D is pipe diameter, V is velocity of the fluid, δ is density of the fluid, and μ is viscosity of the fluid (all expressed in any consistent absolute system of units). Williams, *supra* note 161, at 197. In streamline flow, all the liquid particles follow paths generally parallel to the walls of the pipe. Wiliams draws the analogy to an unfolding telescope or collapsible drinking cup. Turbulent flow is characterized by whirls and eddies.

[163] ZABA & DOHERTY, PRACTICAL PETROLEUM ENGINEERS' HANDBOOK 445 (2d ed. 1939); Williams, *supra* note 161, at 197. Velocities giving a Reynolds number of 2,000 to 2,500 are said to be "critical velocities."

[164] Fowler & Brown, *supra* note 161, at 127.

[165] Birge, *supra* note 159, at 178.

[166] *Id.* at 179, 280. The conclusions of Fowler & Brown do not conflict necessarily with Birge's. They experimented with mixtures at Reynolds numbers under 20,000, whereas Birge was concerned with Reynolds numbers above 20,000. According to Williams' graph of relative velocities plotted against the logarithms of Reynolds numbers (Williams, *supra* note 161, at 198), it would seem that the contamination would decrease from Reynolds numbers 3160 to 20,000, but there would be little change thereafter. This apparently would confirm both Birge's and Fowler & Brown's conclusions. Since commercial pipe lines are operated within the range examined by Birge, his conclusion is more significant than that reached by Fowler and Brown.

Another important question is the effect of line length on contamination. We must distinguish the *rate* of spread, which decreases with the distance traveled,[167] from the length (*ergo* volume) of contamination spread, which increases with the distance traveled. In 1933, Kashcheev, observing gasoline-kerosene contacts pumped from Baku to Batum, concluded that the amount of contamination did not increase *proportionally* to the length of the line.[168] Birge's observations of the Plantation Pipe Line indicate that the length of the line influences the normal contamination in a logarithmetric ratio.[169] This slight increase in normal contamination is augmented by the artificial or induced contamination caused by the "dead fluid" in station by-passes and equipment mentioned previously.[170] Tests indicate that after the initial station, the spread of contamination is proportional to the number of stations through which the products are handled.[171]

The data assembled from pilot models[172] and field tests[173] make possible the construction of graphs showing the contamination to be expected from various interfaces.[174] We may proceed from this information to product scheduling. Formerly, it was believed that a greater mixing took place when a lighter product preceded a heavier product (lower Reynolds num-

[167] Birge, *Contamination Control in Products Pipe Lines,* THE OIL & GAS JOURNAL, Sept. 20, 1947, p. 276.

[168] Cited in Fowler & Brown, *supra* note 161, at 121.

[169] Birge, *supra* note 167, at 278. For example, the gasoline-kerosene contamination equation is $Y = 1.93X^{0.529}$, where Y is the contamination spread in feet and X is the line distance traveled in feet. For a graphical representation of this relation, see *Id.* at 177. Smith & Schulze also found a logarithmetric ratio. SMITH & SCHULZE, INTERFACIAL MIXING CHARACTERISTICS OF PRODUCTS PIPE LINES 63, 64 (1947).

[170] Birge estimates this figure to be eleven percent for Plantation's main line. Birge, *supra* note 167, at 278.

[171] Roach, *Factors Influencing Commingling in a Products Pipe Line,* WORLD OIL, January, 1948, p. 172.

[172] Williams obtained his primary data from $\frac{1}{2}$ inch pyrex glass tubing erected on uprights in such a manner as to reproduce the profile elevations of the Keystone line. The correlation between the data obtained from this model, that from the actual 8-inch Keystone line, and the "Little Big Inch" line is extremely close. WEP, BIG INCH AND LITTLE INCH 39, plate 12 (1946). Smith & Schulze also obtained fine agreement between pilot model and field observations. SMITH & SCHULZE, *op. cit. supra* note 169.

[173] Birge's data are based on five years observation on Plantation Pipe Line operations.

[174] Birge plotted contamination in feet against length of line for various interfaces. On this same graph he superimposed contamination in barrels against the same contamination-in-feet scale for different pipe diameters so that the barrel figure could be readily obtained. Birge, *supra* note 167, at 177. Smith & Schulze went one step further and plotted the barrels of mixture against specific gravities, showing the different percentages of each product in the same graph. The desired cut can be made simply by instructing the operator to cut when the specific gravity of the incoming stream reaches a designated figure. SMITH & SCHULZE, *op. cit. supra* 169, at 68–69. Williams correlated percentage contamination with the ratio of average velocity to maximum velocity. Williams, *Pumping Various Products Through the Same Pipe-Line System,* THP OIL & GAS JOURNAL, Sept. 22, 1945, pp. 198, 308.

ber) than that which resulted from the reverse order. This belief has been dispelled by Smith and Schulze who found that the characteristic curves differed only slightly, and the spread of contamination was practically the same.[175] Another notion which hampered the scheduler was the assumption that line shut-downs with gasoline and kerosene, or other relatively dissimilar products, in contact with each other would cause excessive spread of contamination. Experiments conducted by the Plantation Pipe Line have proved this to be incorrect.[176] Operations may be suspended for reasonable periods without fear of prohibitive spread of contamination.[177]

The determination of the proper product cycle is dependent upon the needs of the shippers, the capacity of the line, and the spread of contamination as shown by data similar to that discussed previously. Based on these factors, products may be scheduled in cycles which are usually multiples of five days.[178] Once the cycles have been established, the next problem is the proper positioning of each product with respect to other products within the cycle. The basic rule governing this location is to place products adjacent to each other which will be disposable into one or the other product or into some other product being handled currently.[179] This brings us to the main reason for examining the subject of contamination, i.e., minimum batch size for contamination control. At this point the expression

[175] SMITH & SCHULZE, op. cit. supra note 169, at 60. In fact, the authors found their data applicable, despite the fact that the Reynolds number of the heavier products was one which would give heavy intermixing. This would seem to indicate that only one product needs to be well into the turbulent range to avoid excessive contamination. Id. at 64.

[176] Plantation pumped a kerosene-diesel fuel interface into their 4-inch Bremen-Macon lateral line and shut it down at 225 psi. for 57 hours. After the shut down period, the line was started up and the kerosene arrived in Macon with only normal contamination. Birge, Contamination Control in Products Pipe Lines, THE OIL & GAS JOURNAL, Sept. 20, 1947, p. 282.

[177] Plantation shuts down its laterals regularly over the weekend with fuel in them, without prohibitive spread of contamination. Id. at 284. Apparently the normal topography has little effect on spread of contamination in the shutdown lines. Id. at 282.

[178] For a complete description of this process, see Birge, supra note 176, and Dreyer, Scheduling and Dispatching: Description of the Procedures at Plantation Pipe Line, THE OIL & GAS JOURNAL, Oct. 6, 1949, p. 178. The cycles are planned one month in advance.

[179] Ibid. Frequently "buffer" batches are inserted to separate two products, the properties of which render disposal of their mixture difficult. For example, Product A has a low flash and high end point, Product B has a high flash and a low end point. Very small amounts (.25%) of Product A will reduce the flash of Product B as much as 25° or 30° F, which is extremely undesirable as it renders use of Product B dangerous. At the same time the contamination of A by small amounts of B will lower disproportionately the end point of Product A, an important specification of A. Under these facts we could not cut sharply at either end for fear of spoiling one product, nor at the middle because to do so would ruin both. The answer is to insert a buffer slug of Product C which has a high flash and a high end point. The contamination buffer can be cut both ways since the resultant contamination between A and C will not affect A's high end point nor will the contamination between B and C affect adversely the high flash point of B.

"percentage contamination" has real significance. Although the length (or volume) of the batch does not affect the quantity of contamination, it does have a definite affect on disposability of the contaminated products. For example, the spread of contamination between kerosene and diesel fuel through Plantation's main line is said to be approximately 800 barrels on either end. One half of the total contamination, roughly 800 barrels, is kerosene to be disposed into the diesel fuel. But 3 percent kerosene is the limit that specifications will permit to be introduced into the diesel. Therefore, to absorb the 800 barrels of kerosene into the diesel fuel and still remain within specifications, there must be 800 x 100/3 or 26,667 barrels of diesel in the batch. Hence the requirement of a 25,000 barrel minimum.[180] It is important to note that this minimum batch is "correct" for Plantation's operations only, and if the spread of contamination is greater, the minimum batch necessarily would have to be larger. Conversely, if the contamination is less, the minimum can be set at a lower figure. Thus it seems that minimum batches will vary according to the particular operation, and it is impractical, if not impossible, to establish an arbitrary minimum batch for all lines or products.

In addition to the contamination aspect, the balance of the line must be considered. Great differences in viscosity of adjacent products will cause waste of horsepower unless proper scheduling of heavy product batches keeps the line in balance.[181]

Finally, if the pipe line furnishes tanks at the origin, and their location is such that booster pumps must be installed to move the products into the pipe line, the cost of facilities will be an economic factor tending to compel large minimums.[182]

(d) *Conclusions.* The first need is one of definition. People have been using the word "tender" to mean several different things.[183] It is small wonder that arguments are rampant in this field. If a tender is simply an accounting document used to designate the aggregate of daily shipments for a convenient period of time, there would seem to be no reason to limit the minimum. Rather it should be determined by the pipe line company

[180] Birge, supra note 176, at 288–291. See discussion of this problem in Petroleum Rail Shippers' Ass'n v. Alton & Southern R.R., 243 I.C.C. 589, 657 (1941).

[181] *Id.* at 291.

[182] *Ibid.*

[183] The standard joke circulating in pipe line circles today is the question, "what is a tender?" A few of the responses were given in the foregoing discussion. It is apparent that the prevalent notion among laymen (most legal and economic writers fall in this classification) is that a minimum tender refers to the minimum amount accepted in a single shipment. Cook, Control of the Petroleum Industry by Major Oil Companies 23, 39 (TNEC Monograph 39, 1941) ; Prewitt, *The Operation and Regulation of Crude Oil and Gasoline Pipe Lines*, 56 Q. J. Econ. 177, 184 (1942) ; 9 U. of Chi. L. Rev. 503, 504 (1942).

and the shipper, according to how frequently they wish to close out accounts. If it is to mean the quantity of a designated product which must be delivered for a single shipment, then a further analysis must be made. If the carrier is a crude pipe line furnishing "common-stream" transportation service, there would seem to be no reason for any minimum shipment to be received by the pipe line, other than the limitation mentioned in respect to the feasibility of making a connection. The point of strain is in the delivery end of the transportation. Admittedly, there are few data on this point, and the following suggestion must be labelled a "horseback opinion," but it is submitted that a 5,000-barrel minimum delivery limit would be a good prima facie rule, subject to being set aside by respectable evidence that it is unsatisfactory.[184]

Where the shipper desires segregation of his product, and this is applicable both to crude lines and products lines, the spread of contamination and disposability of the contaminated product should be the basis for the establishment of minimum shipments on an individual line operation basis. Certainly a shipper who requires segregation of his product cannot be heard to protest against a *reasonable* minimum arrived at by a process similar to the one suggested above.[185] In the event that the carrier furnishes storage at the origin, the effect of this should also be an element in determining what is reasonable. Finally, because of the early history of minimum tender abuse, and due to the inherent frailties of human nature,[186] it seems necessary to provide for review of the reasonableness of these minimum shipments by a disinterested and unbiased tribunal.

2. IDENTITY OF PRODUCT SHIPPED. The inherent nature of pipe line transportation precludes delivery of the identical shipment received by the pipe line. Therefore, to expedite prompt handling of shipments, it is com-

---

[184] This estimate is based on the fact that consignees of crude shipments invariably are refiners. Even the smallest "tea-kettle" refinery has sufficient crude storage capacity to handle 5,000 barrels. Moreover, the 5,000 barrel figure was asserted to be a reasonable shipping requirement by the numerous small-refiner complainants in Petroleum Rail Shippers' Ass'n v. Alton & Southern R.R., 243 I.C.C. 589, 657 (1941). On the other hand, it is believed that this figure is sufficiently large that deliveries under this rule will not unduly hamper pipe line operation. See Service Pipe Line Company, Proposed Rules and Regulations, March 31, 1950, Item No. 25(b).

[185] Any such protest on the part of a shipper who had requested the segregation could be brought under the old adage of "biting the hand that feeds you," since the segregation is maintained for his benefit. CONWAY, PIPE LINE DIVORCEMENT 50 (unpublished thesis in University of Oklahoma Law School Library, 1950).

[186] "It is too much of a strain of human good intentions to expect that the owner of a line, chiefly interested in his own shipments, will to his own disadvantage deal with a rival who wishes to use his common-carrier line." Address before the American Petroleum Institute on Nov. 9, 1948, by Clyde B. Aitchison of the Interstate Commerce Commission, cited in SEN. REP. No. 25, 81st Cong., 1st Sess. 21 (1949).

mon for crude line tariffs to provide that crude received for shipment is subject to being mixed with other shipments and to the resultant changes in gravity and quality. Moreover, the tariffs specify that the pipe line company is not obliged to deliver the identical petroleum received, but may make delivery out of its common stock.[187] However, many crude line tender rules provide that the carrier will endeavor to segregate shipments which differ from the common stream. The pipe line companies will make every attempt to maintain the quality and gravity of the batch. But the rules provide that the carrier will not be liable for any variation or contamination of the segregated shipment, nor held to deliver the identical shipment.[188] The products lines do not undertake to deliver the identical product shipped, but permit tonnage substitution of the same product meeting approximately the same specifications.[189]

(3) QUALITY OF PRODUCT ACCEPTED. (a) *Crude Lines.* The basic requirement is that all crude oil accepted for shipment must be "marketable" or "merchantable." These terms generally mean that crude must be properly settled and contain less than a certain percentage of BS&W at a specified distance below the pipe line connection. The quality of the oil must not have been seriously impaired in storage. Some tariffs limit the temperature at which oil will be accepted.[190] Others place limits on gravity and viscosity so as to permit easier handling and transportation.[191]

Where natural gasoline or liquified petroleum gases are shipped, the tariffs specify the ratio (by volume) of these "indirect" products to "direct" products (crude) that will be accepted for mixed shipments. Upper limits are set for the Reid vapor pressure of the pure "indirect" product and for that of the resulting mixture.

(b) *Products Lines.* Specifications on products lines include color number, A.S.T.M. distillation specifications (I.P., 50 percent, and end point), flash point, and viscosity.[192] Because these are so numerous and

[187] Reduced Pipe Line Rates and Gathering Charges, 243 I.C.C. 115, 135, 136 (1940); FTC, REPORT ON PIPE-LINE TRANSPORTATION OF PETROLEUM 21, 22, 453 (1916); Emerson, *Salient Characteristics of Petroleum Pipe Line Transportation,* 26 LAND ECON. 27, 30 (No. 1, 1950). See Atlantic Pipe Line Company, I.C.C. Tariff No. 84, Aug. 1, 1949, Item No. 40; Humble Pipe Line Company, I.C.C. Tariff No. 448, Sept. 16, 1947, Item No. 12; Phillips Pipe Line Company, I.C.C. Tariff No. 10, Dec. 1, 1949, Item No. 6.

[188] Humble Pipe Line Company, I.C.C. Tariff No. 485, Sept. 28, 1949, Item No. 35; Shell Pipe Line Corporation, I.C.C. Tariff No. 294, April 20, 1950, Item No. 20; Service Pipe Line Company, Proposed Rules and Regulations, March 31, 1950, Item 30(c).

[189] Humble Pipe Line Company, Local Tariff (Texas) No. 126, Jan. 20, 1950, Item 10; Phillips Petroleum Company, I.C.C. Tariff No. 86, Jan. 10, 1948, Item No. 20. See Emerson, *supra* note 187, at 31.

[190] Humble Pipe Line Company, I.C.C. Tariff No. 448, Sept. 16, 1947, Item No. 4.

[191] Atlantic Refining Company, I.C.C. Tariff No. 84, Aug. 1, 1949, Item No. 10.

[192] Keystone Pipe Line Company, Pa. P.U.C. Tariff No. 16, May 10, 1946, Item No. 5.

varied, tariffs sometimes provide that products will be accepted for transportation only when storage facilities for the particular commodity tendered are available at the destination, and products of the same quality and specifications currently are being handled through the line.[193]

4. LOSS IN TRANSIT. Tariffs provide that the carrier shall not be liable for any loss, damage, or delay caused by act of God, public enemy, war, quarantine, authority of law, strikes, fires, riots, acts of default of shipper or owner,[194] or for any cause not due to the negligence of the carrier.[195] These provisions present two questions, one of law, the other of policy. There would seem to be little dispute concerning the defenses of act of God[196] and public enemy, which traditionally were allowed to common-law common carriers.[197] The same is true of the more recent exceptions to a common-carrier's liability as an insurer, such as losses caused by acts or defaults of the shipper or owner,[198] or by intervening acts under authority of law.[199] Acts committed by citizens of a hostile nation engaged in war are covered by the public enemy exception.[200] Losses and delays due to quarantine restrictions apparently are included in the authority-of-law defense.[201]

In addition to these implied exceptions to a common carrier's liability, express exceptions may be created by special contract between the carrier

[193] Phillips Petroleum Company, I.C.C. Tariff No. 88, Dec. 1, 1949, Item No. 10.

[194] FTC, REPORT ON PIPE-LINE TRANSPORTATION OF PETROLEUM 456 (1916); Atlantic Pipe Line Company, I.C.C. Tariff No. 84, Aug. 1, 1949, Item No. 70; Phillips Pipe Line Company, Texas Tariff No. 4, Nov. 1, 1948, tem No. 19; Shell Pipe Line Corporation, Texas Tariff No. 110, Jan. 30, 1950, Item No. 19.

[195] Humble Pipe Line Company, I.C.C. Tariff No. 485, Sept. 28, 1949, Item No. 95; Keystone Pipe Line Company, Pa., P.U.C. Tariff No. 16, May 10, 1946, Item No. 60; Phillips Pipe Line Company, Oklahoma Tariff No. 2, Aug. 15, 1949, Item No. 65; Shell Pipe Line Corporation, I.C.C. Tariff No. 294, April 20, 1950, Item No. 60. See Emerson, *Salient Characteristics of Petroleum Pipe Line Transportation,* 26 LAND ECON. 27, 31 (No. 1, 1950).

[196] Seaboard Air Line Ry. v. Mullin, 70 Fla. 450, 70 So. 467, L.R.A. 1916 D, 982 (1915); St. Louis & San Francisco R.R. v. Dreyfus, 42 Okla. 401, 141 Pac. 773, L.R.A. 1915 D, 547 (1914); cf. Interstate Commerce Commission v. Tank Car Oil Corp., 151 F.2d 834, 836 (5th Cir. 1945).

[197] Holladay v. Kennard, 12 Wall. (U.S.) 254, 20 L.Ed. 390 (1870); Pittsburgh, Cincinnati & St. Louis Ry. v. Hollowell, 65 Ind. 188, 32 Am.Rep. 63 (1879); American Cigarette & Cigar Co. v. Garner, 229 N.C. 173, 47 S.E.2d 854 (1948).

[198] McCarthy & Baldwin v. Louisville & Nashville R.R., 102 Ala. 193, 14 So. 370, 48 Am.St.Rep. 29 (1893); American Cigarette & Cigar Co. v. Garner, 229 N.C. 173, 47 S.E.2d 854 (1948).

[199] Southern Express Co. v. Sottile Brothers, 134 Ga. 40, 67 S.E. 414, 28 L.R.A. (N.S) 139 (1910); Chesapeake & Ohio Ry. v. Williams, 156 Ky. 114, 160 S.W. 769, 49 L.R.A. (N.S.) 347 (1913); Abasi Brothers v. Louisville & Nashville R.R., 115 Miss. 803, 76 So. 665, L.R.A. 1918 B, 652 (1917).

[200] See note 197 *supra.*

[201] See note 199 *supra.*

and the shipper.[202] Under this rule, common carriers have successfully stipulated against losses caused by strikes,[203] fires,[204] and riots beyond their control.[205] This limitation of liability must not be unjust, unreasonable, or contrary to public policy.[206] But limiting liability to damage caused by the carrier's negligence normally is not considered unreasonable nor unjust.[207] Tariffs filed with, and approved by, the Interstate Commerce Commission are deemed to be essential and controlling provisions of the contract between shipper and carrier.[208] Therefore, the shipper will be bound by the express exceptions spelled out in the tariff, in the absence of special facts rendering them unjust or unfair. On the other hand, the policy question might well be resolved the other way. It seems more equitable for the carrier to bear the loss, for it is in an excellent position to spread the burden to *all* shippers using the line. Under the present arrangement, the loss is borne ratably by the owners of shipments in the line at the time the loss occurs.

Another common tariff clause provides that the carrier will not receive oil which is involved in litigation, or the ownership of which is encumbered by any lien or charge, unless the shipper furnishes sufficient indemnity to protect the pipe line company. Coupled with this requirement usually is a provision that a tender by the shipper shall be deemed a warranty of title.[209]

In general, the tariff requirements dealing with identity of product shipped, quality of product accepted, and loss in transit appear to facilitate free movement through the lines and they do not act as restrictions upon common-carrier use of the lines.[210]

---

[202] Railroad Co. v. Lockwood, 17 Wall. (U.S.) 357, 21 L.Ed. 627 (1873); Express Co. v. Kountze Brothers, 8 Wall.(U.S.) 342, 19 L.Ed. 457 (1869); Grogan & Mertz v. Adams Express Co., 114 Pa. 523, 60 Am.Rep. 360 (1886).

[203] Jonesboro, Lake City & Eastern R.R. v. Maddy, 157 Ark. 484, 248 S.W. 911 (1923); American Fruit Distributers v. Hines, 55 Cal.App. 377, 203 Pac. 821 (1921); Leavens v. American Express Co., 86 Vt. 342, 85 Atl. 557 (1913).

[204] Werthheimer v. Pennsylvania R.R., 1 Fed. 232 (C.C.S.D.N.Y. 1880); Hall v. Pennsylvania R.R., 1 Fed. 226 (C.C.W.D.Pa. 1880).

[205] American Fruit Distributers v. Hines, 55 Cal.App. 377, 203 Pac. 821 (1921); Southern Ry. v. John T. Barbee & Co., 190 Ky. 63, 226 S.W. 376, 20 A.L.R. 257 (1920).

[206] See note 202 *supra*.

[207] Express Co. v. Kountze Brothers, 8 Wall. (U.S.) 342, 19 L.Ed. 457 (1869); Grogan & Mertz v. Adams Express Co., 114 Pa. 523, 60 Am.Rep. 360 (1886).

[208] Davis v. Henderson, 266 U.S. 92, 45 Sup.Ct. 24, 69 L.Ed. 182 (1924); Davis v. Cornwell, 264 U.S. 560, 44 Sup.Ct. 410, 68 L.Ed. 848 (1924); American Railway Express Co. v. American Trust Co., 47 F.2d 16 (7th Cir. 1931).

[209] Shell Pipe Line Corporation, I.C.C. Tariff No. 294, April 20, 1950, Item No. 15.

[210] Prewitt, *The Operation and Regulation of Crude Oil and Gasoline Pipe Lines,* 56 Q. J. Econ. 177, 188 (1942); *but cf.* Cook, Control of the Petroleum Industry by Major Oil Companies 39 (TNEC Monograph 39, 1941); Comment, 51 Yale L. J. 1338, 1344 n.38 (1942); 9 U. of Chi. L. Rev. 503, 504 n.14 (1942).

5. STORAGE FACILITIES. As a general rule, interstate pipe lines do not
furnish storage at both terminals or along their lines.[211] Pipe line tariffs
frequently provide that oil will not be received unless provision is made
for its prompt acceptance by the consignee at destination.[212] Another common provision calls for separate pipeage agreements with shippers. The
purpose of this clause is to assure the carrier that adequate facilities have
been provided to permit receipt by the carrier and delivery to the consignee in quantities and at pressures satisfactory to the pipe line before
the duty[213] to transport will arise.[214] These provisions have been criticized
by some people who consider them designed to reserve the pipe lines for
private use by their shipper-owners.[215] At this point a distinction must be
made. Undeniably, common carriers are bound to furnish adequate facilities for public service, including proper depots or terminals for the recep-
tion and discharge of freight (and passengers).[216] But the business of a
common carrier is transportation, not storage.[217] Storage of the goods
being transported is a transportation service only to the extent that it is
necessarily incidental to the transportation, and a carrier's duty is co-
extensive with that limitation.[218] Consequently, most pipe lines only main-

[211] H.R. REP. No. 2192, 72d Cong., 2d Sess. LXVIII (1933) ; Prewitt, *supra* note 210, at
186.

[212] *Ibid.;* FTC, REPORT ON PIPE-LINE *T*RANSPORTATION OF PETROLEUM 22, 457, 458
(1916) ; See Service Pipe Line Company, Proposed Rules and Regulations, March 31, 1950,
Item No. 35.

[213] According to the late Professor Hohfeld, a carrier labors under a *liability* until a
member of the public makes a proper application and sufficient tender, at which time a *duty*
of carriage arises. HOHFELD, FUNDAMENTAL LEGAL CONCEPTION 57, 58 (1923). Where the
tariff rules provide for separate pipeage contracts, it would seem that these must be made
before the *duty* would arise.

[214] Emerson, *Salient Characteristics of Petroleum Pipe Line Transportation,* 26 LAND
ECON. 27, 31 (No. 1, 1950) ; Atlantic Pipe Line Company, I.C.C. Tariff No. 84, Aug. 1, 1949,
Item No. 20; Humble Pipe Line Company, I.C.C. Tariff No. 485, Sept. 28, 1949, Item No. 65 ;
Keystone Pipe Line Company, Pa. P.U.C. Tariff No. 16, May 10, 1946, Item No. 30; Phillips
Petroleum Company, I.C.C. Tariff No. 88, Dec. 1, 1949, Item No. 35.

[215] Complaint, p. 38, United States v. American Petroleum Institute, Civil No. 8524,
D. D.C. Sept. 30, 1940; *Hearings before Special Committee Investigating Petroleum Resources
pursuant to S. 36,* 79th Cong., 2d Sess. 559 (1946) ; Prewitt, *supra* note 210, at 186.

[216] Merchants Warehouse Co. v. United States, 283 U.S. 501, 51 Sup.Ct. 505, 75 L.Ed.
1227 (1931) ; Atchison, Topeka & Santa Fe Ry. v. Railroad Comm., 173 Cal. 577, 160 Pac. 828,
2 A.L.R. 975 (1916) ; *error dismissed,* 245 U.S. 638, 38 Sup.Ct. 191, 62 L.Ed. 525 (1918) ; State
v. Republican Valley R.R., 17 Neb. 647, 24 N.W. 329, 52 Am.Rep. 424 (1885).

[217] State v. Southern Pacific Co., 52 La.Ann. 1822, 28 So. 372 (1900) ; Propriety of
Operating Practices—New York Warehousing, 216 I.C.C. 291 (1936) ; Reconsignment and
Storage of Lumber and Shingles, 27 I.C.C. 451 (1913) ; *In re* Demurrage Investigation, 19
I.C.C. 496 (1910) ; see H.R. REP. No. 2192, 72d Cong., 2d Sess. LXVII, LXVIII (1933).

[218] Propriety of Operating Practices—New York Warehousing, 216 I.C.C. 291 (1936) ;
Idem., 198 I.C.C. 134 (1933) ; American Warehousemen's Ass'n v. Inland Waterways Corp.,
188 I.C.C. 13 (1932) ; *TNEC Hearings* 8299.

tain sufficient "working" tankage to receive deliveries from the shipper or connecting carriers. In addition, where local laws[219] or tariffs provide for the service, carriers furnish tankage at destination for the use of the consignee during a specified period of time.[220] Provision is made for a demurrer charge for subsequent delay in accepting delivery from the carrier's tanks at destination.[221]

In judging the merits of pipe line storage rules, we must bear in mind that pipe lines are a transportation agency. Moreover, the movement of fluid through a pipe line is governed by the principle of successive volume displacements, and any restriction in rate of delivery or acceptance can retard the movement of all products in the line, thus reducing the load factor (*ergo* efficiency) of the pipe line.[222] The provisions discussed in the last paragraph are reasonably calculated to maintain uninterrupted flow at high percentages of capacity. It is believed that they do not impose undue hardship on shippers[223] and, therefore, must be considered proper terms for rendering pipe line service.

C. Ratable Taking

A survey of the record discloses sporadic complaints against "pipe line proration,"[224] selective buying,[225] and allegations of non-ratable taking.[226] The circumstances which make possible "pipe line proration" exist where the supply of crude oil available for sale exceeds purchasers' requirements. The practice itself consists in purchasers selecting certain

[219] For example, Rule 5 of Oil & Gas Circular No. 10, Railroad Commission of Texas, provides that pipe lines shall furnish, without additional charge, sufficient storage, such as is incidental and necessary to the transportation of oil, including storage at destination or so near thereto as to be available for prompt delivery to destination point, for five days from the date of offer of delivery at destination.

[220] Phillips Petroleum Company, I.C.C. Tariff No. 88, Dec. 1, 1949, Item No. 30; Humble Pipe Line Company, I.C.C. Tariff No. 448, Sept. 16, 1947, Item No. 10; *cf.* Birge, *Contamination Control in Products Pipe Lines,* THE OIL & GAS JOURNAL, Sept. 20, 1947, p. 291.

[221] These charges vary from ⅛ to one cent per barrel per day delay.

[222] Emerson, *Salient Characteristics of Petroleum Pipe Line Transportation,* 26 LAND. ECON. 27, 31 (No. 1, 1950).

[223] *But cf.* Prewitt, *The Operation and Regulation of Crude Oil and Gasoline Pipe Lines,* 56 Q. J. ECON. 177, 186 (1942).

[224] *E.g.,* Complaint, pp. 35, 36, United States v. American Petroleum Institute, Civil No. 8524, D. D.C., Sept. 30, 1940; *TNEC Hearings* 7561, 7609, 8303; *Hearings before Subcommittee of Committee on Interstate and Foreign Commerce on H.R. 290 & H. R. 7372,* 76th Cong., 3d Sess., Part 4, 1880 (1940) ; SEN. REP. No. 25, 81st Cong., 1st Sess. 20 (1948).

[225] *E.g., TNEC Hearings* 7308, 7562; *Hearings, supra* note 224, Part 3, at 1416, Part 4, at 1880, 1881.

[226] *E.g., Hearings before Special Committee to Study Problems of American Small Business pursuant to S. 20,* 80th Cong., 1st Sess., Part 9, 1069 (1947) ; *TNEC Hearings* 8156, 8158, 8172, 8173; Comment, 51 YALE L. J. 1338, 1344 (1942).

wells to furnish all their requirements, thereby permitting the favored wells to operate at capacity or at "allowable"[227] as the case may be. The wells not selected usually must be shut down for lack of storage capacity, which exposes them to underground drainage by the operative wells. The reason for this discrimination is alleged to be an interest held by purchasers in the selected producing wells. A more logical reason is that convenience favors obtaining crude requirements from those leases already connected to the pipe line, rather than making additional connections. Whatever the reason, the result is discrimination. Selective buying follows essentially the same pattern except that the purchaser discriminates between pools or areas rather than between leases within a pool.

State legislatures have provided a remedy by enacting "common purchaser" statutes which require equitable distribution of purchases within the state.[228] Largely due to the influence of these laws, discriminatory buying practically has ceased.[229] Another factor limiting discrimination is the matter of good business policy. Purchasers know that the neglected field today may well be the source of much-needed crude oil tomorrow. Consequently, they endeavor to avoid discrimination by equitably distributing their purchases, in order to enjoy continuing good relations with the producers in the field.[230] Apart from this development, it is pertinent to observe that the blame for abuse properly should lie at the door of the crude oil *purchaser* and not the pipe line company, which generally acts only as a transporter.[231]

There remains the question of ratable taking by pipe lines. The laws making pipe lines common carriers prohibit carriers from discriminating between shippers by giving any undue preference or advantage to any shipper.[232] Accordingly, tariffs filed with the Interstate Commerce Commission[233] and state regulatory bodies provide that, when tenders of oil

---

[227] The allowable is the limit set by the State conservation authorities.

[228] *E.g.*, 52 OKLA. STAT. § 54 (1941); TEX. CIV. STAT. ANN., art. 6049a § 8 (Vern. 1949).

[229] *Hearings before Special Committee Investigating Petroleum Resources pursuant to S. 36*, 79th Cong., 2d Sess. 80 (1946); *TNEC Hearings* 7308, 7322–7324, 8304; *but cf. Hearings, supra* note 224, Part 3, at 1416.

[230] BALL, THIS FASCINATING OIL BUSINESS 174 (1940).

[231] Reduced Pipe Line Rates and Gathering Charges, 243 I.C.C. 115, 122 (1940); *Hearings, supra* note 226, Part 10, at 1237; *TNEC Hearings* 8303, 8304; H.R. REP. No. 2192, 72d Cong., 2d Sess. XLIII (1933); SEN. DOC. No. 61, 70th Cong., 1st Sess. 8, 101, 105 (1928); BALL, THIS FASCINATING OIL BUSINESS 174 (1940); API, SURVEY 52 (1935); Prewitt, *The Operation and Regulation of Crude Oil and Gasoline Pipe Lines*, 56 Q. J. ECON. 177, 183 n.5 (1942).

[232] *E.g.*, 24 STAT. 380 (1887), as amended, 49 U.S.C. § 3(1) (1946); 52 OKLA. STAT. § 56 (1941); TEX. CIV. STAT. ANN., art. 6045 (Vern, 1949).

or gasoline exceed the capacity of a pipe line, the transportation furnished by the carrier shall be apportioned among all shippers ratably.[234] The charges of non-ratable taking which were raised in the *TNEC* and *Small Business Hearings*[235] consisted of statements that the major pipe lines were loaded to capacity, and that the witnesses believed that independents could not obtain space in the lines.[236] This seems scant evidence upon which to predicate a finding of abusive practices, particularly when the same witness who had raised the point in the *TNEC Hearings*,[237] and other witnesses at the same hearing, testified that no outside shipper had ever tendered a shipment over the lines in question.[238] In fact, the evidence points strongly toward ratable taking practices.[239] In view of this testimony, and the readily available remedy at the hands of the Interstate Commerce Commission or state regulatory bodies, the conclusion seems inevitable that the problem of ratable taking is well under control.[240]

D. Shippers' Use of Pipe Lines

During the course of most debates over availability of major-company owned pipe lines to independent shippers, it is asserted that very few "outside" shipments are being transported by the lines. Thus, in the famous "Splawn Report,"[241] it was noted that in 1931 over 60 percent of the large integrated companies carried no outside oil in their gathering lines, and about one-half of these companies made the same report on their trunk

---

[233] Atlantic Pipe Line Company, I.C.C. Tariff No. 84, Aug. 1, 1949, Item No. 50; Humble Pipe Line Company, I.C.C. Tariff No. 485, Sept. 28, 1949, Item No. 15(c); Shell Pipe Line Corporation, I.C.C. Tariff No. 294, April 20, 1950, Item No. 20.

[234] Humble Pipe Line Company, Local (Texas) Tariff No. 125, Dec. 1, 1949, Item No. 16; Phillips Pipe Line Company, Oklahoma Tariff No. 2, Aug. 15, 1949, Item No. 35; Shell Pipe Line Corporation, Texas Local Tariff No. 110, Jan. 30, 1950, Item No. 16.

[235] See note 226 *supra*.

[236] One exception to this statement appears in *TNEC Hearings* 8158, but the allusion there was to pipe line operation in 1904.

[237] *TNEC Hearings* 8179.

[238] *TNEC Hearings* 9758.

[239] *E.g., Hearings, supra* note 226, Part 10, at 1235, 1251; *Hearings before Special Committee Investigating Petroleum Resources pursuant to S. 36,* 79th Cong., 2d Sess. 80 (1946); *TNEC Hearings* 8304, 9585, 8596; FARISH & PEW, REVIEW AND CRITICISM ON BEHALF OF STANDARD OIL CO. (N.J.) AND SUN OIL CO. OF MONOGRAPH NO. 39 WITH REJOINDER BY MONOGRAPH AUTHOR 24 (TNEC Monograph 39–A, 1941); Emerson, *Salient Characteristics of Petroleum Pipe Line Transportation,* 26 LAND ECON. 27, 31 (No. 1, 1950).

[240] In fact, some states require pipe lines to refuse to accept shipments of oil produced in violation of state conservation laws, and hold the companies responsible for knowing the quotas for each district. See TEX. CIV. STAT. ANN. art. 6049a § 8a (Vern. 1949).

[241] H.R. REP. No. 2192, 72d Cong., 2d Sess. (1933).

lines.[242] The remaining 40 percent served only 129 shippers.[243] The Interstate Commerce Commission found that one to six non-affiliated shippers were served in 1935 by twenty out of thirty-seven respondent pipe line companies.[244] In 1936, the Independent Petroleum Association made a study of oil transported by major pipe line companies for shippers having no interest in the line.[245] The Association found that ten companies transported an average of only 8.73 percent of the total oil transported from non-affiliated companies, and three of the pipe lines reported that they operated only as plant facilities, carrying no outside oil.[246]

This subject again was considered in the *TNEC Hearings*. The compilation of the statistics obtained from industry's answers to the Committee's questionaires[247] revealed that, for the period 1929–1938, less than 10 percent of the crude oil,[248] and less than 20 percent of the gasoline transported by pipe lines belonged to non-affiliated shippers.[249] During the period of fuel "shortage" in 1947, the matter was treated again, this time by the "Wherry" Committee.[250] The testimony tended to show an increase in outside use of pipe lines. For example, Sohio Pipe Line transported more oil for non-affiliated shippers than it carried for its own account during the period 1941–1946.[251] Ajax Pipe Line devoted slightly less than half of its service to outsiders.[252] Stanolind Pipeline Company (now Service Pipe Line Company) was somewhat lower, transporting 68 percent for its par-

[242] *Id.* at LXIII. Only 5.1 percent of the gathering lines, and ten percent of the trunk lines carried over fifty percent of outside oil. *Ibid.*

[243] Prewitt, *The Operation and Regulation of Crude Oil and Gasoline Pipe Lines*, 56 Q. J. ECON. 177, 182 (1942).

[244] Reduced Pipe Line Rates and Gathering Charges, 243 I.C.C. 115, 121 (1940). Seven of the carriers served from ten to thirty-seven shippers. The remaining ten pipe lines did not carry outside oil. *Ibid.*

[245] INDEPENDENT PETROLEUM ASSOCIATION OF AMERICA, PIPE-LINES-IMPORTS-PRICES 10 (1938), cited in COOK, CONTROL OF THE PETROLEUM INDUSTRY BY MAJOR OIL COMPANIES 23, 24 (TNEC Monograph 39, 1941).

[246]. *Ibid.*

[247] The questionnaire is reproduced in *TNEC Hearings* 7426–7434.

[248] *TNEC Hearings* 7724. The president of Sun Oil Company, Mr. J. Howard Pew, testified that eighty-four percent of the oil carried by Sun's crude lines was their own oil. Substantially all of the sixteen percent balance was transported for the accounts of major integrated companies. *Id.* at 7200.

[249] *TNEC Hearings* 7728. Sun Oil Company's figures were 91.2 percent of own gasoline, the balance divided between three major companies. *Id.* at 7200, 7728. See list of outside shippers. *Id.* at 8115–8118.

[250] *Hearings before Special Committee to Study Problems of American Small Business pursuant to S. 20*, 80th Cong., 1st Sess. (1947).

[251] *Id.*, Part 10, at 1248, 1249.

[252] 1945: deliveries to affiliates—58.64%, deliveries to non-affiliates—41.36%; 1946: affiliates—50.13%, non-affiliates—49.87%; first half of 1947: affiliates—51.83%, non-affiliates —48.17%. Id., Part 10, at 1252.

ent, Standard Oil Company (Ind.), and 32 percent for 15 other shippers.[253] No percentages were given for Ohio Oil Company's pipe line which had twenty-four shippers,[254] or for the Great Lakes Pipe Line Company, which had forty-seven shippers.[255] However, Shell's products lines from Wood River, Illinois, to East Chicago and Columbus, Ohio, were operated as plant facilities and did not transport outside shipments except over part of the system on a special deal with three majors.[256]

Looking at the evidence, it seems that there has been an increase in the amount of outside use of major company pipe lines within the past eight years. However, the percentage of outside shipments remains significantly lower than that which ordinarily would be expected of a transportation service rendered as legal common carriage. This fact has been asserted to be logically compelling proof that pipe lines companies have not functioned as common carriers, but have been operated in such a manner as to deny independents use of the lines.[257] But such reasoning transcends, rather than follows, logic. The hiatus in the process is the absence of curiosity concerning the reasons *why* outside shipments are so minute.

Let us investigate the crude line situation. Due to the fact that crude oil must be refined before it can be marketed to the consuming public,[258] there are only three groups of potential shippers: refiners, purchasing companies affiliated with refiners, and crude oil producers. Eliminating the major companies and their affiliated purchasing organizations, there remain only independent refiners and independent producers. The great majority of independent refiners are located in the producing areas[259] and have their own gathering lines or short pipe lines.[260] Thus they are at the wrong end of the line and have little need to use the common carrier crude lines. But how about the few independent refiners located at tidewater or in populous areas, who purchase crude in the field and need transportation to their

---

253 *Id.,* Part 10, at 1263.

254 *Id.,* Part 10, at 1235, 1236.

255 *Id.,* Part 10, at 1259, 1260.

256 *Id.,* Part 10, at 1256, 1257.

257 COOK, CONTROL OF THE PETROLEUM INDUSTRY BY MAJOR OIL COMPANIES 23 (TNEC Monograph 39, 1941); Prewitt, *The Operation and Regulation of Crude Oil and Gasoline Pipe Lines,* 56 Q. J. ECON. 177, 182 (1942); Comment, 51 YALE L. J. 1338, 1340–1341 (1942); *but cf.* HAMILTON *et al.,* PRICE AND PRICE POLICIES 150 (1938).

258 H.R. Doc. No. 812, 59th Cong., 1st Sess. 36 (1906); 40 CONG. REC. 9254 (1906); KEMNITZER, REBIRTH OF MONOPOLY 6, 65 (1938); Black, *Oil Pipe Line Divorcement by Litigation and Legislation,* 25 CORN. L. Q. 510, 526 (1940).

259 *Hearings before Special Committee Investigating Petroleum Resources pursuant to S. 36,* 79th Cong., 2d Sess. 77, 197 (1946); *TNEC Hearings* 7201, 8156–8159, 8544–8545; ROSTOW, A NATIONAL POLICY FOR THE OIL INDUSTRY 58, 67 (1948); COOK, *op. cit. supra* note 257, at 21; Comment, 51 YALE L. J. 1338, 1341 (1942).

260 *TNEC Hearings* 8332, 8616–8618, 9708; COOK, *op. cit. supra* note 257, at 21.

refineries? Why don't they use the common carrier lines? In the first place, they face a transportation time lag and a tie-up of capital. Because movement through a pipe line consists of a continuous series of successive volume displacements, the line must be full at all times before a barrel taken in the line can force a barrel out of the line. This line fill-up, termed "inventory," usually consists of undelivered tenders. So when our independent refiner seeks to move his crude from the field to his refinery, he must first supply his portion of the line fill. For example, assume that he was able to close a deal for 2000 barrels daily production in East Texas which he desires to be transported to his refinery in Michigan. Before he can receive the first 2000 barrel delivery at his refinery he must deliver to the pipe line an amount of oil equal to his daily run times the number of days required for the oil to move through the line. Thus, if it takes 15 days from East Texas to his receiving point at Earhart Station, Michigan, he must deliver 30,000 barrels for line fill. He has a capital investment tied up in 30,000 barrels of crude oil until he ceases shipment and another shipper's line fill permits delivery of his balance. In addition to the money involved, he has a time lag. Pipe lines must schedule ahead in order to keep their lines full at all times. Therefore, thirty days advance notice is due the pipe line to permit scheduling of the shipment. The earliest possible delivery date would be after thirty days notice plus the transportation time of fifteen days, or forty-five days. It could easily be longer.

Another problem confronting our independent refiner was mentioned in the discussion of contamination. If his crude has a higher gravity than the common stream he stands to lose the value of the resulting drop in gravity. If he desires segregated shipment, then he must meet the pipe line's minimum shipment requirements.

A fourth problem associated with the process of buying in the field and tendering to a pipe line is that of division payments to all producing and royalty interests. This involves some very complicated bookkeeping, particularly where communitized leases are involved.

Because of these main problems, and other incidental aspects such as scheduling, storage, and making up the shipments, most independent refiners prefer to sell their oil in the field and buy at delivery points. In normal times, this represents an advantage to them, for they are guaranteed delivery of a specified amount at a certain time, the bookkeeping is simple, and frequently the large companies are very cooperative where sudden changes of conditions render it impossible for the small refiners to receive the specified amount during a certain period. It is only during periods of shortage that independent refiners are unable to arrange for such purchases, and at that time they must go out and "beat the bushes" for crude. This very situation occurred in 1947, which probably accounts for the increase in outside use of the lines. It is pertinent to note that those refiners who actually were able to secure production and were in a position to utilize the large crude lines, found the lines generally observing the rules of common carriage.[261] All the lines were crowded to capacity during this shortage,[262] and this fact may have deterred some outside use. The pipe lines must take ratably, but where an independent tries to tender 800 barrels per day to a pipe line crammed full at 400,000 barrels per day, he is going to be discouraged, to say the least. The trouble involved in prorating all the large shipments just to squeeze in the 800 barrels is prohibitive.

Another factor deterring independent use of the common carrier crude lines is that refineries are not always located sufficiently close to the lines to utilize them. An independent refiner testified before the Wherry Committee in 1947 that the reason for a shut-down of his refinery at Fall City, Nebraska, was not unavailability of Stanolind's pipe line but the prohibitive rail rate for transshipment from Stanolind's terminal at Washington, Kansas, to his refinery.[263]

This brings us to the position of the producer. It may be stated categorically that the producer has no market at the refinery, and prefers to sell in the field.[264] There are several reasons for this. Primarily, because the crude must be refined before it is merchantable,[265] the producer ultimately must sell to a refiner or to his agent. The bargaining position of the producer would be no better, and possibly not as good, if he sought to sell the crude at the refinery gates. Moreover, his capital would be tied up during the period he was looking for a purchaser, which would preclude further investment in producing properties until he had consummated the

---

[261] *Hearings before Special Committee to Study Problems of American Small Business pursuant to S. 20,* 80th Cong., 1st Sess., Part 9, 1094, 1096, Part 10, 1237, 1251, 1264, 1265, 1271, 1272 (1947). The prime example of this occurred in Cotton County, Oklahoma, where independent shippers used premium payments to "steal connections" from one of the major purchasing companies and then tendered that same oil to the pipe line company (an affiliate of the purchasing company) which ran the oil without a murmur.

[262] *Hearings before Special Committee to Study Problems of American Small Business pursuant to S. 20,* 80th Cong., 1st Sess., Part 9, 1069, 1098, 1103, 1151, Part 10, 1244, 1245 (1947).

[263] *Hearings, supra* note 262, Part 9, at 1094–1096.

[264] Reduced Pipe Line Rates and Gathering Charges, 243 I.C.C. 115, 122, 140 (1940); *TNEC Hearings* 7309, 8343–8344; 40 Cong. Rec. 9253, 9254 (1906); Sen. Rep. No. 25, 81st Cong., 1st Sess. 20 (1949); Farish & Pew, Review and Criticism on Behalf of Standard Oil Co. (N.J.) and Sun Oil Co. of Monograph No. 39 with Rejoinder by Monograph Author 27, 32 (TNEC Monograph 39–A, 1941); Hamilton *et al.,* Price and Price Policies 151 (1938); *but cf.* Complaint, p. 37, United States v. American Petroleum Institute, Civil No. 8524, D. D.C., Sept. 30, 1940.

[265] See note 258 *supra.*

sale.[266] He must face the other problems discussed above in connection with independent refiners' use of pipe lines. Thus, convenience and security have been largely instrumental in the creation of the present structure whereby the producer sells in the field. The producer is assured of reasonably prompt pipe line connections in new fields, prompt connections to all properties within fields, a steady and continuous market, and ratable takings.[267]

It is axiomatic that the independent refiner cannot use a gasoline pipe line without having marketing facilities at the destination.[268] This creates one limitation on outside use of major gasoline lines. The main restriction, however, seems to be that most gasoline lines have been built as plant facilities and run from the refinery of the shipper-owner directly to the market with no thought of any connections to outside shippers.[269] This is true also of independent products lines.[270] Some of these lines bluntly call themselves "plant facilities" and refuse even to file valuation reports with the Interstate Commerce Commission, much less file tariffs or accept outside shipments. But even where the products lines are operated as common carriers, there still remains the problem of getting to and from the pipe lines. We have already seen that transshipment costs may be prohibitive.[271]

Summarizing the evidence, the limited extent of outside shippers' use of crude lines is due largely to abuses committed many years ago when the present structure of the petroleum industry was in its early formative period. It does not denote present default in performance of common carrier duties. Insofar as the products lines are concerned, many continue to be operated as private lines. But the legality of this practice has not been finally determined. The present case of *Champlin Refining Company v. United States*[272] appears to support the private carrier concept but the antitrust ramifications remain unresolved.[273]

[266] For discussion of a producer's desire to avoid tie-up of assets, see *TNEC Hearings* 8343–8344.

[267] *Hearings before Special Committee Investigating Petroleum Resources pursuant to S. 36,* 79th Cong., 2d Sess. 80 (1946).

[268] *TNEC Hearings* 7177, 8159, 8180, 8545.

[269] Exceptions to this statement are the Great Lakes Pipe Line and the Plantation Pipe Line, which were constructed as common carriers.

[270] The classic example is Champlin's 6-inch line from Enid, Oklahoma, to Rock Rapids, Iowa. This line has no physical connection for tie-in anywhere but at Champlin's Enid refinery and its three terminals along the line.

[271] See note 263 *supra*, and related textual material.

[272] 71 Sup.Ct. 715 (1951).

[273] The legal questions will be discussed in Part II of this book. The economic aspect will be treated in the section immediately following this paragraph.

II. INEQUALITIES OF COMPETITION ENGENDERED BY MAJOR COMPANY PIPE LINE OWNERSHIP

The great bulk of the nation's crude supply is produced in the southwestern states of Texas, Oklahoma, Arkansas, Louisiana, and New Mexico.[274] The greatest gasoline consumption is concentrated along the Atlantic Coast and in the North Central states.[275] Some of the needs of the North Central states can be supplied by the Rocky Mountain states, and California can furnish part of the Atlantic Coast requirements,[276] but it is obvious that the Southwestern states must furnish most of the crude oil and gasoline used in the Atlantic coastal states and a substantial part of that required by the North Central states. The great distances separating the producing fields from the consuming areas make transportation vitally important.[277]

Shortly after pipe lines were introduced in 1865, they demonstrated their superior efficiency and economy as a means of transporting crude oil to the refinery.[278] By 1937, crude lines had taken the bulk of the traffic away from the railroads.[279] In 1940 their tariff rates were roughly one-third the rail rates.[280] Since that time, crude line rates have decreased and rail rates have increased[281] to the extent that crude pipe lines and rail

[274] *TNEC Hearings* 7704, 7772; Rostow, A National Policy for the Oil Industry 9 (1948); The Petroleum Engineer, The Petroleum Data Book, E–43 to E–61 (1947); Comment, 51 Yale L. J. 1338, 1339 (1942). Kansas is close enough to this area to make the point even stronger. Illinois, after a boom culminating in 10.9 percent of American production in 1940, has declined rapidly due to wide-open production methods.

[275] *TNEC Hearings,* 7704, 7772; Rostow, A National Policy for the Oil Industry 9 (1948); The Petroleum Engineer, The Petroleum Data Book I–63 (1947); Comment, 51 Yale L. J. 1338, 1339.

[276] Although California ranks second highest in individual state crude production it is also one if the greatest consuming states. Moreover, it is the chief supplier for the Pacific Coast marketing area, consisting of California, Washington, Oregon, Arizona, Nevada and a small section of western Idaho. This "regional sub-market area" is isolated by transportation costs. Through a practice of price discrimination, California does maintain an export balance, but most of this goes to Pacific Ocean markets. Occasionally, when Gulf Coast crude is extremely high, California crude will appear in Atlantic Coast markets. See 1 Bain, The Economics of the Pacific Coast Petroleum Industry 1–24 (1944).

[277] *TNEC Hearings* 8675, 9352.

[278] H.R. Rep. No. 2192, 72d Cong., 2d Sess. LXXII (1933); Sen. Doc. 61, 70th Cong., 1st Sess. 33 (1928); FTC, Report on Pipe-Line Transportation of Petroleum XXV, XXVI, 12 (1916).

[279] *TNEC Hearings* 8274, 8592, 8602.

[280] Reduced Pipe Line Rates and Gathering Charges, 243 I.C.C. 115, 124 (1940); see Sen. Rep. No. 25, 81st Cong., 1st Sess. 11, 20 (1949); Pogue, *Economics of the Petroleum Industry* in Elements of the Petroleum Industry 453, 476 (1940); Comment, 51 Yale L. J. 1338, 1339 (1942).

[281] Reduced Pipe Line Rates and Gathering Charges, 272 I.C.C. 375, 380 (1948); Sen. Rep. No. 25, 81st Cong., 1st Sess. 20 (1949).

transportation can not even be considered competitive.[282] The products lines, although starting as late as 1931, quickly duplicated the record of the crude lines.[283] The situation had become so clear-cut by 1944 that the railroads admitted that they could not compete on equal terms with either crude or refined products lines.[284] It is apparent that free access to pipe lines is a competitive necessity.[285]

Earlier in this book the concentration of pipe line ownership in the hands of twenty-two "majors" was discussed.[286] The ability of these companies to ship through their own lines creates a distinct competitive advantage over independent companies attempting to reach the same marketing areas. The proponents of pipe line divorcement claim that this shipper-owner relationship is exactly the same as the old coal-railroad tie-up which prompted the passage of the Commodities Clause of the Hepburn Act,[287] making it unlawful for any railroad company to transport in interstate or foreign commerce any commodity (except timber and its products, and that used in the business of carriage) which the railroad had made or in which it had any interest.[288] The seriousness of this charge and the tenacity displayed by its advocates[289] make imperative its detailed examination.

In the early days of the industry, the Standard Oil Trust monopolized[290] pipe line transportation,[291] and contracted with the railroads to

[282] See notes 33–34 *supra;* Petroleum Rail Shippers' Ass'n v. Alton & Southern R.R., 243 I.C.C. 589, 655 (1941); FTC, Report on Pipe Line Transportation of Petroleum 465 (1916); Pogue, *supra* note 280, at 476; *cf.* Williams, *The ICC and the Regulation of Intercarrier Competition,* 63 Harv. L. Rev. 1349 n.1 (1950).

[283] See note 35 *supra;* Petroleum Rail Shippers' Ass'n v. Alton & Southern R.R., 243 I.C.C. 589, 601, 605, 626, 674 (1941); Comment, 51 Yale L. J. 1338, 1339 (1942).

[284] Ass'n of American Railroads, Report by Subcommittee on Pipe Line Transport 2 (1949).

[285] FTC, Report on Pipe-Line Transportation of Petroleum 466 (1916); Cook, Control of the Petroleum Industry by Major Oil Companies 19–23 (TNEC Monograph 39, 1941); Prewitt, *The Operation and Regulation of Crude Oil and Gasoline Pipe Lines,* 56 Q. J. Econ. 177, 179 (1942); Comment, 51 Yale L. J. 1338, 1347 (1942).

[286] See notes 37–39 *supra* and related textual material.

[287] 34 Stat. 585 (1906), 49 U.S.C. § 1(8) (1946).

[288] *TNEC Hearings* 7377; Sen. Rep. No. 25, 81st Cong., 1st Sess. 20 (1949). Rostow, A National Policy for the Oil Industry 63 (1948); Wilcox, Competition and Monopoly in American Industry 89 (TNEC Monograph 21, 1940); Kemnitzer, Rebirth of Monopoly 90 (1938); Black, *Oil Pipe Line Divorcement by Litigation and Legislation,* 25 Corn. L. Q. 510 (1940) *passim.*

[289] See note 4 *supra* for a brief resumé of their efforts.

[290] A deliberate effort has been made up to this point to use the word "monopoly" only in the generic sense. It exists when a single seller controls the entire supply of a commodity or service. Wilcox, Competition and Monopoly in American Industry 9 (TNEC Monograph 21, 1940). It will be necessary to plunge into the realm of economic concepts in the section

maintain rail rates at a high level,[292] "rebating" a substantial portion to Standard.[293] The combination of technological and contractural advantages enabled Standard Oil Company to deliver Pennsylvania crude oil to New York for ten cents a barrel, whereas its competitors were charged forty-five cents.[294] The resulting differential was so large that it made Standard Oil Company master of the oil fields. This economic duress permitted Standard to dictate the crude oil purchase price.[295] Later, the collusive agreements between the Standard Oil Company and the railroads were stricken down, and the differential was lowered. But the leverage still was so great that pressure was applied to Congress to open up the pipe lines to independent shippers. This movement culminated in the "oil amendment" of the Hepburn Act, which impressed common carrier status on pipe lines engaged in interstate commerce.[296] After a preliminary skirmish with the Interstate Commerce Commission to avoid the impact of the Hepburn Act,[297] the large companies filed tariffs with the Commission and transported outside oil. However, the early rates tended to match the rail rates,[298] so the immediate effect of making pipe lines common carriers was only a Pyrrhic victory for the independent.[299]

devoted to discussion of monopoly in the oil industry, but until that time an attempt will be made to avoid this additional complication.

[291] The Pipe Line Cases, 234 U.S. 548, 34 Sup.Ct. 956, 58 L.Ed. 1459 (1914).

[292] Handy v. Cleveland & Marietta R.R., 31 Fed. 689 (C.C.S.D.Ohio 1887); 21 Cong. Rec. 2457 (1890); United States Industrial Commission, Preliminary Report on Trusts and Industrial Combinations, Vol. 1, pp. 663–667, cited by Beard, Regulation of Pipe Lines as Common Carriers 14 (1941).

[293] Standard Oil Company of New Jersey v. United States, 221 U.S. 1, 42–43, 31 Sup.Ct. 502, 509, 55 L.Ed. 619, 638 (1911); Handy v. Cleveland & Marietta R.R., 31 Fed. 689 (C.C. S.D.Ohio) 1887); 21 Cong. Rec. 2457 (1890); Laidler, Concentration of Control in American Industry 16 (1931); Stocking, The Oil Industry and the Competitive System 24 (1925); Tarbell, The History of the Standard Oil Company cc. 2, 3, 11 (1904); Black, *Oil Pipe Line Divorcement by Litigation and Legislation,* 25 Corn. L. Q. 510, 526 (1940).

[294] See note 292 *supra.*

[295] See note 291 *supra.*

[296] 34 Stat. 584 (1906), 49 U.S.C. § 1 (1946). The development of pipe line common carrier status under the Hepburn Act will be treated in Part II of this book. It is predicted that those products lines which attain a position in the seller's market comparable to that held in the buyer's market by the large lines in the *Pipe Line Cases* also will be declared common carriers by the court. See Whitesel, *Recent Federal Regulation of the Petroleum Pipe Line as a Common Carrier,* 32 Corn. L. Q. 337, 348–349 (1947).

[297] In the Matter of Pipe Lines, 24 I.C.C. 1 (1912); Prairie Oil and Gas Co. v. United States, 204 Fed. 798 (Comm.Ct. 1913); The Pipe Line Cases, 234 U.S. 548, 34 Sup.Ct. 956, 58 L.Ed. 1459 (1914).

[298] Reduced Pipe Line Rates and Gathering Charges, 243 I.C.C. 115, 124 (1940). See discussion of prohibitive rates *supra.*

[299] Black, *Oil Pipe Line Divorcement by Litigation and Legislation,* 25 Corn. L. Q. 510 1940; see also Rostow, A National Policy for the Oil Industry 58, 59 (1948).

The basic fact is that until pipe line tariffs provide for "cost rates," or the lines are completely divorced, the shipper-owners will realize *some* competitive advantage over outside shippers to the extent of the difference btween the cost and the rate.[300] The reason for this is that shipper-owners necessarily ship at cost,[301] whether the line is operated as a department of the corporate shipper,[302] as a wholly-owned subsidiary,[303] or as a joint adventure,[304] while outside shippers must pay the tariff rate. In addition to this differential, shipper-owners obtain a further advantage by realizing a profit for carrying their competitors' goods.[305] During the early formulative period of petroleum industry development, the tremendous competitive differential in the transportation phase enabled the large companies possessing extensive pipe line systems to locate their refineries near tidewater or large marketing areas, while the smaller outfits were forced to construct their plants near the producing fields.[306]

[300] See notes 74–82 *supra*, EDWARDS, MAINTAINING COMPETITION 172–173 (1949). Thus in Complaint, p. 7, United States v. Phillips Petroleum Company and Phillips Pipe Line Company, Civil No. 182, D. Del., Sept. 30, 1940, it was alleged that this amounted to 1.4 cents per gallon on shipments from Borger, Texas, to Kansas City, Kansas, and 1.3 cents per gallon on shipments from Borger to East St. Louis. These sums represent approximately twenty-five percent of the refinery value of such gasoline. On shipments from Tulsa, Oklahoma, to Kansas City, Kansas; Des Moines, Iowa; Omaha, Nebraska; Chicago, Illinois; and Minneapolis, Minnesota, the differentials were alleged to be 1.4 cents, 1.6 cents, 1.45 cents, 1.3 cents, and 1.75 cents, respectively, per gallon. These sums represent approximately thirty percent of the refinery value of such gasoline. Complaint, p. 11, United States v. Great Lakes Pipe Line Company, Civil No. 183, D. Del., Sept. 30, 1940. An analysis of some of the Interstate Commerce Commission data for 1947 shows that the average *cost* for eight large crude trunk lines was about 2⅜ cents per barrel per 100 miles while the tariff rate was about 4⅛ cents per barrel per 100 miles. For seven of the large products lines, the *cost* was about 4⅜ cents per barrel per 100 miles and the *rate* was 7½ cents per barrel per 100 miles. Emerson, *Salient Characteristics of Petroleum Pipe Line Transportation*, 26 LAND ECON. 27, 32 (No. 1, 1950).

[301] *TNEC Hearings* 7234, 8167–8168, 8290, 9716, 9757; H.R. REP. No. 2192, 72d Cong., 2d Sess. LXXII (1933); Black, *Oil Pipe Line Divorcement by Litigation and Legislation*, 25 CORN. L. Q. 510, 512–513 (1940); Comment, 51 YALE L. J. 1338, 1341 (1942); 9 U. OF CHI. L. REV. 503, 504 (1942); *but cf.* Adelman, *Integration and Antitrust Policy*, 63 HARV. L. REV. 27, 42 (1949); Hale, *Vertical Integration: Impact of the Antitrust Laws Upon Combinations of Successive Stages of Production and Distribution*, 49 COL. L. REV. 921, 937–938 (1949); see note 317 *infra*.

[302] Complaint, p. 10, United States v. Phillips Petroleum Company and Phillips Pipe Line Company, Civil No. 182, D. Del., Sept. 30, 1940.

[303] Complaint, pp. 4–5, United States v. Standard Oil Company (Ind.), Civil No. 201, N.D. Ind., Sept. 30, 1940.

[304] Complaint, pp. 10–11, United States v. Great Lakes Pipe Line Company, Civil No. 183, D. Del., Sept. 30, 1940.

[305] SEN. REP. No. 25, 81st Cong., 1st Sess. 20 (1949); EDWARDS, MAINTAINING COMPETITION 196 (1949); ROSTOW, A NATIONAL POLICY FOR THE OIL INDUSTRY 63 (1948); BEARD, REGULATION OF PIPE LINES AS COMMON CARRIERS 82, 111 (1941); Comment, 51 YALE L. J. 1338, 1341 (1942); 9 U. OF CHI. L. REV. 503, 505 (1942).

The monopolistic potential[307] created by an extreme spread between pipe line costs and tariff rates was brought to the attention of the Interstate Commerce Commission during the hearings in the *Reduced Pipe Line Rates* case.[308] The cost-rate differential was discussed at several points during the *TNEC Hearings*. The members of the Committee from the Department of Justice[309] and the Federal Trade Commission[310] felt that payment by the carrier to the shipper-owner of *any part* of the difference between cost and tariff rate constituted a rebate (on shipper-owner movements) or a draw-back (on outside shipments).[311] Industry's spokesmen agreed that exorbitant rates created an unfair advantage[312] but insisted that a reasonable rate would not create an unfair advantage because the independent shipper would be availing himself of the benefits of the shipper-owner's capital to do more business on less capital than he could have done if he had constructed his own line.[313]

---

306 *TNEC Hearings* 7201, 8157–8159; FTC, REPORT ON PIPE-LINE TRANSPORTATION OF PETROLEUM XXXI (1916); ROSTOW, A NATIONAL POLICY FOR THE OIL INDUSTRY 58 (1948); COOK, CONTROL OF THE PETROLEUM INDUSTRY BY MAJOR OIL COMPANIES 20 (TNEC Monograph 39, 1941); HAMILTON *et al.*, PRICE AND POLICIES 147, 151 (1938); KEMNITZER, REBIRTH OF MONOPOLY 80 (1938). This accounts for the situation described in text at note 259 *supra*.

307 "It is obvious that no more powerful instrument of monopoly could be used than an advantage in the cost of transportation." Swift & Co. v. United States, 196 U.C. 375, 402, 25 Sup.Ct. 276, 281–282, 49 L.Ed. 518, 527 (1905); *cf.* Meeker & Co. v. Lehigh Valley R.R., 21 I.C.C. 129 (1911); Coxe Brothers & Co. v. Lehigh Valley R.R., 4 I.C.C. 535 (1891).

308 "The margin between the costs of pipe line transportation and the published rates must be narrowed, or else those refiners who do not own pipe lines will be forced out of existence." Joint brief filed by The Standard Oil Co. (Ohio) and National Refining Company, Reduced Pipe Line Rates and Gathering Charges, 243 I.C.C. 115 (1940), cited in COOK, CONTROL OF THE PETROLEUM INDUSTRY BY MAJOR OIL COMPANIES 22 (TNEC Monograph 39, 1941).

309 *TNEC Hearings,* 7235–7236 (Wendell Berge), 7203–7204, 7256–7257 (F. B. Berquist), 7251–7352 (Hugh B. Cox).

310 *TNEC Hearings* 7233–7234, 7256–7257, 7261–7262, 8166–8168 (Willis J. Ballinger).

311 This feeling was the basis for the three complaints (see notes 302–304) which subsequently were filed under the Elkins Act. 32 STAT. 847–848 (1903), as amended, 34 STAT. 587–589 (1906), 49 U.S.C. § 41 (3) (1946). It is widely held among government officials and writers. *E.g.*, SEN. REP. No. 25, 81st Cong., 1st Sess. 21 (1949); ROSTOW, A NATIONAL POLICY FOR THE OIL INDUSTRY 63 (1948); BEARD, REGULATION OF PIPE LINES AS COMMON CARRIERS 110–111 (1941); Prewitt, *The Operation and Regulation of Crude Oil and Gasoline Pipe Lines,* 56 Q. J. ECON. 177, 200 (1942); Black, *Oil Pipe Line Divorcement by Litigation and Legislation,* 25 CORN. L. Q. 510 (1940) *passim;* Comment, 51 YALE L. J. 1338, 1351 (1942).

312 *TNEC Hearings* 7233–7234, 7251–7253, 7256, 7261–7262 (J. Howard Pew), 8289–8290 (Fayette B. Dow).

313 *TNEC Hearings,* 7251–7253, 7256, 7261–7262. This statement is true only up to the point where large-scale movement would pay-out a new line. However, it is valid for our purposes, because the shipments made by the independent refiner do not reach this magnitude. Obviously, if they did, he would build his own line. *Cf.* Stocking, Book Review, 1 VAND. L. REV. 490, 492 (1948).

At first blush, the principle of equality among shippers[314] appears to clash with the common carrier's constitutional right to a reasonable rate of return upon the value of his property used to render the carriage.[315] But "equality" under the Interstate Commerce Act and the Elkins Act does not mean equalization of fortune, opportunity or abilities.[316] Thus, a "fair and reasonable" rate charged an outside shipper includes operating expense, overhead, depreciation, taxes, and a *reasonable return on investment*.[317] Differences of opinion exist on what constitutes a reasonable return.[318] However, the Interstate Commerce Commission has primary jurisdiction over the reasonableness of returns,[319] and those approved by the Commission are deemed presumptively fair.[320] Conceding that they are, a

[314] New York, New Haven & Hartford R.R. v. Interstate Commerce Commission, 200 U.S. 361, 26 Sup.Ct. 272, 50 L.Ed. 515 (1906) ; *cf.* Louisville & Nashville R.R. v. Mottley, 219 U.S. 467, 31 Sup.Ct. 265, 55 L.Ed. 297 (1911) ; Armour Packing Co. v. United States, 209 U.S. 56, 28 Sup.Ct. 428, 52 L.Ed. 681 (1908) ; 3–B SHARFMAN, THE INTERSTATE COMMERCE COMMISSION 359–370 (1941) ; Black, *Oil Pipe Line Divorcement by Litigation and Legislation*, 25 CORN. L. Q. 510, 518 (1940) ; 9 U. OF CHI. L. REV. 503, 505 (1942).

[315] Denver Union Stock Yard Co. v. United States, 304 U.S. 470, 58 Sup.Ct. 990, 82 L.Ed. 1469 (1938) ; Vandalia R.R. v. Schnull, 255 U.S. 113, 41 Sup.Ct. 324, 65 L.Ed. 539 (1921) ; Northern Pacific Ry. v. North Dakota, 236 U.S. 585, 35 Sup.Ct. 429, 59 L.Ed. 735 (1915) ; The Minnesota Rate Cases, 230 U.S. 352, 33 Sup.Ct. 729, 57 L.Ed. 1511 (1913) ; Willcox v. Consolidated Gas Co., 212 U.S. 19, 29 Sup.Ct. 192, 53 L.Ed. 382 (1909).

[316] Ellis v. Interstate Commerce Commission, 237 U.S. 434, 445, 35 Sup.Ct. 645, 647, 59 L.Ed. 1036, 1041 (1915) ; Interstate Commerce Commission v. Diffenbaugh, 222 U.S. 42, 46, 32 Sup.Ct. 22, 24, 56 L.Ed. 83, 87 (1911) ; Penn Refining Co. v. Western New York & Pennsylvania R.R., 208 U.S. 208, 221, 28 Sup.Ct. 268, 273, 52 L.Ed. 456, 462 (1908) ; 9 U. OF CHI L. REV. 503, 506; *but cf.* Assigned Car Cases, 774 U.S. 564, 583, 47 Sup.Ct. 727, 734, 71 L.Ed. 1204, 1217 (1927).

[317] Minnelusa Oil Corp. v. Continental Pipe Line Co., 258 I.C.C. 41, 57 (1944) ; Petroleum Rail Shippers' Ass'n v. Alton & Southern R.R., 243 I.C.C. 589, 663 (1941) ; Reduced Pipe Line Rates and Gathering Charges, 243 I.C.C. 115, 142–144 (1940) ; *TNEC Hearings* 7235, 7252, 8166–8168; Adelman, *Integration and Antitrust Policy*, 63 HARV. L. REV. 27, 42 (1949). Another way of stating this would be to say that the shipper-owner's "cost" would include a reasonable return on his investment. *TNEC Hearings* 7235, 7252; Adelman, *supra*, at 42 ; Hale *supra* note 301, at 938; Note, 58 YALE L. J. 969, 978 (1949).

[318] United States v. Atlantic Refining Co., Civil No. 14060, D. D.C., Dec. 23, 1941 (7%) ; Petroleum Rail Shippers' Ass'n v. Alton & Southern R.R., 243 I.C.C. 589, 663 (1941) (10% on products lines) ; Reduced Pipe Line Rates and Gathering Charges, 243 I.C.C. 115, 142 (1940) (8% on crude lines) ; *TNEC Hearings* 7253 (9%) ; FTC, REPORT ON PIPE-LINE TRANSPORTATION OF PETROLEUM XXIX, 18 (1916) (6%).

[319] El Dorado Oil Works v. United States, 328 U.S. 12, 66 Sup.Ct. 843, 90 L.Ed. 1053 (1946) ; General American Tank Car Corp. v. El Dorado Terminal Co., 308 U.S. 422, 60 Sup. Ct. 325, 84 L.Ed. 361 (1940) ; Texas & Pacific Ry. v. American Tie & Timber Co., 234 U.S. 138, 34 Sup.Ct. 885, 58 L.Ed. 1255 (1914) ; Mitchell Coal & Coke Co. v. Pennsylvania R.R., 230 U.S. 247, 33 Sup.Ct. 916, 57 L.Ed. 1472 (1913) ; Texas & Pacific Ry. v. Abilene Cotton Oil Co., 204 U.S. 426, 27 Sup.Ct. 350, 51 L.Ed. 553 (1907).

[320] Hudson & Manhattan R.R. v. United States, 313 U.S. 98, 61 Sup.Ct. 884, 85 L.Ed.

larger question is raised whether public policy should endorse an arrangement which permits a shipper-owner to realize even a reasonable profit from carriage of his competitor's goods. It is alleged that the financial union of shipper and pipe line is productive of discrimination among shippers and tends toward monopoly.[321] Certainly this was true in the coal-railroad set-up.[322] But can an analogy safely be made between railroads and pipe lines? It hardly seems so. "Accepting the risk of obscuring the obvious by discussing it,"[323] the following fundamental differences between the two methods of transportation preclude the analogy:[324] (1) pipe lines were built by the shippers who use them—the oil companies themselves; (2) pipe lines were built to serve one industry whereas railroads were built to serve all industries, as well as passengers; (3) the typical crude line was laid from a particular refinery or terminal to a producing field for the purpose of obtaining a supply of crude oil for that refinery. The typical products line was constructed from the refinery to a specific marketing area desired to be reached by the shipper-owner. Consequently, the public served by these lines is limited to the producers and shippers in origin areas and to the refineries at their termini, or along their established routes. Railroads, on the other hand, were built for the purpose of engaging in the business of transportation, for a transportation profit. Within the limits of their trackage, they have available a vast number of potential customers

1212 (1941); Mississippi Valley Barge Line Co. v. United States, 292 U.S. 282, 54 Sup.Ct. 692, 78 L.Ed. 1260 (1934); *TNEC Hearings* 7235; see text at note 102 *supra*. But there must be substantial evidence supporting the Commission's decision. Interstate Commerce Commission v. Mechling, 330 U.S. 567, 67 Sup.Ct. 894, 91 L.Ed. 1102 (1947); see Davis, *Scope of Review of Federal Administrative Action*, 50 Col. L. Rev. 559 (1950).

321 See note 311 *supra*.

322 United States v. Reading Co., 253 U.S. 26, 40 Sup.Ct. 425, 64 L.Ed. 760 (1920); New York, New Haven & Hartford R. R. v. Interstate Commerce Commission, 200 U.S. 361, 26 Sup.Ct. 272, 50 L.Ed. 515 (1906); Meeker & Co. v. Lehigh Valley R.R., 21 I.C.C. 129 (1911); Cedar Hill Coal & Coke Co. v. Atchison, Topeka & Santa Fe Ry., 15 I.C.C. 73 (1909); Coxe Brothers & Co. v. Lehigh Valley R.R., 4 I.C.C. 535 (1891); Haddock v. Delaware, Lackawanna & Western R.R., 4 I.C.C. 296 (1890); Attorney-General v. Great Northern Ry., 1 Drew. & Sm. 154, 29 L.J.Ch. (N.S.) 794 (1860).

323 United States v. Reading Co., 253 U.S. 26, 61, 40 Sup.Ct. 425, 434, 64 L.Ed. 760, 780 (1920).

324 *TNEC Hearings* 8593–8595; H.R. Rep. No. 2192, 72d Cong., 2d Sess. LXXVIII (1933); Beard, Regulation of Pipe Lines as Common Carriers 158–159 (1941); Dow, The Issue of Pipe Line Divorcement 6–9 (1939); A.P.I., Survey 55–56 (1935); Mills, The Pipe Line's Place in the Oil Industry 15–17 (1935); Francis, Divorcement of Pipe Lines 11–12 (1935); Conway, Pipe Line Divorcement 25–27 (unpublished thesis in University of Oklahoma Law School Library, 1950); *cf.* Shuman, The Petroleum Industry 114 (1940); but *cf. TNEC Hearings* 7646–7657; Rostow, A National Policy for the Oil Industry 63, 120–121 (1948); Black, *Oil Pipe Line Divorcement by Litigation and Legislation*, 25 Corn. L. Q. 510 (1940) *passim*.

from the public at large; (4) pipe lines carry only petroleum products in one direction.[325] Railroads haul all kinds of commodities in as many directions as their lines run; (5) a pipe line either transports crude oil from the field to the refinery, or refined products from the refinery to the marketing area. It cannot carry crude to the refinery and then transport the refined product back to the producing territory. By contrast, a railroad, hauling some products predominantly in one direction, has the advantage of return hauls of other products; (6) crude pipe lines have a limited expectancy. Every barrel of oil transported reduces the amount remaining to be carried. But the typical railroad can expect increasing traffic as the community being served continues to expand with the passage of time; (7) pipe line capacity is limited. Unlike a railroad, it cannot run additional trains or add cars. To obtain greater capacity, additional lines or pumping stations must be added at great cost; (8) pipe lines are extended to the property where the crude is produced and will make the necessary connections to the shipper's tanks without additional charge. A railroad will construct sidetracks only at the shipper's expense. These do not exhaust the many differences between railroads and pipe lines, but they serve to show that the problems involved in regulating pipe lines and railroads are not the same.[326]

The Commodities Clause was enacted to end railroad discrimination in rates and service which could not be remedied by the Interstate Commerce Commission at that time (1906) due to its lack of jurisdiction over these matters. Since then, full power over every type of discrimination has been vested in the Commission with the result that the underlying reason— lack of remedy—no longer is present.

The contrast between the function of the pipe line as a working constituent in a single productive scheme and the complete economic entity of the railroad engaged in the business of transportation service led to the conclusion in the "Splawn" report that pipe lines were "plant facilities" in an integrated industry, and that application of the Commodities Clause to pipe lines seemed difficult.[327] The consistent position taken by Congress

[325] Occasionally the direction of flow through a line has been reversed. This requires a re-setting of pumping stations to conform to the new hydraulic design. Also, lines have been changed from crude service to products, and from products lines to crude lines. But these changes are very infrequent and the statement is valid for any single operating period.

[326] The closest approach to a pipe line-railroad analogy is the resemblance between a crude pipe line and a logging spur built into a forest to carry logs to a central saw mill where they are cut into manufactured products. Significantly, these "tap" lines were expressly excluded from the Commodities Clause. Tap Line Cases, 234 U.S. 1, 34 Sup.Ct. 741, 58 L.Ed. 1185 (1914).

[327] H.R. REP. No. 2192, 72d Cong., 2d Sess. LXXVIII (1933); cf. POGUE, ECONOMICS OF PIPE LINE TRANSPORTATION IN THE PETROLEUM INDUSTRY (1932).

in defeating decisively the numerous attempts to extend the Commodities Clause to pipe lines evidences its rejection of the alleged analogy.[328] This is not to say that monopolistic conditions do or do not exist in the petroleum industry, but merely that divorcement of the component branches cannot be accomplished through a Trojan Horse maneuver by analogy to the coal-railroad structure. Instead, an independent investigation of the present behavior of the petroleum industry necessarily must furnish the yardstick for formulation of divorcement policy.

Another facet of the same problem is the allegation that "profits" realized in the transportation phase are utilized by the major integrated companies to "subsidize" the refining and marketing branches, thereby enabling the major companies to enjoy an unfair competitive advantage over the independent who must show a profit on his business of refining or marketing or go out of business.[329] This favorite argument of petroleum industry critics is the result of an incomplete analysis. When an integrated company transports oil for itself, any "profit" realized is strictly a "paper profit,"[330] since the charges merely are a matter of corporate bookkeeping.[331] Actually, what has happened is that the refining branch has received the crude at a lower cost.[332] To charge the refinery with operating at a loss because it *would have* suffered a loss had it paid the full tariff is to distort the fundamental truth, *i.e.*, that the integrated company has realized one of the efficiencies peculiar to integration.[333] The complaint must be recog-

[328] See note 4 *supra.*

[329] Complaint, pp. 39, 57, United States v. American Petroleum Institute, Civil No. 8524, D. D.C., Sept. 30, 1940; *TNEC Hearings* 7107, 7262, 7271, 7309, 7315, 7318, 7377, 7581–7582, 8845, 8864–8865, 8871, 8879, 8898, 9151, 9181, 9210, 10039; 3 BAIN, THE ECONOMICS OF THE PACIFIC COAST PETROLEUM INDUSTRY 5–8 (1947); COOK, CONTROL OF THE PETROLEUM INDUSTRY BY MAJOR OIL COMPANIES 6, 22–23, 28 (TNEC Monograph 39, 1941); Whitesel, *Recent Federal Regulation of the Petroleum Pipe Line as a Common Carrier,* 32 CORN. L. Q. 337, 374 (1947); Prewitt, *The Operation and Regulation of Crude Oil and Gasoline Pipe Lines,* 56 Q. J. ECON. 177, 199–201 (1942); Black, *Exclusive Dealer Devices in the Marketing of Petroleum Products,* 29 GEO. L. J. 439, 442 (1941); *cf.* H. R. REP. No. 2465, 80th Cong., 2d Sess. 6 (1948); H.R. REP. No. 2192, 72d Cong., 2d Sess. LXXVII (1933).

[330] *TNEC Hearings* 7234, 8290, 9757; H.R. REP. No, 2192, 72d Cong., 2d Sess. LXXII (1933); ROSTOW, A NATIONAL POLICY FOR THE OIL INDUSTRY 59 (1948); *cf.* Adelman, *The A & P Case: A Study in Applied Economic Theory,* 63 Q. J. ECON. 238, 245 (1949). See United States v. New York Great Atlantic & Pacific Tea Co., 173 F.2d 79, 86 (7th Cir. 1949) for a parallel situation in the grocery trade.

[331] See note 98 *supra.*

[332] See notes 301–304 *supra.*

[333] *TNEC Hearings* 7234, 7240, 9716; Adelman, *Integration and Antitrust Policy,* 63 HARV. L. REV. 27, 43 (1949). Professor Rostow, who could hardly be called a friend of integration, was one of the first to call attention to this. ROSTOW, A NATIONAL POLICY FOR THE OIL INDUSTRY 65 (1948). See also Adelman, *The A & P Case: A Study in Applied Economic Theory,* 63 Q. J. ECON. 238, 245–246 (1949); Note, 58 YALE L. J. 969, 978 (1949).

nized for its true nature, an attack against vertical integration. Vertical integration has not yet been judicially declared to be monopolistic *per se*.[334] Its legality depends upon the purpose or intent with which it was conceived, *or,* the power it creates *and* the attendant purpose or intent.[335] Therefore, further discussion of this aspect will be found in the next section of this book devoted to an examination of trade restraining and monopolistic characteristics of the petroleum industry.

There remains the question of the profit obtained from the carriage of outside shipments. Formerly, this question was rendered moot by the fact that few, if any, outside shippers used the lines.[336] But increased utilization of the common carrier pipe lines by outside shippers has revived the issue. On principle there is little difference between an integrated company earning a reasonable rate of return on its pipe line investment and realizing the same quantity from a dissociated line of endeavor such as shipbuilding.[337] The advantage would be the same.[338] Here, too, the hue and cry of "subsidizing" is raised.[339] This constitutes an attack on conglomerate integration, and like that on vertical integration, must be evaluated in terms of trade restraint or monopolization rather than by a declaration of illegality *per se.*

---

[334] United States v. Columbia Steel Co., 334 U.S. 495, 68 Sup.Ct. 1107, 92 L.Ed. 1533 (1948) ; United States v. Paramount Pictures, Inc., 334 U.S. 131, 68 Sup.Ct. 915, 92 L.Ed. 1260 (1948) ; *cf.* United States v. New York Great Atlantic & Pacific Tea Co., 67 F.Supp. 626, 676 (E.D.Ill. 1946) ; Adelman, *Integration and Antitrust Policy*, 63 HARV. L. REV. 27, 43 (1949) ; Note, 58 YALE L. J. 764, 769 (1949) ; *cf.* Oppenheim, *A New Look at Antitrust Enforcement Trends* in N.Y. BAR ASS'N ANTITRUST LAW SYMPOSIUM 69, 76 (1950) ; Comment, 43 ILL. L. REV. 523, 530 (1948) ; *but cf.* ROSTOW, A NATIONAL POLICY FOR THE OIL INDUSTRY 123–144 (1948) ; Rostow, *Monopoly Under the Sherman Act, Power or Purpose?*, 43 ILL. L. REV. 745 (1949) passim.

[335] *Ibid.*

[336] See section devoted to Shippers' Use of Pipe Lines *supra.*

[337] *TNEC Hearings* 7234–7235, 7240, 7262. This practice is more prevalent among independents than among major oil companies.

[338] Adelman, *Integration and Antitrust Policy,* 63 HARV. L. REV. 27, 43 (1949).

[339] "If you are in the grocery business and you also own an undertaking establishment and a theater and a fleet of ships and you take the profits from those other businesses and route them on the grocery front, you may win the battle but it isn't because of your efficiency as a grocer; it is because you are calling in other allies and other sources, so that your efficiency there on the grocery front is not determined, as I say, by your efficiency as a groceryman. In this integrated movement you are calling on profits from other businesses, you have got them available to route on the competitive front where you sell the gas and oil, and it looks to me like the independent hasn't got much chance when you call in three or four other guys to help you." *TNEC Hearings* 7234.

III. ALLEGED CREATION OF MONOPOLY IN THE OIL INDUSTRY THROUGH THE INSTRUMENTALITY OF PIPE LINE CONTROL

A. The Charge

A combination of two quotations from the current legal literature presents a concise statement of the charge of monopolistic conditions in the oil industry. "Control of the pipe lines now appears to be the nerve center of the oil empires, and the key to monopoly power in the industry."[340] "In the market for crude oil, the majors are monopsonistic or oligopsonistic buyers; in the markets for refined products they are oligopolists. In both phases of the process they are concerned to limit the potential scope of independent refiners in an industry where entry would be relatively easy, in the absence of such economic pressures."[341] This charge has encountered the objection that it has confused laymen due to the esoteric use of economic "gobble-degook."[342] It has been suggested also that careful analysis should be substituted for epithets and blanket condemnation.[343] These criticisms underscore the fact that before we can determine whether there is a monopoly in the oil industry, we must understand what is meant by the term "monopoly" and how it is measured. The need for definition and the formulation of a yardstick is apparent. Accordingly, at the risk of repeating what already is familiar to many readers, a brief restatement of some existing definitions will be made so that economic terms may aid analysis rather than confuse it.

B. Economic Concepts[344]

The importance of economic terms and theory is becoming increasingly apparent in antitrust law. More and more, economic doctrine is being

[340] Comment, 51 YALE L. J., 1338, 1347 (1942). Permission to quote granted by the publisher, the Yale Law Journal. *Cf.* ROSTOW, A NATIONAL POLICY FOR THE OIL INDUSTRY 117–118 (1948).

[341] ROSTOW, A NATIONAL POLICY FOR THE OIL INDUSTRY 66 (1948). Permission to quote granted by the publishers, the Yale University Press.

[342] HARDWICKE, ANTITRUST LAWS, ET AL. *v.* UNIT OPERATION OF OIL OR GAS POOLS 176, n. 168 (1948). See Recent Books, 46 MICH. L. REV. 860 (1948).

[343] Kulp, Book Review, 1 OKLA. L. REV. 329 (1948); Kahn, Book Review, 34 CORN. L. Q. 284 (1948); MacLachlan, Book Review, 13 LAW & CONTEMP. PROB. 715, 717 (1948); *cf.* Stigler, Book Review, 57 YALE L. J. 1322 (1948).

[344] The debt owed to WILCOX, COMPETITION AND MONOPOLY IN AMERICAN INDUSTRY (TNEC Monograph 21, 1940) is patent. Other general sources include CHAMBERLIN, THE THEORY OF MONOPOLISTIC COMPETITION (6th ed. 1948); STIGLER, THE THEORY OF PRICE (1947); BOWMAN & BACH, ECONOMIC ANALYSIS AND PUBLIC POLICY (1946); BURNS, THE DECLINE OF COMPETITION (1936); ROBINSON, THE ECONOMICS OF IMPERFECT COMPETITION (1934). When additional specific sources are drawn upon, they will be cited.

assimilated by court decisions and administrative action. The following concepts have become necessary tools of legal analysis. It is believed that their restatement in this book accords with prevalent usage.

1. PERFECT COMPETITION. This theoretical concept requires five conditions. First, the product must be plentiful and sufficiently homogeneous to permit instantaneous shifting of buyers from one seller to another in order to secure the advantage of a lower price. Second, the market organization must be such that every unit sold at one instant of time will be sold at the same price. Third, sellers must be so great in number and so small in size that the quantity produced by each is so insignificant a part of the total supply that no increase or decrease by any one of them can affect appreciably the market price. Likewise, the buyers must be numerous, small, and purchase so insignificant a portion of the total demand, that no increase or decrease in the purchase of any of them can affect appreciably the market price. Given these conditions, it follows that a seller who raises his price above that of the market will sell nothing, and one selling below the market price will sell his capacity (which is limited by hypothesis). Thus, the market price determines the policy of buyers and sellers, and not vice versa.[345] Fourth, there must be freedom from restraint on the independent action of any seller or buyer.[346] Each must act in his own interest, disre-

---

[345] This sets up the classical "equilibrium" theory. Each seller will produce up to the point where the cost of producing an additional unit (marginal cost) will equal the additional income that the market price permits him to derive from the sale (marginal revenue). Each buyer will purchase up to the point where the cost of acquiring an additional unit is equal to the desirability or satisfaction involved in the additional unit. It is interesting for lawyers to note the counterpart of their "reasonable man" in the mythical "economic man" who rationally equates marginal cost to marginal revenue. However, the "economic man" apparently has far greater knowledge than his legal cousin. The "irrational passion for dispassionate rationality" has caused the danger of abstraction becoming distraction to be quite real in the economic world, as will be developed later.

[346] Restraint includes custom, contract, collusion, threats or fear of retaliation, and governmental regulation.

[347] Capital must *instantaneously* shift from one industry to another, from product to product, from firm to firm, in constant pursuit of the economic Grail, *i. e.,* profit. Buyers and sellers must freely enter and leave the market arena in continuous procession. Professor Chamberlin says this is the feature which serves to distinguish perfect competition from pure competition. CHAMBERLIN, THE THEORY OF MONOPOLISTIC COMPETITION 6 (6th ed. 1948). His distinction is said not to have impressed writers on the subject. White, *A Review of Monopolistic and Imperfect Competition Theories,* 26 AM. ECON. REV. 637, 641 (1936). But a later article termed it "felicitous." Machlup, *Monopoly and Competition: A Classification of Market Positions,* 27 AM. ECON. REV. 445, 448 (1937).

[348] Fly, *Observations on the Anti-Trust Laws, Economic Theory and the Sugar Institute Decisions, I,* 45 YALE L. J. 1339, 1342 (1936). Economists express this by saying the individual demand curve is perfectly elastic. Wright, *Imperfect Competition, Oligopoly, and Monopoly-Discussion,* 38 AM. ECON. REV. 30 (No. 2, May, 1948) ; Machlup, *Monopoly and Competition:*

garding that of his competitors. Fifth, the market price must be dynamic, constantly responding to changes in supply and demand. The mechanism must be frictionless and timeless.[347] It is evident that these conditions do not exist concurrently in the real world, so this concept must be recognized for what it is—simply an instrument of economic analysis.

2. PURE COMPETITION. Here a tangential contact between theory and reality is accomplished. Information concerning present and future supply and demand conditions is unequally distributed. Independence of action is affected by custom. Movement of capital no longer hovers between industries, products, and firms like a bee seeking nectar, but is impeded by friction. Access and withdrawal from the market are retarded by minor obstacles. But two indicia of perfect competition must be present, *viz.*, a homogeneous or standardized product, and numerous small buyers and sellers, none of whom has any degree of control over the price. Under these conditions, the consumer is perfectly indifferent between sellers, and the individual seller believes that, acting alone, he cannot affect the price.[348] The term "pure" simply connotes an absence of human control over prices. The organized commodities markets and the securities exchanges are said to be examples of pure competition. But even in these markets, manipulation rears its [ugly] head upon occasion. So, pure competition does exist, but its occurrence is rare.

3. IMPERFECT COMPETITION.[349] In this concept, recognition is accorded to the many elements in real life which negate the frictionless and timeless conditions assumed in defining perfect competition. Information

---

A Classification of Market Positions, 27 AM. ECON. REV. 445, 448 (1937); Robinson, *What is Perfect Competition?*, 49 Q. J. ECON. 104, 105 (1934). A demand curve is the locus of points each representing the maximum quantity saleable at a specific price. It is an objective concept, viewed from the point of the seller. Elasticity of demand is the responsiveness of demand to price changes. If a small drop in price increases sales by an equally proportionate amount, the elasticity is said to be unity or one. If the proportionate increase in sales is less than the proportionate decline in price (the ratio is less than one), the demand is said to be inelastic. If it is greater (the ratio is more than one), the demand is elastic. The modifier "perfect" merely expresses extreme conditions. Thus, a perfectly elastic demand is one where the ratio is infinity, and a perfectly inelastic demand has a ratio of zero. A perfectly inelastic demand curve will be parallel to the price axis and a perfectly elastic demand curve will be parallel to the quantity axis. See MARSHALL, PRINCIPLES OF ECONOMICS 96, 99, 102 n.1, 839–840 (8th ed. 1949); ROBINSON, THE ECONOMICS OF IMPERFECT COMPETITION 17–18 (1934); Lerner, *Geometrical Comparison of Elasticities*, 37 AM. ECON. REV. 191 (1947); Henderson, *Geometrical Note on Elasticity of Demand*, 36 AM. ECON. REV. 662 (1946). The elasticity concept finds use as an index of the total amount that consumers are willing to spend (sellers will receive) in response to price changes.

[349] The leading work on this topic is ROBINSON, THE ECONOMICS OF IMPERFECT COMPETITION (1934). With due deference to Mrs. Robinson, however, the author disagrees with her implied thesis that imperfect competition does not involve a blend of monopolistic and competitive factors. Indeed, that is exactly what "imperfect competition" implies.

concerning the quality and price of products is hidden from traders. Individual freedom of action is inhibited by restrictive covenants, custom, and fear of reprisal. Mobility of capital, as well as ease of entry and departure, may be curtailed sharply. Sellers differentiate their products so as to build up consumer preference, thereby avoiding instantaneous shifting due to price differences. Non-price competition abounds.[350] The numbers of buyers and sellers may be so small or their proportionate part of the market so great that their business policies will determine the market price instead of the converse situation specified in perfect competition. The concept, as used in this text, essentially denotes a market condition which departs from pure or perfect competition. Since these conditions exist today in greater or less degree in most markets, it is obvious that imperfect competition is a commonplace.

4. MONOPOLISTIC COMPETITION.[351] In its narrow, more precise meaning, this is a form of imperfect competition which is marked by product heterogeneity.[352] There may be numerous sellers and no one of them able to control a major part of the supply of the commodity offered for sale. But each seller differentiates his product from that of the other sellers so that buyers will be insensitive to *small* differences in price. Within this extremely limited range, the seller is czar. However, competition in the guise of substitution constantly presses the perimeter of his monopoly monarchy. Needless to say, monopolistic competition characterizes the majority of manufactured consumer's goods markets. It manifests itself in the oil industry in gasoline and motor oil marketing. Phillips "66," Texas "Fire Chief," and Sunoco "Dynalube" all have their enthusiastic devotees. "Monopolistic Competition" also is used in a more general sense (as in "The

---

[350] Non-price competition takes the form of rivalry in quality, style, advertising and sales technique.

[351] The original, and still standard, work on this subject is CHAMBERLIN, THE THEORY OF MONOPOLISTIC COMPETITION (1st ed. 1933). For a further development of spatial competition, brand competition, competition in product specifications and terms of sale, see Copeland, *Competing Products and Monopolistic Competition*, 55 Q. J. ECON. 1 (1940). See also Meriam, *Bigness and the Economic Analysis of Competition*, 28 HARV. BUS. REV. 109 (No. 2, 1950); Chamberlin, *Monopolistic or Imperfect Competition?*, 51 Q. J. ECON. 557 (1937).

[352] This dissimilarity may be based upon certain characteristics of the product itself, *viz.*, trade-mark or trade name; exclusive patented features; special wrapping; or singularity of style, color, design, or quality. It may be due to the conditions under which the sale was made, *e.g.*, the location and atmosphere of the retailer's establishment, his manner of dealing with customers, his reputation for reliability and fair dealing, and all the other personal attractions which influence people. CHAMBERLIN, THE THEORY OF MONOPOLISTIC COMPETITION 56–70 (6th ed. 1948). Professor Chamberlin originally called this "product differentiation." But due to the custom of misinterpreting his theory by treating product differentiation as abnormal rather than normal, he has changed the name to "product heterogeneity." Chamberlin, *Product Heterogeneity and Public Policy*, 40 AM. ECON. REV. 85 (No. 2, May, 1950).

Theory of Monopolistic Competition") to describe the blending of monopolistic and competitive elements in real life economy.

5. CUTTHROAT COMPETITION.[353] Competition becomes cutthroat when prices drop to, and remain for some time at, a point where no seller can recover his costs plus a fair return on his investment. This arises when there is excess capacity of the fixed factors in the industry.[354] The popular name for competition which threatens to become cutthroat competition is price warfare. The point at which price warfare becomes cutthroat competition is difficult to ascertain. A detailed analysis of the costs of price reducers and a determination of a fair rate of return is necessary before the distinction can be drawn. The importance of cutthroat competition is its causal relation to industrial instability.

6. PREDATORY AND DISCRIMINATORY COMPETITION. When a seller cuts his price with the prime purpose of driving another out of the market, he is said to be engaged in predatory competition. When the reduction is confined to the portion of his sales in competition with another, his action is deemed both discriminatory and predatory. An example is the pricing policies of the old Standard Oil Trust which maintained its prices in localities where it had control, and drastically reduced its prices in areas where competitors were active. After eliminating these local rivals, the company raised its prices back to the pre-combat level.

Discriminatory competition can be practiced by utilizing a "fighting brand" to compete with lower-priced rivals, while maintaining the price of the leading or standard brands. Bain[355] describes the use of a "third structure" gasoline by the Pacific Coast majors to fight price-wise the independent refiners, while maintaining the price structure of "regular" and "premium" (ethyl) grades.

The crux of predatory competition is motive or purpose, which subjectively is known only to the price-cutter. Many sellers who cannot meet the price of their more efficient competitors ascribe to their rivals a predatory intent. More often than not, this is biased suspicion, not objective proof. The problem of ascertaining intent makes difficult the distinction between bona fide "hard" and predatory competition.

---

[353] See Reynolds, *Cutthroat Competition*, 30 AM. ECON. REV. 736 (1940).

[354] Adelman, *Effective Competition and the Antitrust Laws*, 61 HARV. L. REV. 1289, 1328 (1948) ; Reynolds, *Cutthroat Competition*, 30 AM. ECON. REV. 736, 737 (1940). Excess capacity exists when, if all plants in the industry were to produce at capacity, the profit ratio of the industry would be subnormal. The economic definition of capacity of a plant is that operational rate which achieves the minimum average cost. Cassels, *Excess Capacity and Monopolistic Competition*, 51 Q. J. ECON. 426 (1937).

[355] 1 BAIN, THE ECONOMICS OF THE PACIFIC COAST PETROLEUM INDUSTRY 121–124 (1944) ; 2 BAIN, THE ECONOMICS OF THE PACIFIC COAST PETROLEUM INDUSTRY 256–258 (1945).

7. Potential Competition. The function of potential competition essentially is that of a regulatory device. It either supplements or supplants actual competition in restraining firms from overcharging for their products or underpaying for their purchases. Because of the "imperfect"[356] nature of competition as it actually exists in our present economy, potential competion is an extremely important concept. Freedom of entry (and departure) constitutes the *sine qua non* of its existence. An example of potential competition in the oil industry takes the form of Mid-continent and Gulf Coast crude oil and gasoline constantly looming on the horizon of the Pacific Coast market, poised for entry whenever the transportation cost is equalized by price differential between the areas.

8. Effective or Workable Competition.[357] In this concept lies the greatest hope for a realistic appraisal of American industry as it exists today. The concept itself is in a state of flux, only recently having been articulated.[358] Its development very aptly illustrates the diversity of views among economists. At the risk of oversimplification, a broad classification into two types of approach may be made. The first is that of the "structuralists" who emphasize *market structure* on the theory that, given the proper market mechanism, the limitations on the market position or scope of action of firms necessarily will produce a form of competition best calculated to serve the public welfare. Thus, J. M. Clark visualizes a ". . . rivalry in selling goods, in which each selling unit normally seeks maximum net revenue, under conditions such that the price or prices each seller can charge are effectively limited by the free option of the buyer to buy from a rival seller or sellers of what we think of as 'the same' product, necessitating an effort by each seller to equal or exceed the attractiveness of the others' offerings to a sufficient number of sellers to accomplish the end in view."[359]

---

[356] This merely denotes deviation from the theoretically "perfect" perfect competition.

[357] See Edwards, Maintaining Competition (1949) ; Learned, Integration in American Industry (paper presented before the A.P.I. on Nov. 9, 1949) ; Meriam, *Bigness and the Economic Analysis of Competition*, 28 Harv. Bus. Rev. 109 (No. 2, 1950) ; Bain, *Workable Competition in Oligopoly: Theoretical Considerations and Some Empirical Evidence*, 40 Am. Econ. Rev. 35 (No. 2, May, 1950) ; Mason, *The Current Status of the Monopoly Problem in the United States*, 62 Harv. L. Rev. 1265 (1949) ; Rodgers & Luedicke, *Dynamic Competition*, 27 Harv. Bus. Rev. 237 (1949) ; Adelman, *Effective Competition and the Antitrust Laws*, 61 Harv. L. Rev. 1289 (1948) ; Stigler, *The Extent and Bases of Monopoly*, 32 Am. Econ. Rev. 1 (Supp., June, 1942) ; Clark, *Toward a Concept of Workable Competition*, 30 Am. Econ. Rev. 241 (1940).

[358] Dean Mason credits J. M. Clark, *supra* note 357, with being the first writer to use the term "workable competition" in his article of 1940.

[359] Clark, *Toward a Concept of Workable Competition*, 30 Am. Econ. Rev. 241, 243 (1940). Permission to quote granted by the publishers, the American Economic Association. This is not to imply that J. M. Clark is a "structuralist"; it only means that his 1940 article stressed structure.

Clair Wilcox abbreviated this to ". . . the availability to buyers [and sellers] of genuine alternatives in policy among their sources of supply [and distribution]."[360] This abbreviation was "too loose" for George Stigler, who felt that "[a]n industry is workably competitive when (1) there are a considerable number of firms selling closely related products in each important market area, (2) these firms are not in collusion, and (3) the long run average cost curve for a new firm is not materially higher than for an established firm."[361] Corwin Edwards[362] lists seven conditions of workable competition, including numerous buyers and sellers, effective profit motivation, absence of collusion, freedom of entry, and the absence of a dominant firm.[363]

The second approach is that of the "behaviorists," who feel that emphasis on mere structure is misplaced. They hold that actual firm behavior in the market is more significant. They look to see if products and processes constantly are being improved, costs reduced, prices cut concomitantly with cost reductions, maintenance of proper firm size-efficiency relationship, and avoidance of waste of resources in production and distribution. Under the leadership of Dean Mason, of the Harvard Graduate School of Public Administration, the two approaches are being brought together to form a cohesive concept of measurement. There is no fundamental difference in the end desired; there is simply a divergence in means.

The concept of workable competition is evolving toward a realistic standard against which individual industries can be measured in the public interest.

9. MONOPOLY AND MONOPSONY.[364] Just as there are gradations of competition, so there are different meanings of "monopoly." In the strictest sense, what will be termed "perfect monopoly" (the antithesis of perfect

---

[360] Wilcox, *Competition and Monopoly in American Industry* 8 (TNEC Monograph 21, 1940). The remark made in note 359 *supra* is applicable here.

[361] Stigler, *The Extent and Bases of Monopoly*, 32 AM. ECON. REV. 1, 2–3 (Supp., June, 1942). Permission to quote granted by the publishers, the American Economic Association. The first two conditions are designed to eliminate monopoly, explicit collusion, and tacit avoidance of price competition due to fear of retaliation. The third condition insures free entry into the market. Note Stigler's remark that the necessary number of firms is an adjunct of "trust-busting" and has no relation to the deviation of an industry from workable competition. *Id.* at 3.

[362] Director of the Bureau of Industrial Economics, Federal Trade Commission.

[363] EDWARDS, MAINTAINING COMPETITION 9–10 (1949).

[364] See Mason, *The Current Status of the Monopoly Problem in the United States*, 62 HARV. L. REV. 1265 (1949); Knauth, *Monopoly Reconsidered*, 60 POL. SCI. Q. 563 (1945); Harbeson, *The Present Status of the Sherman Act*, 39 MICH. L. REV. 189 (1940); Harbeson, *The Public Interest Concept in Law and in Economics*, 37 MICH. L. REV. 181 (1938); Mason, *Monopoly in Law and Economics*, 47 YALE L. J. 34 (1937); Sweezy, *On the Definition of Monopoly*, 51 Q. J. ECON. 362 (1937).

competition) denotes absolute control by a single seller over the entire supply of a product for which no substitute is available. Another condition of perfect monopoly is the absence of any threat of governmental regulation. It is obvious that under these conditions, the monopolist has absolute control over the quantity of product to be marketed or, alternatively, over the price at which it will be sold. Just as patently, there never can exist such a situation, and the concept is one of analysis only. A second type of "monopoly," which herein will be referred to as "imperfect monopoly,"[365] exists where a single seller attains a degree of important, continuing control over the supply of a product for which there are no close substitutes,[366] thus rendering the purchaser practically without any freedom of choice. The monopolist has control over output or price up to the point of substitution.[367] This is the most common type of "monopoly," and will be the meaning of monopoly used in this book. Some economists also use the term "monopoly" to denote this measure of control attained by a group of sellers acting in concert. In order to clarify the use of terms, it is submitted that such a situation might better be termed "group monopoly." Finally, "monopoly" sometimes is used very loosely to designate any firm or group of firms which possesses sufficient power over production and prices to establish market conditions dissimilar to those resulting from perfect competition. Rather than call this "monopoly," it should be termed imperfect competition.[368]

The foregoing paragraph described conditions from the sellers' side of the market. Where similar conditions exist on the buyers' side of the market, the suffix "poly" is changed to "psony," thus making monopsony.[369] An example of an 1895 monopsonist is the Seep Purchasing Company of Oil City. Seep was Standard Oil Company's purchasing affiliate. Because it bought 80 percent of the Pennsylvania crude oil production (and Standard had absolute control over all pipe lines in the area), the Company was able virtually to set its own price.[370]

[365] See Machlup, *Monopoly and Competition: A Classification of Market Positions*, 27 AM. ECON. REV. 445, 450 (1937).

[366] Stigler expresses this as a product whose cross-elasticity of demand with respect to other products is small. STIGLER, THE THEORY OF PRICE 221 (1947). Joan Robinson says it is bounded on all sides by a marked gap in the chain of substitutes. ROBINSON, THE ECONOMICS OF IMPERFECT COMPETITION 5 (1934).

[367] This has been expressed as the ability to exploit a trade position without the necessity of maintaining it. Knauth, *Monopoly Reconsidered*, 60 POL. SCI. Q. 563, 576 (1945).

[368] WILCOX, COMPETITION AND MONOPOLY IN AMERICAN INDUSTRY 10 (TNEC Monograph 21, 1940); *but cf.* STIGLER, THE THEORY OF PRICE 198 (1947).

[369] Mrs. Robinson tells us that the term is derived from ὀψωνεῖν, to go marketing. ROBINSON, THE ECONOMICS OF IMPERFECT COMPETITION 215 n.1 (1934).

[370] SEN. Doc. No. 61, 70th Cong., 1st Sess. 101 (1928); EDWARDS, MAINTAINING COM-

10. Duopoly and Duopsony.[371] Where two sellers, instead of one, attain sufficient control over the supply of a product to manipulate prices, the situation is termed duopoly. There must be no actual, or tacit, agreement between them concerning production or price, for such a situation would be a group monopoly rather than duopoly. However independent their actions may be, their fortunes are indissolubly linked together. Each must take into account the policy of his rival in determining his own policy.[372] Where the sellers are of unequal strength, there is a strong tendency toward price leadership.[373] The real test of independence is whether buyers are presented with a genuine alternative. This is a market behavior test rather than pure structure.[374]

Again, the term duopoly is converted to duopsony to indicate the corresponding situation in the buyers' market.

11. Oligopoly and Oligopsony. The term oligopoly is used to describe the situation where sellers are few in number and any one of them

PETITION 95 n.6 (1949); Cook, Control of the Petroleum Industry by Major Oil Companies 25 (TNEC Monograph 39, 1941).

[371] See Chamberlin, The Theory of Monopolistic Competition, c. 3 (6th ed. 1948); Lewis, *Some Observations on Duopoly,* 38 Am. Econ. Rev. 1 (No. 2, May, 1948); Stigler, *Notes on the Theory of Duopoly,* 48 J. Pol. Econ. 521 (1940). The early work in this field was performed by the mathematical economists, Cournot, Bertrand, and Edgeworth. As early as 1838, Cournot demonstrated that duopoly competition would give different results than would ensue from pure competition. Unfortunately, his teachings wore the mantle of mathematical equations. Because of this, and the dogmatic belief of the neo-classicists in the relative unimportance of monopoly, Cournot's analysis became largely a mental chess game enjoyed by the other mathematical economists. Nicholls, *Social Biases and Recent Theories of Competition,* 58 Q. J. Econ. 1, 8 (1943).

[372] See Adelman, *Effective Competition and the Antitrust Laws,* 61 Harv. L. Rev. 1289, 1297 (1948) for a description of their behavior. For an interesting analogy between the market behavior of duopolists and two players engaged in a game, see Morgenstern, *Oligopoly, Monopolistic Competition, and the Theory of Games,* 38 Am. Econ. Rev. 10 (No. 2, May, 1948). See also Smithies, *Optimum Location in Spatial Competition,* 49 J. Pol. Econ. 423 (1941).

[373] Price leadership is the phenomenon where all sellers (or buyers) adapt their prices to that of a dominant competitor, known as the recognized price leader. Edwards, Maintaining Competition 35–36 (1949); see Comer, *Price Leadership,* 7 Law & Contemp. Prob. 61 (1940); Comment, 29 Calif. L. Rev. 507 (1941). This is a familiar practice to the oil industry where the leading marketer (formerly?) posted prices for the tank car, tank wagon, and, often, the service station market in its territory. Also the leading crude purchaser posts the crude price in the field. 2 Bain, The Economics of the Pacific Coast Petroleum Industry 107–108, 114, 291–292 (1945); Burns, The Decline of Competition 93–109 (1936). However, this is by no means the "automatic" mechanism that critics of the petroleum industry allege it to be. Burns, *op. cit. supra;* Learned, *Pricing of Gasoline: A Case Study,* 26 Harv. Bus. Rev. 723 (1948); see Rodgers & Luedicke, *Dynamic Competition,* 27 Harv. Bus. Rev. 237 (1949).

[374] This illustrates Dean Mason's idea that structure and market behavior approaches are not so far apart. Here, by definition, to get the proper definitive conditions to satisfy the structure concept, the proper behavior pattern is met.

is of such a size that his policies affect appreciably the market price. Products may be either homogeneous or heterogeneous. The hallmark is the ability of a seller or sellers to affect the market price. It is characterized by an awareness of the other sellers and of the *indirect* effect of one's pricing policies as reflected by the reactions of the other sellers.[375] Sometimes, price leadership and "conscious parallelism" are among its progeny.[376] Oligopoly is the meeting ground of competitive and monopolistic elements in industry. Consequently, it is of common occurrence, particularly in the mass production industries where capital investment is large.

The same situation in the buyers' side of the market is called oligopsony.

C. Mores, Economic Theory and the Law on Monopoly

At the outset, two factors which have affected the development of American antitrust law must be mentioned. The first of these is caused by a failure critically to appraise innovations in economic theory. The result is that one dogma is replaced by another, with little appreciable improvement in methods of analysis. The second factor is the time lag between changes in social institutions and economic theory, and between changed economic thinking and assimilation of the new concepts into legal doctrine.

In the early days of both economic theory[377] and antitrust law,[378] the English economy consisted of manorial estates, local markets, gilds, and

[375] This feature has been considered so significant by one writer that he based a classification of competition on it. Machlup, *Monopoly and Competition: A Classification of Market Positions*, 27 AM. ECON. REV. 445 (1937).

[376] "Conscious parallelism" is the term used to describe the situation where a number of firms follow a parallel course of action *with knowledge* and in contemplation of the fact that other concerns are adhering to it also. It received judicial acceptance in Triangle Conduit & Cable Co. v. Federal Trade Commission, 168 F.2d 175 (7th Cir. 1948), *aff'd by equally divided court, sub nom.*, Clayton Mark & Co. v. Federal Trade Commission, 336 U.S. 956, 69 Sup.Ct. 888, 93 L.Ed. 1110 (1949). The Court of Appeals for the Seventh Circuit held that where it acted to eliminate price competition, it was *per se* a violation of Section 5 of the Federal Trade Commission Act. Apparently it is not in and of itself a violation of the Sherman Act, but undoubtedly it furnishes cogent probative circumstantial evidence from which a conspiracy may be inferred under certain circumstances. See Rahl, *Conspiracy and the Anti-Trust Laws*, 44 ILL. L. REV. 743, 761 (1950). If collusion justifiably may be inferred, the oligopoly becomes a "group monopoly."

[377] Stigler sets the birth date of economics at 1776, when Adam Smith's *Wealth of Nations* was published. STIGLER, THE THEORY OF PRICE 12 (1947). But the ideas which Smith collated and published were being formed well before this date.

[378] Perhaps a good date would be 1415, the year of the renowned dictum in The Dyer's Case, Y. B. 2 Hen. V, f. 5, pl. 26 (1415) ("Per Dieu, if the plaintiff were here, he should go to prison till he had paid a fine to the King"). Professor Oppenheim says this dictum was echoed in Atlantic Cleaners and Dyers, Inc. v. United States, 286 U.S. 427, 52 Sup.Ct. 607, 76 L.Ed. 1204 (1932). OPPENHEIM, CASES ON FEDERAL ANTI-TRUST LAWS 8 (1948).

borough corporations. The monopolies of the times were exclusionary royal grants made to favorites of the crown.[379] Market competition, as the focus of economic forces, had not come into being. Business regulation laws were directed against the practices of forestalling,[380] engrossing,[381] and regrating.[382] Later, the back of the royal monopolies was broken by statute[383] and judicial decisions.[384] The rising "mercantilism" wrested control from the gilds and borough corporations.

By the latter years of the eighteenth century there had emerged a spirit of individualism which completely revamped the relations between government and industry. Adam Smith was the Prophet of a new era, and his *Wealth of Nations* was the Talmud of the times.[385] The old laws against forestalling, engrossing and regrating, necessary to the prior economy, became a drag on the current policy of uninhibited freedom of competition,[386]

[379] Standard Oil Company of New Jersey v. United States, 221 U.S. 1, 51–53, 31 Sup.Ct. 502, 512–513, 55 L.Ed. 619, 641–642 (1911); Darcy v. Allein, 11 Co.Rep. 84b, 77 Eng.Rep. 1260 (Q.B. 1602) (21 year exclusive right to import and manufacture playing cards granted to groom of Queen Elizabeth's privy chamber); The Clothworkers of Ipswich, Godbolt 252, 78 Eng.Rep. 147 (K.B. 1615) (exclusive charter to tailor and make clothes); 3 COKE, INSTITUTES 181 (1797); LOEVINGER, THE LAW OF FREE ENTERPRISE 6–13 (1949); Harbeson, *The Present Status of the Sherman Act*, 39 MICH. L. REV. 189, 204 (1940); Miller, *The Case of the Monopolies—Some of its Results and Suggestions*, 6 MICH. L. REV. 1 (1907). Obviously, the concept of monopoly no longer is confined to a grant of privileges, but includes a condition produced by acts of individuals or combinations. National Cotton Oil Co. v. Texas, 197 U.S. 115, 129, 25 Sup.Ct. 379, 382, 49 L.Ed. 689, 694 (1905).

[380] Forestalling was the practice of purchasing goods on the way to market with the intent to sell them in the market at a higher price. It also took the form of influencing someone else who was bringing such commodities to charge a higher price for his goods, or to dissuade him from coming to the market. LOEVINGER, THE LAW OF FREE ENTERPRISE 8 (1949); Mason, *Monopoly in Law and Economics*, 47 YALE L. J. 34, 38 (1937); Herbruck, *Forestalling, Regrating and Engrossing*, 27 MICH. L. REV. 365 (1929); Jones, *Historical Development of the Law of Business Competition*, 35 YALE L. J. 905, 914 (1926).

[381] Engrossing was dealing with goods in wholesale quantity (in gross) with intent to resell the goods at a profit. It first was restricted to wholesale dealing in victuals, but later the term was applied to any attempt to corner a market. *Ibid.* Thus, it would seem to be the predecessor of the Sherman Act, Section Two, crime of monopolizing or attempting to monopolize. See United States v. Patten, 187 Fed. 664 (C.C.S.D.N.Y. 1911).

[382] Regrating consisted of purchasing any necessities of life in a market and reselling them in the same market or in any other market within four miles of the place of purchase. *Ibid.* The distinction between regrating and engrossing is that the actual resale was necessary to commit the crime of regrating, whereas the purchasing or contracting to purchase with intent to resell constituted the crime of engrossing. Herbruck, *Forestalling, Regrating and Engrossing*, 27 MICH. L. REV. 365, 378 (1929).

[383] The Statute of Monopolies, 1623, 21 JAC. I, c. 3.

[384] See note 379 *supra.*

[385] Hume v. Moore-McCormack Lines, 121 F.2d 336, 338–339 (2d Cir. 1941).

[386] The great Adam Smith himself compared the common fear of engrossing and forestalling to the dread of witchcraft. SMITH, THE WEALTH OF NATIONS 500 (Mod.Lib. ed. 1937).

hence many of them were repealed.[387] The economists produced the concept of free (pure) competition in the market as the automatic regulator of business and the most satisfactory distributor of goods.[388] They conceived the foremost danger to public interest to be combinations in restraint of trade.[389] Apparently the lawyers agreed, for the greatest development of business regulation law was in this field.[390]

The emphasis of both economists and lawyers on the presence of *free competition* was brought to America, where it was well suited to the economy of the expansionist movement. Legal stress was directed against the suppression of individual freedom to compete by agreements among competitors or by predatory competition.[391] Despite the influence of Judge Taft's famous, but questionable,[392] analysis of common law precedents in

[387] Standard Oil Company of New Jersey v. United States, 221 U.S. 1, 55, 31 Sup.Ct. 502, 514, 55 L.Ed. 619, 643 (1911). The action of Parliament in repealing these laws was attributed directly to the influence of Smith and the classical economists. Herbruck, *Forestalling, Regrating and Engrossing*, 27 Mich. L. Rev. 365, 380 (1929).

[388] "In exchanging indeed the different productions of different sorts of labour [sic] for one another, some allowance is commonly made for both. It is adjusted, however, not by any accurate measure, but by the higgling and bargaining of the market, according to that sort of rough equality which, though not exact, is sufficient for carrying on the business of common life." Smith, Wealth of Nations 31 (Mod. Lib. ed. 1937). Permission to quote granted by the publishers, Random House, Inc.

[389] Rahl, *Conspiracy and the Anti-Trust Laws*, 44 Ill. L. Rev. 743, 746 (1950). The propensity of traders to conspire to raise prices was immortalized by Adam Smith: "People of the same trade seldom meet together, even for merriment and diversion, but the conversation ends in a conspiracy against the public, or in some contrivance to raise prises." Smith, Wealth of Nations 128 (Mod. Lib. ed. 1937). Permission to quote granted by the publishers, Random House, Inc. The same theme was present in the Senate debates on the Sherman Act. See 21 Cong. Rec. 2456–2460 (1890).

[390] *E.g.*, Stearns v. Barrett, 1 Pick. 443 (Mass. 1823) (division of territory by joint inventors) ; Pierce v. Fuller, 8 Mass. 223 (1811) (agreement not to run stage on certain route) ; Bunn v. Guy, 4 East 190 (Ch. 1803) (not to practice law within 150 miles of London) ; Mitchel v. Reynolds, I P.Wms. 181, 24 Eng.Rep. 347 (Ch. 1711) (bond not to engage in baker's trade in St. Andrew's Holborn Parish for 5 years) ; Clerk v. Governor & Company of Taylors of Exter, 3 Lev. 241 Ex. (1685) (not to exercise tailor's trade in Exter) ; Prugnell v. Gosse, Aleyn 67 (K.B. 1648) (not to keep shop in Basingstooke) ; Broad v. Jollyfe, Cro.Jac. 596 (K.B. 1620) (not to maintain a mercer's shop in Newport) ; Rogers v. Parrey, 2 Bulst. 136 (K.B. 1614) (not to engage in joiner's trade in London for 21 years) ; Colgate v. Bachelor, Cro.Eliz. 872 (Q.B. 1601) (not to haberdasher in Canterbury or Rochester for 4 years) ; The Blacksmith's Case, 2 Leon. 210 (C.P. 1587) (not to blacksmith in town of South-Mims) ; Anonymous, Moore 115 (K.B. 1578) (not to maintain a mercer's shop in Nottingham for 4 years) ; The Dyer's Case, Y.B. 2 Hen. V, f. 5, pl. 26 (1415) (not to engage in dyer's trade in town for 6 months) ; See Eaton, *On Contracts in Restraint of Trade*, 4 Harv. L. Rev. 128 (1890).

[391] United States v. A. Schrader's Son, Inc., 252 U.S. 85, 98–99, 40 Sup.Ct. 251, 253, 64 L.Ed. 471, 475 (1920) ; United States v. Colgate & Co., 250 U.S. 300, 307, 39 Sup.Ct. 465, 468, 63 L.Ed. 992, 997 (1919) ; Patterson v. United States, 222 Fed. 599, 620 (6th Cir. 1915) ; Harbeson, *The Present Status of the Sherman Act*, 39 Mich. L. Rev. 189, 203–204 (1940).

[392] Peppin, *Price Fixing Agreements Under the Sherman Anti-Trust Law*, 28 Calif. L.

the *Addyston* case,[393] a "rule of reason" for interpreting the Sherman Act was announced in the *Standard Oil case* of 1911.[394] The result was that mere size was declared not to be an offense, nor was the existence of its un-exerted power to be condemned.[395] This led to a distinction between "good" and "bad" trusts,[396] based on the absence or presence of overt abusive acts of industrial giantism.[397]

At this point, the economists, who had thoroughly indoctrinated their legal brethren with the notion that competition and monopoly were anti-thetical and mutually exclusive, began to re-appraise the validity of neo-classical economic theory as applied to the greatly changed economy. They perceived the vastness of the moat separating the neo-classical theory ivory tower from the actual business world, and set about to rectify the situation. The acute observations of Alfred Marshall and Professor Pigou on the "im-perfections" of competition in real life assumed new meaning.[398] The work

REV. 297, 350 (1940); *cf.* Circuit Judge Sanborn's opinion in United States v. Trans-Missouri Freight Ass'n, 58 Fed. 58 (8th Cir. 1893), *rev'd*, 166 U.S. 290, 17 Sup.Ct. 540, 41 L.Ed. 1007 (1897); Foulke, *Restraints on Trade*, 12 COL. L. REV. 220, 235 (1912); Allen, *Criminal Conspiracies in Restraint of Trade at Common Law*, 23 HARV. L. REV. 531, 541 (1910); Evans, *The Supreme Court and the Sherman Anti-Trust Act*, 59 U. OF PENN. L. REV. 61, 65 (1910).

[393] United States v. Addyston Pipe & Steel Co., 85 Fed. 271 (6th Cir. 1898), *aff'd*, 175 U.S. 211, 20 Sup.Ct. 96, 44 L.Ed. 136 (1899). This case is the cornerstone of the spreading *per se* illegality doctrine.

[394] Standard Oil Company of New Jersey v. United States, 221 U.S. 1, 31 Sup.Ct. 502, 55 L.Ed. 619 (1911).

[395] ". . . the law does not make mere size an offense or the existence of unexerted power an offense." United States v. United States Steel Corp., 251 U.S. 417, 451, 40 Sup.Ct. 293, 299, 64 L.Ed. 343, 353 (1920). This was approved by the Court in United States v. International Harvester Co., 274 U.S. 693, 708, 47 Sup.Ct. 748, 753–754, 71 L.Ed. 1302, 1310 (1927), which added ". . . when unaccompanied by unlawful conduct in the exercise of its power." *Ibid.* See Johnston & Stevens, *Monopoly or Monopolization—A Reply to Professor Rostow*, 44 ILL. L. REV. 269, 275–277 (1949).

[396] "Good" trusts—United States v. International Harvester Co., 274 U.S. 693, 47 Sup.Ct. 748, 71 L.Ed. 1302 (1927); United States v. United States Steel Corp., 251 U.S. 417, 40 Sup.Ct. 293, 64 L.Ed. 343 (1920); "Bad" trusts—United States v. American Tobacco Co., 221 U.S. 106, 31 Sup.Ct. 632, 55 L.Ed. 663 (1911); Standard Oil Company of New Jersey v. United States, 221 U.S. 1, 31 Sup.Ct. 502, 55 L.Ed. 619 (1911).

[397] *Ibid.*; United States v. American Can Co., 230 Fed. 859 (D.Md. 1916); Oppenheim, *A New Look at Antitrust Enforcement Trends* in N.Y. BAR ASS'N ANTITRUST LAW SYMPOSIUM 67, 71 (1950); McGrath, *Progress in Enforcing the Sherman Act* in N.Y. BAR ASS'N ANTITRUST LAW SYMPOSIUM 15, 17 (1950); Fleming, *Business and the Antitrust Laws*, 28 HARV. BUS. REV. 97, 99 (No. 3, 1950); Adelman, *Effective Competition and the Antitrust Laws*, 61 HARV. L. REV. 1289, 1307 (1948); Kefauver, *The Supreme Court and Congress versus Monopoly*, 20 TENN. L. REV. 254, 257–258 (1948); Levi, *The Antitrust Laws and Monopoly*, 14 U. OF CHI. L. REV. 153, 158 (1947).

[398] For the view that academic controversy over the solutions to some of the internal inconsistencies of Marshallian theory led to the development of imperfect competition theory, see Nicholls, *Social Biases and Recent Theories of Competition*, 58 Q. J. ECON. 1, 8, 1943).

of the mathematical economists on duopoly ceased to be a mere plaything, becoming instead a springboard for further analysis. Out of these foundations came the constructive contributions of Joan Robinson[399] and Edward Chamberlin.[400] The theory of monopolistic competition [wide sense] swept all before it, like a Genghis Khan of economic thought.[401]

Notwithstanding the patient care which the learned economic writers on the subject have taken to point out its limitations and assumptions, monopolistic competition theory has been widely misunderstood.[402] Part of this has been due to the painless process of substituting one dogma for another, which was described above. Another reason is that too few economists realize the public welfare implications of monopolistic competition theory. As Dean Mason pointed out, economic thinking on the subject of monopoly in the late 1930's was directed toward the shaping of a concept of monopoly as a tool of economic analysis, whereas the law sought [and still seeks] a standard of evaluation by means of which a public policy toward business regulation might be evolved.[403] This dichotomy of ends created a semantic tower of Babel.[404] Economists employed the term "monopoly" to describe control of the market, whereas the legal index of "monopoly" was restriction of competition.[405]

On the economists' side of the picture, it is apparent that, by definition,[406] an industry with an oligopoly structure contains monopolistic elements. The amount of "monopoly power" varies with the individual situation. Product differentiation (monopolistic competition) simply is one of the many factors to be considered.

The petroleum industry is said to come within the economists' definition of an oligopoly.[407] Professor Rostow alleges[408] that the courts recently

[399] Robinson, The Economics of Imperfect Competition (1934).

[400] Chamberlin, The Theory of Monopolistic Competition (1933).

[401] Triffin, Monopolistic Competition and General Equilibrium Theory 17 (1949).

[402] Meriam, *Bigness and the Economic Analysis of Competition*, 28 Harv. Bus. Rev. 109, 113–116 (No. 2, 1950); Rodgers & Luedicke, *Dynamic Competition*, 27 Harv. Bus Rev. 237, 248 (1949). Even Professor Chamberlin has felt constrained to interject a comment in an attempt to dam the tide of misunderstanding. Chamberlin, *Product Heterogeneity and Public Policy*, 40 Am. Econ. Rev. 85 (No. 2, May, 1950).

[403] Mason, *Monopoly in Law and Economics*, 47 Yale L. J. 34 (1937); see also Harbeson, *The Present Status of the Sherman Act*, 39 Mich. L. Rev. 189, 203–205 (1940).

[404] See Meriam, *Bigness and the Economic Analysis of Competition*, 28 Harv. Bus. Rev. 109, 113–115 (No. 2, 1950).

[405] See note 403 *supra*. See also Alexander, Book Review, 61 Harv. L. Rev. 1088, 1089 (1948).

[406] See discussion of oligopoly in section III B 11, *supra*.

[407] *TNEC Hearings*, 7103, 7418–7419, 7706, 9609, 9612, 9961; Rostow, A National

have adopted the test of existence of "monopoly power" as the gist of a Sherman Act (Section Two) violation;[409] that an oligopoly structure *necessarily* produces the same untoward results as the old-style single firm monopoly;[410] and that, therefore, the petroleum industry violates the (Section Two) Sherman Act. Wherefore, Professor Rostow prays that the petroleum industry be disintegrated both vertically and horizontally, and the

Policy for the Oil Industry (1948) passim; Cook, Control of the Petroleum Industry by Major Oil Companies (TNEC Monograph 39, 1941) *passim;* Wilcox, Competition and Monopoly in American Industry 27, 127–129, 135 (TNEC Monograph 21, 1940); Adelman, *Integration and Antitrust Policy,* 63 Harv. L. Rev. 27, 61–62 (1949); Bain, *Rostow's Proposals for Petroleum Policy,* 57 J. Pol. Econ. 55, 59 (1949). One might ask, what is meant by a "few" sellers? In other words, how diffuse must an oligopoly be before it is deemed "safe" in the public interest? Herbert Bergson, head of the Antitrust Division, Department of Justice, testified that he doubted very much that 10 firms would constitute an oligopoly as it "would be rather difficult for them to operate that way." *Hearings before Subcommittee on Study of Monopoly Power of the Committee on the Judiciary,* 81st Cong., 1st Sess., Part 1, 366 (1949). The Supreme Court thought four sellers (two of whom made 90% of the sales) provided effective competition in United States v. National Lead Co., 332 U.S. 319, 67 Sup.Ct. 1634, 91 L.Ed. 2077 (1947). According to the Department of Justice's own classification, there are at least 22 'major" oil companies. Complaint, pp. 6–7, United States v. American Petroleum Institute, Civil No. 8524, D. D.C., Sept. 30, 1940.

[408] For the view that this constitutes an allegation rather than a conclusion, see Book Review, 34 A.B.A.J. 230, 231 (1948); Kahn, Book Review, 34 Corn. L. Q. 284 (1948); Hickman, Book Review, 34 Iowa L. Rev. 155, 158 (1948); MacLachlan, Book Review, 13 Law & Contemp. Prob. 715 (1948); Marshall, Book Review, 57 Yale L. J. 1323 (1948).

[409] Rostow, A National Policy for the Oil Industry xiii, 124–127, 134–137 (1948); Rostow, *Monopoly Under the Sherman Act: Power or Purpose?,* 43 Ill. L. Rev. 745 (1949) *passim;* Rostow, *The New Sherman Act: A Positive Instrument of Progress,* 14 U. of Chi. L. Rev. 567 (1947) *passim.* Nor does Professor Rostow stand alone in this allegation. See Fleming, *Business and the Antitrust Laws,* 28 Harv. Bus. Rev. 97, 99 (No. 3, 1950); Kefauver, *The Supreme Court and Congress versus Monopoly,* 20 Tenn. L. Rev. 254 (1948); Harbeson, *A New Phase of the Antitrust Law,* 45 Mich. L. Rev. 977 (1947); Levi, *The Antitrust Laws and Monopoly,* 14 U. of Chi. L. Rev. 153 (1947); Zlinkoff & Barnard, *The Supreme Court and a Comparative Economy: 1946 Term,* 47 Col. L. Rev. 914 (1947).

[410] Oppenheim, *A New Look at Antitrust Enforcement Trends in* N. Y. Bar Ass'n Antitrust Law Symposium 69, 72 (1950) gives the Rostow writings cited in note 409 *supra* this interpretation. Again, Professor Rostow has his supporters. See Mr. Justice Douglas' dissent in United States v. Columbia Steel Co., 334 U.S. 495, 68 Sup.Ct. 1107, 92 L.Ed. 1533 (1948); *Hearings, supra* note 407, at 76–77 (Mr. Justice Tom Clark, then Attorney General), 366–367 (Ass't Attorney General Bergson); Bergson, *Enforcement and Administration of the Federal Antitrust Laws* in Southwestern Legal Foundation 1950 Institute on Antitrust Laws and Price Regulations, 1, 10 (1950); Bergson, Bigness and the Antitrust Laws 3 (mimeographed address before the Public Relations Society of America, New York City, on Dec. 6, 1949); Address of Corwin Edwards before the American Business Law Institute, New York City, Dec. 28, 1949 (mimeographed); Address of John Blair before Economic Workshop, University of Minnesota, July 12, 1949 (mimeographed).

remainder "atomized" until the oligopoly becomes a polypoly and pure competition is restored.[411]

1. Does the Mere Existence of "Monopoly Power" Violate Section Two of the Sherman Act?[412] Because of the richness of the literature analyzing the cases which have brought a "new look" to anti-trust enforcement,[413] the law will be summarized as much as possible, avoiding extensive discussion of the cases. The language of the Act suggests a logical division of the subject matter into three main topics: monopolization, attempts to monopolize, and conspiracies to monopolize.

(a) *Monopolization.* The crime of monopolization consists of acquiring *or* maintaining monopoly power (present power to raise prices or exclude competition)[414] *with* the intent or purpose to exercise that power.[415]

---

[411] Rostow, A National Policy for the Oil Industry 118 (1948). Professor Rostow later made a fleeting reference to workable competition. Rostow, *Monopoly Under the Sherman Act: Power or Purpose?*, 43 Ill. L. Rev. 745, 785 (1949). But the language in his books smacks of a nostalgia for pure competition. Johnston & Stevens, *Monopoly or Monopolization—A Reply to Professor Rostow*, 44 Ill. L. Rev. 269, 271 (1949); Alexander, Book Review, 61 Harv. L. Rev. 1088, 1090–1091 (1948); Elsbree, Book Review, 42 Am. Pol. Sci. Rev. 577, 578 (1948). Certainly, the notion that firms must be so numerous and so small that no one of them can single out any of its rivals for attack, nor be able to determine its own policies based on its competitors' anticipated reactions thereto, goes beyond workable competition. His demand for impersonal competition identifies the author with the neo-classical school of pure competitive theory. Edwards, Maintaining Competition 124 (1949). Perhaps that was in George Stigler's mind when he wrote that Rostow's chapter on monopoly was inconclusive and fundamentally misdirected because Rostow had followed the (wrong!) economists too closely. Stigler, Book Review, 57 Yale L. J. 1322 (1948).

[412] "Every person who shall monopolize, or attempt to monopolize, or combine or conspire with any other person or persons, to monopolize any part of the trade or commerce among the several States, or with foreign nations, shall be guilty of a misdemeanor, . . ." 26 Stat. 209 (1890), as amended, 15 U.S.C. § 2 (1946).

[413] See *e.g.*, notes 403, 409, and 411 *supra.*

[414] American Tobacco Co. v. United States, 328 U.S. 781, 811, 66 Sup.Ct. 1125, 1140, 90 L.Ed. 1575, 1595 (1946); National Cotton Oil Co. v. Texas, 197 U.S. 115, 129, 25 Sup.Ct. 379, 382, 49 L.Ed. 689, 694 (1905); United States v. Aluminum Company of America, 91 F.Supp. 333, 342 (S.D.N.Y. 1950); United States Steel v. Corn Products Refining Co., 234 Fed. 964, 1012 (S.D.N.Y. 1916); United States v. Patten, 187 Fed. 664, 672 (C.C.S.D.N.Y. 1911); United States v. American Tobacco Co., 164 Fed. 700, 721 (C.C.S.D.N.Y. 1908); see Rostow, *Monopoly Under the Sherman Act: Power or Purpose?*, 43 Ill. L. Rev. 745, 763 (1949). Assistant Attorney General Bergson prefers a wider definition, to wit, the ability to impose unreasonable restraints on competition, to determine prices without substantial regard for competitive market pressures, artificially to allocate and limit production, to divide markets and fields of production, and to exclude competitors. Bergson, *Bigness in Business in* N. Y. Bar Ass'n Antitrust Law Symposium 85, 86 (1950); see also Bergson, Bigness and the Antitrust Laws 3 (1949).

[415] United States v. Paramount Pictures, Inc., 334 U.S. 131, 173, 68 Sup.Ct. 915, 937, 92 L.Ed. 1260, 1301 (1948); Schine Chain Theatres, Inc. v. United States, 334 U.S. 110, 130, 68 Sup.Ct. 947, 958, 92 L.Ed. 1245, 1259 (1948); United States v. Griffith, 334 U.S. 100, 107,

Thus, actual exclusion of existing or potential competitors,[416] or even the exercise of the power to exclude them is not a prerequisite.[417] The distinction between "good" and "bad" trusts no longer is valid.[418] Nor must monopoly power be unlawfully acquired.[419]

As might be expected from the text of the statute,[420] it is unnecessary to show national monopolization, *i.e.,* power and intent to exclude *all* competitors. It is sufficient that an appreciable part of interstate or foreign commerce is monopolized.[421] In each case there must be a judicial delimitation of the relevent competitive market.[422] In the *Alcoa* case it was the "virgin" aluminum ingot market.[423] The domestic leaf market[424] and the

68 Sup.Ct. 941, 945, 92 L.Ed. 1236, 1243 (1948); American Tobacco Co. v. United States, 328 U.S. 781, 809, 66 Sup.Ct. 1125, 1139, 90 L.Ed. 1575, 1593 (1946).

[416] American Tobacco Co. v. United States, 328 U.S. 781, 810, 66 Sup.Ct. 1125, 1139, 90 L.Ed. 1575, 1594 (1946); United States v. New York Great Atlantic & Pacific Tea Co., 173 F.2d 79, 88 (7th Cir. 1949); United States v. Aluminum Company of America, 148 F.2d 416, 431 (2d Cir. 1945); United States v. Aluminum Company of America, 91 F.Supp. 333, 342 (S.D.N.Y. 1950); United States v. Pullman Co., 50 F.Supp. 123, 134 (E.D.Pa. 1943); see Rostow, *supra* note 414, at 763; Kefauver, *The Supreme Court and Congress versus Monopoly,* 20 Tenn. L. Rev. 254, 260 (1948).

[417] United States v. Paramount Pictures, Inc., 334 U.S. 131, 173, 68 Sup.Ct. 915, 937, 92 L.Ed. 1260, 1301 (1948); United States v. Griffith, 334 U.S. 100, 107, 68 Sup.Ct. 941, 945, 92 L.Ed. 1236, 1243 (1948); American Tobacco Co. v. United States, 328 U.S. 781, 810, 66 Sup.Ct. 1125, 1139, 90 L.Ed. 1575, 1594 (1946).

[418] United States v. Aluminum Company of America, 148 F.2d 416, 427 (2d Cir. 1945); United States v. Pullman Co., 50 F.Supp. 123, 134 (E.D.Pa. 1943); Loevinger, The Law of Free Enterprise 215–218 (1949); Fleming, *Business and the Antitrust Laws,* 28 Harv. Bus. Rev. 97, 99 (No. 3, 1950); Bergson, *Bigness in Business* in N. Y.Bar Ass'n Antitrust Law Symposium 85, 89–90 (1950); Rostow, *supra* note 414, at 772.

[419] See note 415 *supra.*

[420] Section Two condemns monopolizing "any part of trade or commerce." See note 412 *supra.*

[421] United States v. Paramount Pictures, Inc., 334 U.S. 131, 173, 68 Sup.Ct. 915, 936–937, 92 L.Ed. 1260, 1300 (1948); United States v. Griffith, 334 U.S. 100, 107, 68 Sup.Ct. 941, 945, 92 L.Ed. 1236, 1243 (1948); United States v. Yellow Cab Co., 332 U.S. 218, 225, 67 Sup.Ct. 1560, 1564, 91 L.Ed. 2010, 2017 (1947); American Tobacco Co. v. United States, 328 U.S. 781, 789, 66 Sup.Ct. 1125, 1129, 90 L.Ed. 1575, 1583 (1946); William Goldman Theatres, Inc. v. Loew's, Inc., 150 F.2d 738, 744 (3d Cir. 1945); *cf.* United States v. Columbia Steel Co., 334 U.S. 495, 519, 68 Sup.Ct. 1107, 1120, 92 L.Ed. 1533, 1550 (1948); Montague & Co. v. Lowry, 193 U.S. 38, 24 Sup.Ct. 307, 48 L.Ed. 608 (1904); Zlinkoff & Barnard, *Mergers and the Anti-Trust Laws: The Columbia Steel Case, The Supreme Court and a Competitive Economy 1947 Term,* 97 U. of Pa. L. Rev. 151, 166–167 (1948).

[422] *Cf.* United States v. Columbia Steel Co., 334 U.S. 495, 68 Sup.Ct. 1107, 92 L.Ed. 1533 (1948); Rostow, *Monopoly Under the Sherman Act: Power or Purpose?,* 43 Ill. L. Rev. 745, 779 (1949); Note, 58 Yale L. J. 764, 766 (1949).

[423] United States v. Aluminum Company of America, 148 F.2d 416, 424–425 (2d Cir. 1945). This choice has been criticized by economists. Meriam, *The Sherman Antitrust Act and Business Economics* in N. Y. Bar Ass'n Antitrust Law Symposium 93, 98 (1950); Mason, *The Current Status of the Monopoly Problem in the United States,* 62 Harv. L. Rev. 1265,

principal product distribution phase were considered separately in the *American Tobacco* suit.[425] The "first-run" exhibition field was the core of the movie cases.[426] The taxicab operating business in four large cities was the scope of the survey in the *Yellow Cab* decision.[427] It is of utmost importance that this definitive task be performed capably, because in and of itself, the delimitation of the market may well determine the outcome of the case.[428] An outstanding example of this is the *Alcoa* case. In the district court, Judge Caffey included "secondary" aluminum and excluded Alcoa's "captive" production in ascertaining the scope of the relevent competitive market.[429] Alcoa's share in that market was only thirty-three percent. But when the case came before the Court of Appeals, Judge Learned Hand excluded "secondary" and included "captive" aluminum. This caused Alcoa's share of the market to be over ninety percent, which the court felt was sufficient to constitute a monopoly.[430]

After defining the market both geographically and by product,[431] the court is confronted with the task of measuring monopoly power. In a much quoted statement,[432] Judge Hand said that a ninety percent share

---

1273–1274 (1949) ; Adelman, *Effective Competition and the Antitrust Laws*, 61 Harv. L. Rev. 1289, 1309–1310 (1948). This does not cast aspersions at Judge Learned Hand, but certainly it illustrates the difficulties which beset a careful determination of the "concentration" cases.

[424] American Tobacco Co. v. United States, 328 U.S. 781, 798, 66 Sup.Ct. 1125, 1134, 90 L.Ed. 1575, 1588 (1946).

[425] *Id.* at 804, 66 Sup.Ct. at 1136, 90 L.Ed. at 1591.

[426] United States v. Paramount Pictures, Inc., 334 U.S. 131, 172–173, 68 Sup.Ct. 915, 936, 92 L.Ed. 1260, 1300 (1948).

[427] United States v. Yellow Cab Co., 332 U.S. 218, 225, 67 Sup.Ct. 1560, 1564, 91 L.Ed. 2010, 2017 (1947).

[428] United States v. Aluminum Company of America, 91 F.Supp. 355–356 (S.D.N.Y. 1950) ; Note, 33 Minn. L. Rev. 398, 404 (1949).

[429] "Secondary" aluminum has been cast before. It is reclaimed and remelted into ingot similar to the virgin aluminum. It comes from two sources: the clippings and trimmings of sheet aluminum which are left after the pattern has been cut, and scrap aluminum which has been recovered from junk. "Captive" aluminum receives its name from the vertically integrated nature of the industry. It is that amount of aluminum ingot which Alcoa absorbs in its fabricating stage.

[430] United States v. Aluminum Company of America, 148 F.2d 416, 424 (2d Cir. 1945).

[431] See note 422 *supra.*

[432] Zlinkoff & Barnard, *supra* note 421, at 176 claim this was an "unsound dictum." But the percentages correspond to the alternative competitive markets being considered. The whole purpose of the discussion of the secondary aluminum depended upon the percentages. Johnston & Stevens, *Monopoly or Monopolization—A Reply to Professor Rostow*, 44 Ill. L. Rev. 269, 275 n.31 (1949). By sheer coincidence, the sixty-four percent figure is the same as that in United States v. International Harvester Co., 274 U.S. 693, 47 Sup.Ct. 748, 71 L.Ed. 1302 (1927), where the Court found effective competition to exist despite the fact that International Harvester held 64.1 percent of the trade in harvesting machines, and had capital and resources in excess of the aggregate of its rivals. See United States v. Aluminum Company of America, 91 F.Supp. 333, 342 (S.D.N.Y. 1950).

". . . is enough to constitute a monopoly; it is doubtful whether sixty or sixty-four percent would be enough; and certainly thirty-three per cent is not."[433] Does this mean that percentage share of the relevant competitive market is the controlling criterion of monopoly power? It would seem not.[434] Percentage share of the market is not a short-cut to decision, but only a short-hand expression of economic power, *viz.*, size, capital, resources, trade, nature of the market, etc.[435] The court will consider the strength of the remaining competition, the probable development of the industry generally, consumer demand trends, and other characteristics of the market.[436] The reason for this is obvious—if products on the periphery of the defined competitive market are close substitutes,[437] if entry into the market is comparatively free, if import supply is elastic with price fluctuations, even a large percentage share of the market is compatible with a small degree of market control.[438] Conversely, under some circumstances, a small share of a particular market held by a conglomerately integrated industrial giant could mask a large degree of market control.[439]

This underscores the need for a yardstick of industrial measurement. At this point the previously mentioned "effective" or "workable" competition concept is particularly apposite, and its articulate use is beginning to filter into the cases.[440] This represents essentially the utilization of a

[433] See note 430 *supra.*

[434] "The relative effect of percentage command of a market varies with the setting in which that factor is placed." United States v. Columbia Steel Co., 334 U.S. 495, 528, 68 Sup.Ct. 1107, 1124, 92 L.Ed. 1533, 1554 (1948) ; see Johnston & Stevens, *Monopoly or Monopolization —A Reply to Professor Rostow,* 44 ILL. L. REV. 269, 273 (1949) ; Rostow, *Monopoly Under the Sherman Act: Power or Purpose?,* 43 ILL. L. REV. 745, 779 (1949) ; Zlinkoff & Barnard, *supra* note 421, at 171–172; Note, 58 YALE L. J. 969, 976 n. 40 (1949).

[435] United States v. Aluminum Company of America, 91 F.Supp. 333, 345 (S.D.N.Y. 1950) ; Rostow, *supra* note 434, at 778–779.

[436] United States v. Columbia Steel Co., 334 U.S. 495, 527, 68 Sup.Ct. 1107, 1124, 92 L.Ed. 1533, 1554 (1948) ; United States v. Aluminum Company of America, 91 F.Supp. 333, 345 (S.D.N.Y. 1950) ; Rostow, *supra* note 434, at 779.

[437] One might ask, if these products are close substitutes, why aren't they included in the relative competitive market? The answer is that substitution is a matter of degree and the court has to scribe the boundary line arbitrarily at some point. See Chamberlin, *Product Heterogeneity and Public Policy,* 40 AM. ECON. REV. 85, 86–87 (No. 2, May, 1950).

[438] Mason, *The Current Status of the Monopoly Problem in the United States,* 62 HARV. L. REV. 1265, 1274 (1949).

[439] *Ibid.;* EDWARDS, MAINTAINING COMPETITION 100 (1949).

[440] *Cf.* United States v. Columbia Steel Co., 334 U.S. 495, 503, 68 Sup.Ct. 1107, 1112, 92 L.Ed. 1533, 1541 (1948) ; United States v. Aluminum Company of America, 91 F.Supp. 333 (S.D.N.Y. 1950) *passim;* United States v. National Lead Co., 332 U.S. 319, 352, 67 Sup.Ct. 1634, 1650, 91 L.Ed. 2077, 2102 (1947) ; see Oppenheim, *A New Look at Antitrust Enforcement Trends* in N. Y. BAR ASS'N ANTITRUST LAW SYMPOSIUM 69, 76–77 (1950).

"rule of reason" technique in an effort to have realities dominate the judgment.[441]

There is considerable controversy concerning the necessity of intent. Professor Rostow feels that once monopoly power has been shown to exist, any requirement of intent is only perfunctory.[442] There is some language in the cases which appears to bear this out.[443] Certainly, it is safe to say that deliberate and specific intent to acquire monopoly power is unnecessary where, as a result of defendant's conduct or business arrangements, monopoly is a *fait accompli*.[444] But note how carefully Judge Hand pointed out that merely because Alcoa had a monopoly of the aluminum ingot market, it did not follow that it had "monopolized" the market.[445] Note, too, the language of Mr. Justice Douglas in the *Griffith*[446] decision when he said: "Anyone who owns and operates the single theatre in a town, or who acquires the exclusive right to exhibit a film, has a monopoly in the popular sense. But he usually does not violate §2 of the Sherman Act unless he has acquired or maintained his strategic position, or sought to expand his monopoly, or expanded it by means of those restraints of trade which are cognizable under §1."

Why have these judges taken such great pains to acknowledge the existence of a "lawful" monopoly,[447] *i.e.*, one that was "thrust on" defend-

[441] *Cf.* Appalachian Coals, Inc. v. United States, 288 U.S. 344, 360, 53 Sup.Ct. 471, 474, 77 L.Ed. 825, 830 (1933); Meriam, *The Sherman Antitrust Act and Business Economics in* N. Y. Bar Ass'n Antitrust Symposium 93, 94–96 (1950).

[442] Rostow, *Monopoly Under the Sherman Act: Power or Purpose?*, 43 Ill. L. Rev. 745, 776 (1949); *cf.* Handler, A Study of the Construction and Enforcement of the Federal Antitrust Laws 78 (TNEC Monograph 38, 1941).

[443] *Cf.* United States v. Columbia Steel Co., 334 U.S. 495, 525, 68 Sup.Ct. 1107, 1123, 92 L.Ed. 1533, 1552 (1948); United States v. Paramount Pictures, Inc., 334 U.S. 131, 173, 68 Sup.Ct. 915, 937, 92 L.Ed. 1260, 1301 (1948); United States v. Griffith, 334 U.S. 100, 105– 107, 68 Sup.Ct. 941, 944–945, 92 L.Ed. 1236, 1242–1243 (1948); United States v. Aluminum Company of America, 148 F.2d 416, 431–432 (2d Cir. 1945).

[444] United States v. Columbia Steel Co., 334 U.S. 495, 525, 68 Sup.Ct. 1107, 1123, 92 L.Ed. 1533, 1552 (1948); United States v. Paramount Pictures, Inc., 334 U.S. 131, 173, 68 Sup.Ct. 915, 937, 92 L.Ed. 1260, 1301 (1948); United States v. Griffith, 334 U.S. 100, 105, 68 Sup.Ct. 941, 944, 92 L.Ed. 1236, 1242 (1948); United States v. Aluminum Company of America, 148 F.2d 416, 431–432 (2d Cir. 1945); *cf.* United States v. Masonite Corp., 316 U.S. 265, 275, 62 Sup.Ct. 1070, 1076, 86 L.Ed. 1461, 1474 (1942); United States v. Patten, 226 U.S. 525, 543, 33 Sup.Ct. 141, 145, 57 L.Ed. 333, 342 (1913); Swift & Co. v. United States, 196 U.S. 375, 396, 25 Sup.Ct. 276, 279, 49 L.Ed. 518, 524 (1905); United States v. Aluminum Company of America, 91 F.Supp. 333, 342 (S.D.N.Y. 1950).

[445] United States v. Aluminum Company of America, 148 F.2d 416, 492 (2d Cir. 1945).

[446] United States v. Griffith, 334 U.S. 100, 106, 68 Sup.Ct. 941, 945, 92 L.Ed. 1236, 1243 (1948); *cf.* United States v. Paramount Pictures, Inc., 334 U.S. 131, 171, 68 Sup.Ct. 915, 936, 92 L.Ed. 1260, 1299–1300 (1948).

[447] See note 445 *supra; cf.* Eastern Wine Corp. v. Winslow-Warren, Ltd., 137 F.2d 955,

ant?[448] Possibly, it was to avoid the absurdity of encouraging competition and forbidding one logical end product.[449] However, it is significant that the statute uses the verb "monopolize," not the noun, to describe the crime.[450] Also, an essentially criminal approach is employed in determining initial guilt, although the remedy aspects is on the equity side of the court.[451] The combination of these two factors would seem to require some form of intent to be present. The criminal law doctrine of a defendant intending the probable consequences of his act is applicable. As Judge Hand stated, ". . . no monopolist monopolizes unconscious of what he is doing."[452]

An inference of wrongful intent is easily drawn where monopoly power has been obtained by a combination of former competitors,[453] or by means of an unlawful conspiracy,[454] or maintained by a determined and

958–959 (2d Cir. 1943); United States v. Trans-Missouri Freight Ass'n, 58 Fed. 58, 82 (8th Cir. 1893); *In re* Greene, 52 Fed. 104, 116–117 (C.C.S.D.Ohio 1892); 21 Cong. Rec. 3151–3152 (1890); Johnston & Stevens, *Monopoly or Monopolization—A Reply to Professor Rostow*, 44 Ill. L. Rev. 269, 278 (1949).

[448] See note 445 *supra*. Judge Hand listed three types of situations where this might occur: (1) where the market is so limited that it is impossible to produce at all and meet the cost of production except by a large scale plant producing enough to supply the whole demand; (2) where changes in cost or taste eliminate all but one firm; (3) where a single producer is the survivor out of a group of active competitors, merely due to superior skill, foresight and industry. *Id.* at 430.

[449] *Cf.* United States v. Aluminum Company of America, 148 F.2d 416, 430 (2d Cir. 1945): ". . . the [Sherman] Act does not mean to condemn the resultant of those very forces which it is its prime object to foster: finis opus coronat. The successful competitor, having been urged to compete, must not be turned upon when he wins." See Adelman, *Effective Competition and the Antitrust Laws*, 61 Harv. L. Rev. 1289, 1310 (1948).

[450] *Cf.* United States v. Aluminum Company of America, 148 F.2d 416, 429 (2d Cir. 1945); National Biscuit Co. v. Federal Trade Commission, 299 Fed. 733, 738 (2d Cir. 1924); Patterson v. United States, 222 Fed. 599, 619 (6th Cir. 1915); United States v. Whiting, 212 Fed. 466, 478 (D.Mass. 1914); United States v. Standard Oil Co., 173 Fed. 177, 196 (C.C.E.D. Mo. 1909); Johnston & Stevens, *Monopoly or Monopolization—A Reply to Professor Rostow*, 44 Ill. L. Rev. 269, 274 (1949).

[451] *Cf.* United States v. Aluminum Company of America, 148 F.2d 416, 430–432 (2d Cir. 1945); Hadlick, Criminal Prosecution Under the Sherman Anti-Trust Act c. II (1939); Rahl, Book Review, 43 Ill. L. Rev. 421, 422–423 (1948).

[452] United States v. Aluminum Company of America, 148 F.2d 416, 432 (2d Cir. 1945).

[453] United States v. Southern Pacific Co., 259 U.S. 214, 42 Sup.Ct. 496, 66 L.Ed. 907 (1922); United States v. Reading Co., 253 U.S. 26, 40 Sup.Ct. 425, 64 L.Ed. 760 (1920); United States v. Union Pacific R.R., 226 U.S. 61, 33 Sup.Ct. 53, 57 L.Ed. 124 (1912); United States v. Terminal Railroad Association of St. Louis, 224 U.S. 383, 32 Sup.Ct. 507, 56 L.Ed. 810 (1912); Northern Securities Co. v. United States, 193 U.S. 197, 24 Sup.Ct. 436, 48 L.Ed. 679 (1904); United States v. Corn Products Refining Co., 234 Fed. 964 (S.D.N.Y. 1916).

[454] American Tobacco Co. v. United States, 328 U.S. 781, 66 Sup.Ct. 1125, 90 L.Ed. 1575 (1946); William Goldman Theatres, Inc. v. Loew's, Inc., 150 F.2d 738 (3d Cir. 1945); *cf.* United States v. Paramount Pictures, Inc., 334 U.S. 131, 170, 68 Sup.Ct. 915, 935, 92 L.Ed. 1260, 1299 (1948).

aggressive program of forestalling competition.[455] *A fortiori,* it can be inferred in the abuse cases.[456] Thus, it would seem that mere existence of monopoly power in and of itself is not enough to constitute a Section Two violation. The intent to exercise the power to raise prices or exclude competitors must be shown. In many instances this intent may readily be inferred. The holder of monopoly power must walk a legal tight-rope in order to avoid acts which would support such an inference.[457] But there is a permitted area of "lawful" monopoly. Its boundaries remain to be pricked out by case-to-case decisions.

(b) *Attempts to Monopolize.* The phrase "attempt to monopolize" denotes acts which are not sufficient in themselves to accomplish monopolization, but which nevertheless produce a dangerous probability that it will occur.[458] In this situation the presence of specific intent to gain a forbidden degree of market control is indispensible.[459] In order to establish the existence of this intent, which goes beyond the mere intent to do the act,[460] a high order of proof has always been required.[461]

Specific intent is spelled out by proof of recourse to business practices

---

[455] United States v. Aluminum Company of America, 148 F.2d 416 (2d Cir. 1945); United States v. Pullman Co., 50 F.Supp. 123 (E.D.Pa. 1943); *cf.* American Tobacco Co. v. United States, 328 U.S. 781, 797, 66 Sup.Ct. 1125, 1133, 90 L.Ed. 1575, 1587 (1946).

[456] United States v. Paramount Pictures, Inc., 334 U.S. 131, 68 Sup.Ct. 915, 92 L.Ed. 1260 (1948); Schine Chain Theatres, Inc. v. United States, 334 U.S. 110, 68 Sup.Ct. 947, 92 L.Ed. 1245 (1948); United States v. Griffith, 334 U.S. 100, 68 Sup.Ct. 941, 92 L.Ed. 1236 (1948).

[457] Consider the following language of Judge Hand in the *Alcoa* case, approved by the Supreme Court in the *American Tobacco* case: ". . . [W]e can think of no more effective exclusion than progressively to embrace each new opportunity as it opened, and to face every newcomer with new capacity already geared into a great organization, having the advantage of experience, trade connections and the elite of personnel. Only in case we interpret 'exclusion' as limited to manoeuvres not honestly industrial, but actuated solely by a desire to prevent competition, can such a course, indefatigably pursued, be deemed not 'exclusionary.' So to limit it would in our judgment emasculate the Act; would permit such consolidations as it was designed to prevent." United States v. Aluminum Company of America, 148 F.2d 416, 431 (2d Cir. 1945).

[458] American Tobacco Co. v. United States, 328 U.S. 781, 785, 66 Sup.Ct. 1125, 1127, 90 L.Ed. 1575, 1581 (1946); Swift & Co. v. United States, 196 U.S. 375, 396, 25 Sup.Ct. 276, 279, 49 L.Ed. 518, 524 (1905); United States v. Aluminum Company of America, 148 F.2d 416, 431–432 (2d Cir. 1945).

[459] United States v. Columbia Steel Co. 334 U.S. 495, 532, 68 Sup.Ct. 1107, 1126, 92 L.Ed. 1533, 1556 (1948); United States v. Griffith, 334 U.S. 100, 105, 68 Sup.Ct. 941, 945, 92 L.Ed. 1236, 1242 (1948); Swift & Co. v. United States, 196 U.S. 375, 396, 25 Sup.Ct. 276, 279, 49 L.Ed. 518, 524 (1905); United States v. Aluminum Company of America, 148 F.2d 416, 432 (2d Cir. 1945); Rahl, *Conspiracy and the Anti-Trust Laws,* 44 ILL. L. REV. 743, 747–748 (1950); Johnston & Stevens, *Monopoly or Monopolization—A Reply to Professor Rostow,* 44 ILL. L. REV. 269, 290 (1949).

[460] United States v. Aluminum Company of America, 148 F.2d 416, 432 (2d Cir. 1945).

[461] Johnston & Stevens, *Monopoly or Monopolization—A Reply to Professor Rostow,* 44 ILL. L. REV. 269, 289 (1949); *cf.* Rahl, *supra* note 459, at 748.

which themselves constitute unreasonable restraints of trade,[462] or which are distasteful to the judges for unexpressed ethical reasons.[463] A long history of acquisitions, especially of potential competitors, will be scrutinized carefully for signs of a "creeping monopoly."[464] Because of the difficulty of proving specific intent, few cases will rest solely on alleged attempts to monopolize. The usual practice in the concentration cases is to "throw the book" at defendants, charging four separate violations: (1) conspiracy to restrain trade (§1), (2) monopolization, (3) attempt to monopolize, and (4) conspiracy to monopolize.[465]

   (c) *Conspiracies to Monopolize.* The *American Tobacco* case[466] restated the necessity of a conspiracy allegation to aggregate independent firms into a group monopolization violation.[467] It is elementary that conspiracies seldom are capable of proof by direct testimony, and may be inferred from the course of conduct of the alleged conspirators.[468] Although proof of an express agreement would, of course, be determinative, formal agreement is not required.[469] Therefore, the proof of conspiracy lies usually

---

[462] United States v. Paramount Pictures, Inc., 334 U.S. 131, 171, 68 Sup.Ct. 915, 936, 92 L.Ed. 1260, 1300 (1948); United States v. Griffith, 334 U.S. 100, 106, 68 Sup.Ct. 941, 945, 92 L.Ed. 1236, 1243 (1948); *cf.* Schine Chain Theatres, Inc. v. United States, 334 U.S. 110, 68 Sup.Ct. 947, 92 L.Ed. 1245 (1948).

[463] Rostow, *Monopoly Under the Sherman Act: Power or Purpose?*, 43 ILL. L. REV. 745, 770 (1949).

[464] United States v. Columbia Steel Co., 334 U.S. 495, 532–534, 68 Sup.Ct. 1107, 1126–1127, 92 L.Ed. 1533, 1556–1557 (1948); see note 453 *supra;* Hale, *Vertical Integration: Impact of the Antitrust Laws upon Combinations of Successive Stages of Production and Distribution*, 49 COL. L. REV. 921, 948 (1949).

[465] See American Tobacco Co. v. United States, 328 U.S. 781, 66 Sup.Ct. 1125, 90 L.Ed. 1575 (1946); United States v. Shapiro, 103 F.2d 775 (2d Cir. 1939); Note, 33 MINN. L. REV. 398, 404–405 (1949).

[466] 328 U.S. 781, 66 Sup.Ct. 1125, 90 L.Ed. 1575 (1946).

[467] Rahl, *Conspiracy and the Anti-Trust Laws*, 44 ILL. L. REV. 743, 748, 754, 756 (1950); Johnston & Stevens, *Monopoly or Monopolization—A Reply to Professor Rostow*, 44 ILL L. REV. 269, 292 (1949); Dession, *The Trial of Economic and Technological Issues of Fact: I*, 58 YALE L. J. 1019, 1023 (1949); Levi, *The Antitrust Laws and Monopoly*, 14 U. OF CHI L. REV. 153, 178 (1947); Rahl, Book Review, 43 ILL. L. REV. 421, 424 (1948).

[468] Interstate Circuit, Inc. v. United States, 306 U.S. 208, 211, 59 Sup.Ct. 467, 472, 83 L.Ed. 610, 617 (1939); Eastern States Retail Lumber Dealers' Ass'n v. United States, 234 U.S. 600, 612, 34 Sup.Ct. 951, 954, 58 L.Ed. 1490, 1499 (1914); Rahl, *Conspiracy and the Anti-Trust Laws*, 44 ILL L. REV. 743, 757 (1950).

[469] United States v. Paramount Pictures, Inc., 334 U.S. 131, 142, 68 Sup.Ct. 915, 922, 92 L.Ed. 1260, 1285 (1948); United States v. United States Gypsum Co., 333 U.S. 364, 394, 68 Sup.Ct. 525, 541, 92 L.Ed. 746, 765 (1948); American Tobacco Co. v. United States, 328 U.S. 781, 809, 66 Sup.Ct. 1125, 1139, 90 L.Ed. 1575, 1594 (1946); United States v. Masonite Corp., 316 U.S. 265, 275, 62 Sup.Ct. 1070, 1076, 86 L.Ed. 1461, 1474 (1942); Interstate Circuit, Inc. v. United States, 306 U.S. 208, 227, 59 Sup.Ct. 467, 474, 83 L.Ed. 610, 620 (1939); Stack v. United States, 27 F.2d 16, 17 (9th Cir. 1928); Fowler v. United States, 273 Fed. 15, 19 (9th Cir. 1921).

in a parade of evidence covering practically all business acts done by defendants over a long period of time. The purpose of this evidence is twofold: first, to establish the alleged collectivism of action, and second, to show the trend toward monopoly or to support the inference of intent to monopolize.

The portrait of conspiracy as a twilight meeting of peaked-hat conspirators is outmoded.[470] It may be inferred from an adherence to a *common* course of action *with knowledge* of its concerted nature.[471] This tacit concert of action may follow a course of startling deviation from the ordinary, or it may be only slightly abnormal. Acts may be themselves unlawful, such as price fixing,[472] division of marketing territory,[473] group boycotts,[474] tying clause arrangements,[475] patent misuse,[476] or *long-term ex-*

[470] William Goldman Theatres, Inc. v. Loew's, Inc., 150 F.2d 738, 743 n. 15 (3d Cir. 1945) ; HAMILTON & TILL, ANTITRUST IN ACTION 15 (TNEC Monograph 16, 1941) ; Rahl, Book Review, 43 ILL. L. REV. 421, 422 (1948).

[471] United States v. Paramount Pictures, Inc., 334 U.S. 131, 142, 68 Sup.Ct. 915, 922, 92 L.Ed. 1260, 1285 (1948) ; United States v. United States Gypsum Co., 333 U.S. 364, 394, 68 Sup.Ct. 525, 541, 92 L.Ed. 746, 765 (1948) ; United States v. Masonite Corp., 316 U.S. 265, 275, 62 Sup.Ct. 1070, 1076, 86 L.Ed. 1461, 1473 (1942) ; Interstate Circuit, Inc. v. United States, 306 U.S. 208, 226, 59 Sup.Ct. 467, 474, 83 L.Ed. 610, 620 (1939) ; American Tobacco Co. v. United States, 147 F.2d 93, 107 (6th Cir. 1944) ; Marino v. United States, 91 F.2d 691, 694 (9th Cir. 1937) ; Fowler v. United States, 273 Fed. 15, 19 (9th Cir. 1921). See note 376 *supra.*

[472] *E.g.,* United States v. Bausch & Lomb Co., 321 U.S. 707, 64 Sup.Ct. 805, 88 L.Ed. 1024 (1944) ; United States v. Socony-Vacuum Oil Co., 310 U.S. 150, 60 Sup.Ct. 811, 84 L.Ed. 1129 (1940) ; Ethyl Gasoline Corp. v. United States, 309 U.S. 436, 60 Sup.Ct. 618, 84 L.Ed. 852 (1940) ; United States v. Trenton Potteries Co., 273 U.S. 392, 47 Sup.Ct. 377, 71 L.Ed. 700 (1927).

[473] Addyston Pipe & Steel Co. v. United States, 175 U.S. 211, 20 Sup.Ct. 96, 44 L.Ed. 136 (1899) ; *cf.* United States v. National Lead Co., 332 U.S. 319, 67 Sup.Ct. 1634, 91 L.Ed. 2077 (1947) ; United States v. Crescent Amusement Co., 323 U.S. 173, 65 Sup.Ct. 254, 89 L.Ed. 160 (1944) ; United States v. Aluminum Company of America, 148 F.2d 416, 427 (2d Cir. 1945).

[474] Associated Press v. United States, 326 U.S. 1, 65 Sup.Ct. 1416, 89 L.Ed. 2013 (1945) ; American Medical Ass'n v. United States, 317 U.S. 519, 63 Sup.Ct. 326, 87 L.Ed. 434 (1943) ; Fashion Originators' Guild of America, Inc. v. Federal Trade Commission, 312 U.S. 457, 61 Sup.Ct. 703, 85 L.Ed. 949 (1941) ; *cf.* Binderup v. Pathe Exchange, Inc., 263 U.S. 291, 44 Sup.Ct. 96, 68 L.Ed. 308 (1923) ; Eastern States Retail Lumber Dealers' Ass'n v. United States, 234 U.S. 600, 34 Sup.Ct. 951, 58 L.Ed. 1490 (1914).

[475] International Salt Co. v. United States, 332 U.S. 392, 68 Sup.Ct. 12, 92 L.Ed. 20 (1947) ; Oppenheim, *A New Look at Antitrust Enforcement Trends* in N. Y. BAR ASS'N ANTITRUST LAW SYMPOSIUM 69, 76 (1950) ; Note 33 MINN. L. REV. 398, 401 (1949).

[476] Mercoid Corp. v. Minneapolis-Honeywell Regulator Co., 320 U.S. 680, 64 Sup.Ct. 278, 88 L.Ed. 396 (1944) ; Mercoid Corp. v. Mid-Continent Investment Co., 320 U.S. 661, 64 Sup.Ct. 268, 88 L.Ed. 376 (1944) ; United States v. Masonite Corp., 316 U.S. 265, 62 Sup.Ct. 1070, 86 L.Ed. 1461 (1942) ; United States v. Univis Lens Co., 316 U.S. 241, 62 Sup.Ct. 1088, 86 L.Ed. 1408 (1942) ; Ethyl Gasoline Corp. v. United States, 309 U.S. 436, 60 Sup.Ct. 618, 84 L.Ed. 852 (1940).

clusive dealing arrangements,[477] in which event their inherent tendency toward monopoly condemns them.[478] On the other hand, acts which are lawful in themselves may form the matrix of a conspiratorial aggregation bent on monopolizing[479] an appreciable segment of interstate or foreign commerce.[480] Thus, it is not the form of the conspiracy, nor the particular acts done but the result sought to be achieved that the statute condemns. Illegality of the conspiracy is not dependent on acquisition of monopoly power.[481]

Economic evidence in the form of market data and analysis has been introduced in the recent cases to demonstrate non-competitive uniformity of action. This information tended to corroborate already substantial quantities of direct evidence of agreement or circumstantial evidence giving rise to a strong inference of formal collusion.[482] Professor Rahl has suggested the possibility that the function of objective economic evidence may shift imperceptibly to the point where it becomes the main proof and subjective

[477] Standard Oil Company of California v. United States, 337 U.S. 293, 69 Sup.Ct. 1051, 93 L.Ed. 1371 (1949); United States v. American Can Co., 87 F.Supp. 18, 31 (N.D.Cal. 1949); cf. Fashion Originators' Guild of America, Inc. v. Federal Trade Commission, 312 U.S. 457, 61 Sup.Ct. 703, 85 L.Ed. 949 (1941); Standard Fashion Co. v. Magrane-Houston Co., 258 U.S. 346, 42 Sup.Ct. 360, 66 L.Ed. 653 (1922); Oxford Varnish Corp. v. Ault & Wiborg Corp., 83 F.2d 764 (6th Cir. 1936); Radio Corporation of America v. Lord, 28 F.2d 257 (3d Cir. 1928); but cf. B. S. Pearsall Butter Co. v. Federal Trade Commission, 292 Fed. 720 (7th Cir. 1923). It is probable that the Pearsall case was not overruled by the Standard Oil Company of California decision, in that the Pearsall Company had only 1% of the market. However, as Mr. Justice Jackson remarked in his dissenting opinion in the Standard Oil Company of California case, the decision virtually amounts to holding requirements contracts to be per se violations. Most oil companies control over 6.7% of their local markets. See Schwartz, Potential Impairment of Competition—The Impact of Standard Oil Company of California v. United States on the Standard of Legality under the Clayton Act, 98 U. OF PA. L. REV. 10 (1949); Comment, 48 MICH. L. REV. 505 (1950).

[478] Dession, The Trial of Economic and Technological Issues of Fact: I, 58 YALE L. J. 1019, 1034 (1949).

[479] Schine Chain Theatres, Inc. v. United States, 334 U.S. 110, 119, 68 Sup.Ct. 947, 952, 92 L.Ed. 1245, 1253 (1948); American Tobacco Co. v. United States, 328 U.S. 781, 809, 66 Sup.Ct. 1125, 1139, 90 L.Ed. 1575, 1594 (1946); United States v. New York Great Atlantic & Pacific Tea Co., 173 F.2d 79, 82, (7th Cir. 1949); United States v. Pullman Co., 50 F.Supp. 123, 135 (E.D.Pa. 1943); cf. United States v. Reading Co., 226 U.S. 324, 357–358, 33 Sup.Ct. 90, 98, 57 L.Ed. 243, 254 (1912); Swift & Co. v. United States, 196 U.S. 375, 396, 25 Sup.Ct. 276, 279, 49 L.Ed. 518, 524 (1905); Aikens v. Wisconsin, 195 U.S. 194, 206, 25 Sup.Ct. 3, 6, 49 L.Ed. 154, 160 (1904).

[480] See note 421 supra.

[481] United States v. Griffith, 334 U.S. 100, 107 n. 9, 68 Sup.Ct. 941, 945, 92 L.Ed. 1236, 1243 (1948); American Tobacco Co. v. United States, 328 U.S. 781, 789, 66 Sup.Ct. 1125, 1129, 90 L.Ed. 1575, 1583 (1946); cf. United States v. Shapiro, 103 F.2d 775, 777 (2d Cir. 1939).

[482] Rahl, Conspiracy and the Anti-Trust Laws, 44 ILL. L. REV. 743, 758 (1950); Dession, The Trial of Economic and Technological Issues of Fact: I, 58 YALE L. J. 1019, 1024–1032 (1949).

evidence of conspiracy would be relegated to a supporting role.[483] The next step in the process seems to be the creation of a rebuttable presumption of conspiracy when certain market conditions have been shown.[484] The burden of overcoming this presumption would be thrust upon defendant, who would have to prove the absence of conspiratorial intent in the "mind" of the corporation. Such a task would be even more difficult to discharge than to envisage, with the result that, for all practical purposes, a new *per se* violation would be created.[485] This expansion of the conspiracy doctrine to the limit of its logic[486] foreshadows "trial by economic ordeal." Professor Rostow asserts that the recent cases have already reached this point, and the finding of conspiracy in antitrust cases is a matter of rote.[487] This calls for an examination of his oligopoly allegations, particularly with reference to the petroleum industry.

2. OLIGOPOLY, INTEGRATION AND THE ANTITRUST LAWS. (a) *Oligopoly as a Per Se Violation.* In recent years, considerable opposition to concentration of economic power has developed. Hostility toward oligopoly structure, and its two prominent companions—size and integration—has reached the stage of outspoken criticism.[488] The attacks have taken two paths: one, that economic concentration is contrary to the genius of a free government,[489] and the other, that oligopoly structure *necessarily* produces market behavior inimical to the public interest.[490] Some hint of the first approach appeared in the reported decisions as early as 1916.[491] It blossomed

---

[483] *Ibid.*

[484] See HANDLER, A STUDY OF THE CONSTRUCTION AND ENFORCEMENT OF THE FEDERAL ANTITRUST LAWS 39–40 (TNEC Monograph 38, 1941). *Quaere,* is this suggested by the Court's language in Interstate Circuit, Inc. v. United States, 306 U.S. 208, 225–226, 59 Sup.Ct. 467, 474, 83 L.Ed. 610, 619–620 (1939)?

[485] Compare the futile efforts of counsel in the *Gypsum* case to prove absence of collusion. United States v. Gypsum Co., 333 U.S. 364, 395–396, 68 Sup.Ct. 525, 542, 92 L.Ed. 746, 766 (1948).

[486] *Cf.* Krulewitch v. United States, 336 U.S. 440, 445, 69 Sup.Ct. 716, 719, 93 L.Ed. 790, 795 (1949); Cardozo, THE NATURE OF THE JUDICIAL PROCESS 51 (1921).

[487] Wood, *The Supreme Court and a Changing Antitrust Concept,* 97 U. OF PA. L. REV. 309, 330 (1949).

[488] See note 410 *supra.*

[489] *Hearings before Subcommittee on Study of Monopoly Power of the Committee on the Judiciary,* 81st Cong., 1 Sess., Part 1, 93, 146, 228, 336, 362 (1949); SEN. DOC. No. 173, 75th Cong., 3d Sess. (1938); Celler, *The Current Antitrust Law Investigation* in N. Y. BAR ASS'N ANTITRUST LAW SYMPOSIUM 35 (1950). The argument goes: big business = big government = statism.

[490] See note 410 *supra.*

[491] United States v. Corn Products Refining Co., 234 Fed. 964 (S.D.N.Y. 1916). "A given organization of industry may be thought to react to the public prejudice, regardless of its directly observeable results." *Id.* at 1012.

out in full strength in the *Alcoa* case where Judge Learned Hand, quoting Senator Sherman,[492] remarked: "Throughout the history of these [anti-trust] statutes it has been constantly assumed that one of their purposes was to perpetuate and preserve, *for its own sake and in spite of possible cost,* an organization of industry in small units which can effectively compete with each other." (Emphasis supplied).[493] The most explicit judicial attack on oligopoly is found in Mr. Justice Douglas' dissent in the *Columbia Steel* case:[494] "Power that controls the economy should be in the hands of elected representatives of the people, not in the hands of an industrial oligarchy [oligopoly?]. Industrial power should be decentralized. It should be scattered into many hands so that the fortunes of the people will not be dependent on the whim or caprice, the political prejudices, the emotional stability of a few self-appointed men."

This feeling rapidly is becoming an article of political faith, but it is not yet the law. The *American Tobacco* decision cannot be cited in its behalf because the actual conspiracy found by the jury was an essential element of the offenses charged.[495] The majority of the court in the *Columbia Steel* case did not consider oligopoly structure in the steel industry sufficient reason to forbid the acquisition of Columbia Steel Company by the United States Steel Corporation. It seems reasonable to suggest that a court which was unwilling to prohibit the junction of yet unconsolidated companies would be even more hesitant to dismember corporate entities which, in general, have served the public well.[496] In the *National Lead* case, the Supreme Court declined to break up an oligopoly of four (virtually a duopoly) where effective competition was shown to exist.[497]

The abstract political theory that concentration of economic power is contrary to the genius of a free government is so vague that a response is difficult. What degree of concentration is meant? What is meant by a "free government"? Economic implications make difficult the acceptance

---

[492] "If the concerted powers of this combination are intrusted to a single man, it is a kingly prerogative, inconsistent with our form of government, and should be subject to the strong resistance of the State and national authorities. . . ." 21 Cong. Rec. 2457 (1890). See also 21 Cong. Rec. 2460, 2598 (1890).

[493] United States v. Aluminum Company of America, 148 F.2d 416, 429 (2d Cir. 1945).

[494] United States v. Columbia Steel Co., 334 U.S. 495, 536, 68 Sup.Ct. 1107, 1128, 92 L.Ed. 1533, 1559 (1948).

[495] American Tobacco Co. v. United States, 328 U.S. 781, 798, 66 Sup.Ct. 1125, 1133, 90 L.Ed. 1575, 1588 (1946). See also *Id.* at 786, 66 Sup.Ct. at 1127–1128, 90 L.Ed. at 1581–1582. See note 467 *supra.*

[496] *Cf.* United States v. Aluminum Company of America, 91 F.Supp. 333, 345 (S.D.N.Y. 1950).

[497] United States v. National Lead Co., 332 U.S. 319, 67 Sup.Ct. 1634, 91 L.Ed. 2077 (1947).

of the notion that the antitrust laws are designed to maintain an economy of small businesses, regardless of the cost to the consuming public. The idea seems retrogressive and inconsistent with the view that the Sherman Act is a "charter of freedom" with a "generality and adaptability comparable to that found to be desirable in constitutional provisions."[498] Present day economy embraces nation-wide and world markets. It is highly unrealistic to plead for atomistic supply without accepting the attendant atomized market.[499] Mass production and large scale distribution economies would be forsaken. It is one thing to argue that the social advantages of multi-firm competition outweigh those of the present structure. It is quite another to urge a radical change in the structure of our basic industries without regard to efficiency, consumer interests, standard of living, and the like, merely for the sake of regaining the atomistic structure of the 1880's.[500] Moreover, recent geopolitical events, such as the action in Korea, have forced a reappraisal of the problem of concentration of economic power and its relation to political objectives. It would be military suicide to disrupt vital defense industries at a time when the aggressor's fist is deterred solely by the industrial potential of this country.[501]

The second corridor of attack on oligopoly structure essentially is economic. Some people have taken in toto the economists' analytical work on monopolistic competition and attempted to transplant it into the law as a device of industrial measurement in the public interest. Without questioning the validity of theoretical assumptions or the applicability of economic theory to real life industrial organization, they misapply terms having innocuous economic connotation to legal situations where the same words denote grevious misbehavior.[502] Economic theory, including monopo-

[498] Appalachian Coals, Inc. v. United States, 288 U.S. 344, 359–360, 53 Sup.Ct. 471, 474, 77 L.Ed. 825, 829 (1933).

[499] Comment, *The Effectiveness of the Federal Antitrust Laws,* 40 AM. ECON. REV. 167, 168 (No. 1, 1950).

[500] "Those who, oversimplifying economic problems, thoughtlessly urge the elimination of virtually all monopolies, not only disregard the unavoidable existence of monopolistic elements in almost all kinds of competition but dangerously invite a program which, by neglecting socially valuable aspects of some industrial integrations ('oligopolies') in some mass production industries, might tragically reduce our living standards." Standard Brands, Inc. v. Smidler, 151 F.2d 34, 42 (2d Cir. 1945). See ARNOLD, THE BOTTLENECKS OF BUSINESS 124 (1940); Meriam, *The Sherman Antitrust Act and Business Economics* in N. Y. BAR ASS'N ANTITRUST LAW SYMPOSIUM 93, 99 (1950).

[501] *Cf.* Robbins & Murphy, *Industrial Preparedness,* 26 HARV. BUS. REV. 329 (1948).

[502] Rodgers, *Dynamic Competition* in SOUTHWESTERN LEGAL FOUNDATION 1950 INSTITUTE ON ANTITRUST LAWS AND PRICE REGULATION 193, 196 (1950); Chamberlin, *Product Heterogeneity and Public Policy,* 40 AM. ECON. REV. 85, 87 (No. 2, May, 1950); Meriam, *Bigness and the Economic Analysis of Competition,* 28 HARV. BUS. REV. 109, 115 (No. 2, 1950); Rodgers & Luedicke, *Dynamic Competition,* 27 HARV. BUS. REV. 237, 238 (1949); Learned, *Pricing of Gasoline: A Case Study,* 26 HARV. BUS. REV. 723, 724 (1948).

listic competition doctrine, unquestionably has a role to play in the formulation of a public interest yardstick. However, the transition from economic to legal analysis requires much caution.[503]

A convenient illustration of the need for a more critical approach lies in the use of the "maximization of profits" assumption from which supposed anti-social characteristics of oligopoly structure are readily derived.[504] Three flaws in the assumption come to mind almost immediately. First, the successful maintenance of a maximum profit spread depends upon a high degree of collusion between the oligopolists, lest secret "price shading" break out and disrupt the scheme.[505] However, the absence of collusion is implicit in the definition of oligopoly.[506] Second, the continuing high prices required for profit maximization would entice new entrants into the market,[507] and this would so diffuse the oligopoly that excess capacity would tend to produce cutthroat competition. Third, the principle of maximizing profits tacitly assumes that business men know their marginal costs and marginal revenue,[508] and utilize marginal analysis to equate them. The plain fact is that business men not only do not use marginal analysis techniques to set price and production policies, but many of them are not even aware of marginal cost or revenue.[509] For the most part, price policies are set by trial and error, with volume of sales (and inventory turnover)

[503] *Cf.* WALKER, FROM ECONOMIC THEORY TO POLICY 54–76 (1943); Meriam, *Bigness and the Economic Analysis of Competition,* 28 HARV. BUS. REV. 109, 115 (No. 2, 1950).

[504] Meriam, *supra* note 503, at 117; Powlison, *The Profit Motive Compromised,* 28 HARV. BUS. REV. 102 (No. 2, 1950), Bain, *A Note on Pricing in Monopoly and Oligopoly,* 39 AM. ECON. REV. 448 (1949); De Scitovszky, *Prices under Monopoly and Competition,* 49 J. POL. ECON. 663, 664 (1941).

[505] Fellner, *Collusion and its Limits under Oligopoly,* 40 AM. ECON. REV. 54 (No. 2, May, 1950); Stigler, *Capitalism and Monopolistic Competition—Discussion,* 40 AM. ECON. REV. 63 (No. 2, May, 1950).

[506] See text at note 372 *supra;* CHAMBERLIN, THE THEORY OF MONOPOLISTIC COMPETITION 106 (6th ed. 1948); *cf.* Rahl, *Conspiracy and the Anti-Trust Laws,* 44 ILL. L. REV. 743, 760 (1950). The structure becomes a group monopoly when collusion is present.

[507] See Johnston & Stevens, *Monopoly or Monopolization—A Reply to Professor Rostow,* 44 ILL. L. REV. 269, 270 n. 6 (1949); Learned, *Pricing of Gasoline: A Case Study,* 26 HARV. BUS. REV. 723, 728 (1948).

[508] See note 345 *supra.*

[509] EITEMAN, PRICE DETERMINATION—BUSINESS PRACTICE VERSUS ECONOMIC THEORY V (University of Michigan Bureau of Business Research Report No. 16, 1949); Rodgers, *Dynamic Competition* in SOUTHWESTERN LEGAL FOUNDATION 1950 INSTITUTE ON ANTITRUST LAWS AND PRICE REGULATIONS 193, 202–203 (1950); Lester, *Shortcomings of Marginal Analysis for Wage-Employment Problems,* 36 AM. ECON. REV. 63 (1946); *cf.* 1 BAIN, THE ECONOMICS OF THE PACIFIC COAST PETROLEUM INDUSTRY 7 (1944); Katona, *Psychological Analysis of Business Decisions and Expectations,* 36 AM. ECON. REV. 44 (1946); *but cf.* Machlup, *Marginal Analysis and Empirical Research,* 36 AM. ECON. REV. 519 (1946).

the primary consideration.[510] Cost of production serves mainly as a check-ing device to keep prices on a realistic plane, or in a few cases, as a base price to which "mark-ups" are added.

The uncritical utilization of monopolistic competition theory to find oligopoly structure inconsistent with the public welfare raises the suspicion that oligopoly antagonists are misapplying monopolistic competition theory in order to promulgate the neo-classical pure competition ideal. The preva-lence of such phrases as "making the American economy more competi-tive," and "increased concentration has caused a decline of competition," adds substance to the suspicion. What these critics fail to realize is that instead of a "decline of competition" since the turn of the century, there has been only a "decline in the *idea* of competition."[511] They have de-veloped a "monopoly-phobia" which makes difficult the formulation of an intelligent public policy toward industry.[512] The idea of prohibiting oligo-poly structure merely because untoward results have sometimes flowed from it is comparable to attempting to solve the problem of domestic quar-rels by forbidding marriage.[513] Nor would atomistic competition be as benevolent as the neo-classicists would have us believe.[514]

The time has come for a realization that monopolistic competition is what most people think of in connection with the word "competition."[515] It may be keener than any other form of competition.[516] In fact, the public interest ideal itself contains a blend of competition and monopoly.[517] More-

---

[510] Eiteman, Price Determination—Business Practice versus Economic Theory (1949) *passim;* Rodgers, *supra* note 509, at 202–203; *Learned, Pricing of Gasoline: A Case Study,* 26 Harv. Bus. Rev. 723, 728–732 (1948).

[511] Adelman, *Effective Competition and the Antitrust Laws,* 61 Harv. L. Rev. 1289, 1296 (1948); Nicholls, *Social Biases and Recent Theories of Competition,* 58 Q. J. Econ. 1, 10 (1943); Wallace, *Monopolistic Competition at Work: A Review,* 51 Q. J. Econ. 374, 379 (1937); *but cf.* Edwards, *Can the Antitrust Laws Preserve Competition?,* 30 Am. Econ. Rev. 164, 165 (Supp., March, 1940).

[512] "Monopoly-phobia, like most phobias, is both a symptom and a cause of a neurotic tendency which, in refusing bravely to face facts, cannot yield intelligent guidance." Standard Brands, Inc. v. Smidler, 151 F.2d 34, 42 (2d Cir. 1945); *cf.* Eastern Wine Corp. v. Winslow-Warren, Ltd., 137 F.2d 955, 958–959 (2d Cir. 1943).

[513] Boulding, *In Defense of Monopoly,* 59 Q. J. Econ. 524, 542 (1945).

[514] *Ibid.* See Arnold, The Bottlenecks of Business 13 (1940); Meriam, *supra* note 503, at 121.

[515] Chamberlin, The Theory of Monopolistic Competition 10 (6th ed. 1948); Johnston & Stevens, *Monopoly or Monopolization—A Reply to Professor Rostow,* 44 Ill. L. Rev. 269 (1949).

[516] Rodgers, *Dynamic Competition* in Southwestern Legal Foundation 1950 Insti-tute on Antitrust Laws and Price Regulations 193, 196 (1950).

[517] Chamberlin, *Product Heterogeneity and Public Policy,* 40 Am. Econ. Rev. 85, 86 (No. 2, May, 1950).

over, this ideal is dynamic and not static in concept.[518] Business behavior and social performance are as (if not more) important as industrial structure.[519] This realistic approach toward accurate measurement of modern industry has resulted in the evolution of the concept of effective or workable competition which rejects many of the assumptions and conclusions of static monopolistic competition theory, but which utilizes the method of analysis developed by monopolistic competition theorists. It neither condemns nor applauds bigness or integration as such, but looks to business behavior and social performance for guidance. It is predicted that the use of this concept as a tool of industrial measurement will find increasing acceptance in the courts and enforcement agencies.

(b) *Fewness and Collusion.* Professor Rostow believes that under an oligopoly structure price, output, and conditions of entry into the market are similar to those obtaining under a single-firm monopoly.[520] His idea is that oligopolists, acting in their own interests, will behave "as if they had combined" in the sense of the *American Tobacco* case, even if they have never enjoyed a "Gary dinner" or the congenial atmosphere of the country club.[521] Because of this, he feels that the courts should (and may) infer the required degree of combination from the fact that the economic power of the separate companies in effect has been aggregated for price policy purposes.[522] Stated baldly, what Professor Rostow suggests is that, *granting the absence of express or even tacit agreement,* conspiracy to monopolize should be inferred whenever firms take parallel action in response to the stimuli of the market. Even more bluntly, there is a conspiracy where there is no conspiracy!

Professor Rostow is guilty of an inconsistency when he relies upon a theory accepting the lack of agreement of any kind to support an inference of conspiracy.[523] Nor does the doctrine of "conscious parallelism" of action

---

[518] Meriam, *Bigness and the Economic Analysis of Competition,* 28 HARV. BUS. REV. 109, 120–123 (No. 2, 1950) ; Rodgers, *supra* note 516, at 208–210; Rodgers & Luedicke, *Dynamic Competition,* 27 HARV. BUS. REV. 237 (1949) passim.

[519] LEARNED, INTEGRATION IN AMERICAN INDUSTRY 3 (paper presented before A.P.I. on No. 9, 1949) ; Meriam, *supra* note 518, at 119–120; Oppenheim, *A New Look at Antitrust Enforcement Trends* in N. Y. BAR ASS'N ANTITRUST LAW SYMPOSIUM 69, 76 (1950) ; Meriam, *The Sherman Antitrust Act and Business Economics* in N. Y. BAR ASS'N ANTITRUST LAW SYMPOSIUM 93, 97 (1950).

[520] See note 410 *supra.*

[521] Rostow, *Monopoly Under the Sherman Act: Power or Purpose?,* 43 ILL. L. REV. 745, 783 (1949).

[522] *Ibid. cf.* Complaint, United States v. Armour & Co., Civil No. 48-C 1351, N.D. Ill., Sept. 15, 1948, paragraph 42 of which is couched in "conscious parallelism" language.

[523] Rahl, *Conspiracy and the Anti-Trust Laws,* 44 ILL. L. REV. 743, 761 (1950).

aid his assertion. The opinion in the *Rigid Steel Conduit*[524] case (which established the doctrine under the Federal Trade Commission Act) explicitly distinguished conspiracy from conscious parallelism. Moreover, the courts will be loath to convict a criminal defendant on a theory which in itself demonstrates that parallelism virtually is unavoidable except by going out of business.[525]

(c) *Bigness and the Sherman Act.* The *United States Steel* and *International Harvester* decisions unequivocally stated that mere size is not an offense under the Sherman Act.[526] This is still the law today. The *Alcoa* and *Pullman* cases did not outlaw size, but banished monopoly power coupled with the intent to use it.[527] Monopoly power and size are not synonymous.[528] The significance of size is relative.[529] Thus, an industrial giant may be engaged in the fiercest competition with other industrial giants and lack the control necessary for monopoly power. On the other hand, a small company may wield monopoly power over a small market.[530] The *Columbia Steel* case clearly demonstrated that monopoly power is something other than the status of a dominant firm in the market.[531] However, it must be recognized that "size carries with it an opportunity for abuse."[532] Be-

[524] Triangle Conduit & Cable Co. v. Federal Trade Commission, 168 F.2d 175 (7th Cir. 1948), *aff'd by equally divided court, sub nom.,* Clayton Mark & Co., 336 U.S. 956, 69 Sup.Ct. 888, 93 L.Ed. 1110 (1949).

[525] Rahl, *supra note* 523, at 762; Johnston & Stevens, *Monopoly or Monopolization—A Reply to Professor Rostow,* 44 ILL. L. REV. 269, 293 (1949).

[526] See note 395 *supra.*

[527] See text at notes 414–416 *supra.*

[528] BERGSON, BIGNESS AND THE ANTITRUST LAWS 3 (1949); Bergson, *Enforcement and Administration of the Federal Antitrust Laws* in SOUTHWESTERN LEGAL FOUNDATION 1950 INSTITUTE ON ANTITRUST LAWS AND PRICE REGULATIONS 1, 11 (1950); see ARNOLD, DEMOCRACY AND FREE ENTERPRISE 24 (1942); ARNOLD, THE BOTTLENECKS OF BUSINESS 124–125 (1940).

[529] EDWARDS, MAINTAINING COMPETITION 120–121 (1949); Meriam, *The Sherman Antitrust Act and Business Economics* in N. Y. BAR ASS'N ANTITRUST LAW SYMPOSIUM 93, 96 (1950); Johnston & Stevens, *Monopoly or Monopolization—A Reply to Professor Rostow,* 44 ILL. L. REV. 269, 273 (1949); see Dession, *The Trial of Economic and Technological Issues of Fact: I,* 58 YALE L. J. 1019, 1036 (1949).

[530] *Ibid.* See also BERGSON, *op. cit. supra* note 528, at 3–4; Bergson, *supra* note 528, at 11; Bergson, *Bigness in Business* in N. Y. BAR ASS'N ANTITRUST LAW SYMPOSIUM 85–86 (1950).

[531] United States v. Columbia Steel Co., 334 U.S. 495, 68 Sup.Ct. 1107, 92 L.Ed. 1533 (1948); United States v. Aluminum Company of America, 91 F.Supp. 333, 346 (S.D.N.Y. 1950).

[532] United States v. Swift & Co., 286 U.S. 106, 116, 52 Sup.Ct. 460, 463, 76 L.Ed. 999, 1006 (1932); *cf.* United States v. Griffith, 334 U.S. 100, 107 n. 10, 68 Sup.Ct. 941, 946, 92 L.Ed. 1236, 1244 (1948); American Tobacco Co. v. United States, 328 U.S. 781, 796, 66 Sup.Ct. 1125, 1133, 90 L.Ed. 1575, 1587 (1946); United States v. New York Great Atlantic & Pacific Tea Co., 173 F.2d 79, 87 (7th Cir. 1949); United States v. Aluminum Company of America, 148 F.2d 416, 430 (2d Cir. 1945); United States v. Aluminum Company of America, 91 F.Supp. 333, 341 (S.D.N.Y. 1950).

cause of this, size is regarded as an earmark or sign of monopoly power.[533] Moreover, frank opposition to size has been expressed by judges,[534] Congressmen,[535] administrative officials [536] and writers.[537] This presents a challenge to big business to so conduct its affairs as to avoid giving any foundation for attack. It may require leaning over backwards at times to prevent abuse. Such a program is not inspired solely by business ethics or statesmanship. In the light of the sentiment of the times, this has become a sound business necessity!

(d) *Integration and the Antitrust Laws.* Earlier in this book, vertical integration was defined as the uniting in one corporate structure the various operations through which the raw material passes in its transformation into refined products ready for the market.[538] As we have seen, vertical integration is a matter of degree. Some firms are fully integrated, while others have combined only a few successive stages. It is very important to note that the goods or services transferred from one stage to another can, as such, be bought or sold in the market.[539] Due to the lack of balance be-

[533] United States v. Griffith, 334 U.S. 100, 107 n. 10, 68 Sup.Ct. 941, 946, 92 L.Ed. 1236, 1244 (1948); United States v. New York Great Atlantic & Pacific Tea Co., 173 F.2d 79, 87, (7th Cir. 1949); United States v. Aluminum Company of America, 91 F.Supp. 333, 344 (S.D.N.Y. 1950); *cf.* United States v. Columbia Steel Co., 334 U.S. 495, 533, 68 Sup.Ct. 1107, 1127, 92 L.Ed. 1533, 1557 (1948).

[534] Compare the language of Mr. Justice Douglas, dissenting in the *Columbia Steel* case: "We have here the problem of bigness. Its lesson should by now have been burned into our memory by Brandeis. The *Curse of Bigness* shows how size can become a menace—both industrial and social." United States v. Columbia Steel Co., 334 U.S. 495, 535, 68 Sup.Ct. 1107, 1128, 92 L.Ed. 1533, 1558 (1948). "The least I can say is that a company that has that tremendous leverage on our economy [51%] is big enough." *Id.* at 540, 68 Sup.Ct. at 1130, 92 L.Ed. at 1561.

[535] Chairman Celler of the Subcommittee on the Study of Monopoly Power speaking: "There seems to be a tendency on the part of most witnesses who appear before us to get a little jittery when they talk about size, as though they were worshipping size as a sort of sacred cow and that you cannot criticize it.

"I am one of those who is unafraid. I am willing to criticize size, and I wonder whether or not we are approaching the time when we must stop, look, and listen as to size; not only as to what size does or does not do, but as to mere size." *Hearings before Subcommittee on Study of Monopoly Power of the Committee on the Judiciary*, 81st Cong., 1st Sess., Part 1, 521 (1949).

[536] Dr. John M. Blair, Chief, Division of Economics, Bureau of Industrial Economics, Federal Trade Commission, testified: "I personally subscribe very wholeheartedly to the view . . . that in many fields, size has far transcended the point required for optimum efficiency, and when size passes beyond that point there remains little economic justification for size." *Hearings, supra* note 535, at 201.

[537] EDWARDS, MAINTAINING COMPETITION 130–131 (1949); ROSTOW, A NATIONAL POLICY FOR THE OIL INDUSTRY (1948); BRANDEIS, THE CURSE OF BIGNESS (1934).

[538] See note 3 *supra; cf.* Hale, *Vertical Integration: Impact of the Antitrust Laws upon Combinations of Successive Stages of Production and Distribution*, 49 COL. L. REV. 921 (1949).

[539] Adelman, *Integration and Antitrust Policy*, 63 HARV. L. REV. 27 (1949).

tween stages, this almost invariably takes place.[540] Horizontal integration refers to the production or sale of more than one product in the same or related line of business, or the combination of firms doing business at different locations. Conglomerate integration refers to firms engaged in the manufacture and/or sale of widely diversified and unrelated products. Since conglomerate integration does not exist to any appreciable extent in the petroleum industry, it will be omitted from discussion.

The main forces behind vertical integration are technological advantages,[541] savings in cost of transfer and elimination of distributive services.[542] Horizontal integration is induced chiefly by the fact that additional increments of production can be added at less than full cost due to the ability to use production or distribution factors already on hand.[543] The test of economically successful integration is that the tasks under consideration are better accomplished by integration than without it. Unfortunately, there is a dearth of information on this question and no authoritative evaluation can be made at this time.[544] Much of the difficulty lies in accounting procedures, as, for example, in handling the problem of common costs.[545] By arbitrarily varying allocations, any department of an integrated company can be made to show a profit (or a loss).[546] The lack of a uniform method of allocation of common costs makes comparison difficult and misleading.[547] However, we may expect voluntary disintegration when

---

[540] EDWARDS, MAINTAINING COMPETITION 130 (1949); LEARNED, INTEGRATION IN AMERICAN INDUSTRY 2 (paper presented before A.P.I. on Nov. 9, 1949); Adelman, *supra* note 539, at 29–30.

[541] Professor Adelman's example of the blast furnace is particularly good. A blast furnace, using coke, produces pig iron + heat + combustible gases. By combining the open hearth stage, much of the pig iron heat is conserved and the coke gases may be utilized. As Professor Adelman says, the saving is obvious. Adelman, *supra* note 539, at 31–32.

[542] Of course these are not the only reasons for vertical integration. The need to spread the risk, the desire to avoid bottlenecks and "squeezes" have all played a part.

[543] Again, there are other motives, such as risk spreading, empire building, relative unavailability of equity capital to small firms, tax advantages in using internal sources of capital, etc.

[544] Adelman, *Integration and Antitrust Policy,* 63 HARV. L. REV. 27, 30 (1949); Rostow, *A Reply,* 57 J. POL. ECON. 60, 64 (1949); Handler, *Industrial Mergers and the Anti-Trust Laws,* 32 COL. L. REV. 179, 271 (1932). About all that can be stated positively is that each case must stand on its own merits.

[545] 1 BAIN, THE ECONOMICS OF THE PACIFIC COAST PETROLEUM INDUSTRY 92–93, 96–99 (1944); Adelman, *supra* note 544, at 30–31; Hale, *supra* note 538, at 941–945.

[546] *TNEC Hearings* 9398, 9750, 9941; Hale, *supra* note 538 at 941; *Sun Oil,* FORTUNE, Feb., 1941, pp. 116–117.

[547] Take, for example, the determination of gasoline costs. Gasoline is the "main" product, but it is impossible to produce gasoline without also producing a variety of other hydrocarbons. At the *TNEC Hearings* it was disclosed that several different methods were used to prorate costs: (1) "sales-value" method—the total costs of crude oil and refining operations are

direct costs or other reliable data indicate that a department is not going to pay its own way.[548]

The accounting problem bears on another subject of inquiry, that of "buying below cost" or its reciprocal, "subsidizing" one phase with the "profits" of another. The charge of buying below cost fails to take into account the return on investment in the prior phase,[549] and the subsidizing charge is based on the arbitrary allocation of costs.[550]

The *Columbia Steel* and *Paramount Pictures* cases squarely rejected the government's contention that vertical integration is illegal *per se*.[551] These decisions held that the legality of vertical integration depends upon (1) the purpose or intent with which it was conceived, or (2) the power it creates and the attendant purpose or intent.[552] The first condition relates to the specific intent requirement of "attempts to monopolize," and the second has to do with "monopoly power plus intent to use it" which is the definition of the crime of monopolizing. Thus, integration is a neutral thing,[553] neither good nor bad in the eyes of the law, and the legality of defendant's

allocated among the jointly produced products in proportion to their average refinery sales price. This method was employed by the Atlantic Refining Co. (10,047), Cities Service Co. (10,049–10,054), Consolidated Oil Corp. (10,055), Gulf Oil Corp. (10,056), Ohio Oil Co. (10,059), Skelly (10,064), Pan American Petroleum & Transport Co. (10,069); (2) "by products" method—all revenue from products other than gasoline are deducted from total costs of crude and refining operations, and the balance is assumed to be gasoline costs. Continental (10,055), Phillips (10,059), Pure (10,060), Standard Oil (Ind.) except for Pan American (10,065–10,072). This can sometimes lead to absurd results where the value of the by-products exceeds total cost, the cost of gasoline would be less than nothing; (3) "gasoline-value" or "replacement value" method—the costs of all stocks and distillates, except heavy fuel oil, are assumed to equal their value as potential sources of gasoline. The revenue from heavy fuel oil and the "gasoline value" of the rest are deducted from total costs of crude and refining operations, and the remainder is considered the gasoline cost. Standard Oil (N.J.) group (10,073–10,092); (4) "sales realization" or "gallonage" method—total cost prorated on basis of ratio of sales of each product to total sales. Sun Oil Co. (10,092), Texas Co. (10,094). All of the companies stressed the arbitrary nature of all methods of allocation.

[548] When rising costs of operating retail stations, climaxed by the adoption of anti-chain store taxes, made this phase of integration unsound economically, most stations were disintegrated under the "Iowa Plan" of leasing to independents. *TNEC Hearings* 8427–8428, 8699, 9938.

[549] *TNEC Hearings* 7233–7234, 7251–7252, 8167–8168, 8290; Adelman, *Integration and Antitrust Policy,* 63 HARV. L. REV. 27, 42 (1949); Hale, *supra* note 538, at 938; Note, 58 YALE L. J. 969, 978 (1949).

[550] See note 546 *supra;* see also Adelman, *The A & P Case: A Study in Applied Economic Theory,* 63 Q. J. ECON. 238, 244–246 (1949); Note, 58 YALE L. J. 969, 978 (1949); *but cf. TNEC Hearings* 10,039.

[551] See note 334 *supra.*

[552] United States v. Columbia Steel Co., 334 U.S. 495, 524–525, 68 Sup.Ct. 1107, 1123, 92 L.Ed. 1533, 1552 (1948); United States v. Paramount Pictures, Inc., 334 U.S. 131, 174, 68 Sup.Ct. 915, 937, 92 L.Ed. 1260, 1301 (1948).

conduct is determined by the standards previously discussed in this book.[554] Factors bearing on the question whether monopoly power is created by a particular integration are the *nature of the market to be served* and the *leverage on the market* which the integration creates or makes possible.[555] The former is the "relevant competitive market" concept discussed above. "Leverage" is defined by Adelman as the use of a monopoly position [monopoly power] at one stage to acquire it at an earlier or later stage (vertical leverage); or to extend it into an adjacent market area (horizontal leverage).[556] This clearly is embraced by the definition of monopolization previously developed.

Due to the antitrust laws and a change in business *modus operandi*, leverage seldom is applied these days. Instead, a "squeeze" tactic sometimes is employed. The lack of balance between stages and the concomitant buying and selling in the market has been mentioned previously.[557] If a firm sells at one stage to firms which are its competitors in the succeeding stage, a "squeeze" potential may be created. Simply by raising the price at which it sells to its rivals and lowering its price at the competitive stage, an integrated company can narrow its competitors' profit margin. This tactic has been used occasionally to teach independent non-integrated firms who was master, and, by so doing, to implement the price leadership mechanism in maintaining price structures deemed favorable by the integrated company. However, this behavior also is apt to result in competitors complaining to the government, and, for this reason, is not too prevalent.

A far more probable type of conduct is that of a dominant firm permitting its competitors to remain in the market and exploiting its position by allowing the high prices it charges its competitors to be passed on to the consuming public.[558]

A novel legal doctrine of comparatively recent origin has arisen to plague integrated corporations. The *General Motors*,[559] *Yellow Cab*,[560] and *A & P*[561] cases have given rise to a "bath-tub" conspiracy doctrine,[562]

---

[553] Adelman, *Effective Competition and the Antitrust Laws*, 61 HARV. L. REV. 1289, 1321 (1948).

[554] See Section III C 1 *supra*. This analysis is concurred in by Hale, *supra* note 538, at 949.

[555] See note 552 *supra*.

[556] Adelman, *Integration and Antitrust Policy*, 63 HARV. L. REV. 27, 44 (1949).

[557] See text at note 540 *supra*.

[558] Adelman, *Integration and Antitrust Policy*, 63 HARV. L. REV. 27, 45 (1949).

[559] United States v. General Motors Corp., 121 F.2d 376 (7th Cir. 1941), *cert. denied*, 314 U.S. 618, 62 Sup.Ct. 105, 86 L.Ed. 497 (1941).

[560] United States v. Yellow Cab Co., 332 U.S. 218, 67 Sup.Ct. 1560, 91 L.Ed. 2010 (1947).

[561] United States v. New York Great Atlantic & Pacific Tea Co., 173 F.2d 79 (7th Cir. 1949).

i.e., an illegal conspiracy may exist between the corporate members of a commonly owned enterprise.[563] Conspiracy has been found to exist between affiliated companies,[564] between a parent and wholly-owned subsidiaries,[565] and between combinations of the two.[566] It is still open to question whether this theory will be extended to a finding of conspiracy between a single corporation and two or more of its officers. It has been held that an unlawful conspiracy cannot be formed between a corporation and a single officer without the knowledge or participation of another officer or agent of the corporation.[567] Several state cases have satisfied the requirement of multiplicity of parties by finding a conspiracy among the individual officers, thereby making a single corporation liable as a co-conspirator due to the acts of its officers.[568] Contrary to the predictions of legal commentators on the subject,[569] a recent federal district court memorandum, denying a motion for preliminary injunction, distinguished an "intra-corporate agreement from an "intra-enterprise" conspiracy and refused to sustain a charge of conspiracy between a single corporation and its officers.[570]

At first, the tenor of the "bath-tub" conspiracy cases seemed to indicate a change in the present policy of strict application of the Sherman Act

[562] The expression is borrowed from Searls, *The Antitrust Laws from the Viewpoint of a Private Practitioner* in Southwestern Legal Foundation 1950 Institute on Antitrust Laws and Price Regulation 71, 86 (1950).

[563] Rahl, *Conspiracy and the Anti-Trust Laws*, 44 Ill. L. Rev. 743, 762–768 (1950); Adelman, *Effective Competition and the Antitrust Laws*, 61 Harv. L. Rev. 1289, 1314–1317 (1948); Notes, 43 Ill. L. Rev. 551 (1948); 47 Col. L. Rev. 786, 788–791 (1947).

[564] See note 560 *supra.* See also Tooke & Reynolds v. Bastrop Ice & Storage Co., 172 La. 782, 135 So. 239 (1931) for a case based on a state statute copied from the Sherman Act.

[565] See note 559 *supra.*

[566] Schine Chain Theatres, Inc. v. United States, 334 U.S. 110, 68 Sup.Ct. 947, 92 L.Ed. 1245 (1948); United States v. New York Great Atlantic & Pacific Tea Co., 173 F.2d 79 (7th Cir. 1949); *cf.* United States v. Crescent Amusement Co., 323 U.S. 173, 65 Sup.Ct. 254, 89 L.Ed. 160 (1944).

[567] Union Pacific Coal Co. v. United States, 173 Fed. 737, 745 (8th Cir. 1909); *cf.* Rahl, *supra* note 563, at 765 n. 72.

[568] Note, 47 Col. L. Rev. 786, 791 (1947), citing Dunshee v. Standard Oil Co., 152 Iowa 618, 132 N.W. 371 (1911); Tooke & Reynolds v. Bastrop Ice & Storage Co., 172 La. 782, 135 So. 239 (1931); Schoedler v. Motometer Gauge & Equipment Corp., 134 Ohio St. 78, 15 N.E.2d 958 (1938).

[569] See notes, 43 Ill. L. Rev. 551, 553 (1948); 47 Col. L. Rev. 786, 791 (1947).

[570] United States v. The Lorain Journal Co., CCH Trade Reg. Rep. ¶ 62,531 (N.D.Ohio 1949). "However, no case has been brought to the attention of the Court or has been disclosed by independent research—at least where the corporation has been joined as a party defendant—which holds that there may be a conspiracy between the corporation and its employees and officers acting in its behalf." This is somewhat surprising in the face of a previous Court of Appeals decision, White Bear Theatre Corp. v. State Theatre Corp., 129 F.2d 600 (8th Cir. 1942). Professor Rahl expresses difficulty in perceiving the substance of the distinction between an intra-enterprise conspiracy involving two corporations and a conspiracy involving only one. Rahl, *Conspiracy and the Anti-Trust Laws*, 44 Ill. L. Rev. 743, 765 n. 72 (1950).

to loose-knit combinations and lax treatment of the close-knit, integrated corporations. The idea was advanced that a combination of the *Yellow Cab* intra-enterprise conspiracy doctrine and the *International Salt Company*[571] holding that it is unreasonable, *per se*, to foreclose competitors from any substantial market, would provide a potent weapon of attack upon integrated firms,[572] since "the essence of integration is the elimination of competition."[573] This proposition was short-lived as the *Columbia Steel* case rejected the *per se* approach in favor of the rule of reason where integration is present. Despite generally expressed opinion that the *Columbia Steel* case must be "canalized in the narrow channel which the facts in the case established,"[574] it is submitted that integrated combination cases will continue to be judged on their facts, and not disposed of summarily through the application of the illegality *per se* dogma.

3. THE REMEDY ASPECT. The application of remedies imposes a different standard of measurement than that utilized to determine illegality in the first instance.[575] The recent developments in remedy cases demonstrate first of all an awareness that strong measures may be required to restrain a tendency on the part of monopolizers toward recidivism.[576] A second common thread discernible in the cases is the requirement that the "fruits" of monopolistic practices or restraints of trade be disgorged.[577] A third point was brought out by the *Schine* decision,[578] *i.e.*, the purpose

[571] International Salt Co. v. United States, 332 U.S. 392, 396, 68 Sup.Ct. 12, 15, 92 L.Ed. 20, 26 (1947).

[572] See Kefauver, *The Supreme Court and Congress versus Monopoly*, 20 TENN. L. REV. 254, 261 (1948); Berge, *Problems of Enforcement and Interpretation of the Sherman Act*, 38 AM. ECON. REV. 172, 178–179 (No. 2, May, 1948); Zlinkoff & Barnard, *The Supreme Court and a Competitive Economy: 1946 Term*, 47 COL. L. REV. 914, 931 (1947); Note, 33 MINN. L. REV. 398, 399 (1949).

[573] Zlinkoff & Barnard, *supra* note 572, at 931. Professor Adelman calls this "the doctrine of compartmentalization." Adelman, *Integration and Antitrust Policy*, 63 HARV. L. REV. 27, 52–53 (1949).

[574] United States v. Standard Oil Company of California, 78 F.Supp. 850, 879 (S.D.Cal. 1948), aff'd, 337 U.S. 293, 69 Sup.Ct. 1051, 93 L.Ed. 1371 (1949); Notes, 58 YALE L. J. 764, 773 (1949); 43 ILL. L. REV. 523, 534 (1948).

[575] United States v. Aluminum Company of America, 91 F.Supp. 333, 346 (S.D.N.Y. 1950); see text at note 451 *supra;* see also Mason, *The Current Status of the Monopoly Problem in the United States*, 62 HARV. L. REV. 1265, 1272 (1949).

[576] United States v. Aluminum Company of America, 91 F.Supp. 333, 343 (S.D.N.Y. 1950); cf. United States v. Crescent Amusement Co., 323 U.S. 173, 65 Sup.Ct. 254, 89 L.Ed. 160 (1944); United States v. Swift & Co., 286 U.S. 106, 117, 52 Sup.Ct. 460, 463, 76 L.Ed. 999, 1007 (1932).

[577] United States v. Paramount Pictures, Inc., 334 U.S. 131, 68 Sup.Ct. 915, 92 L.Ed. 1260 (1948); Schine Chain Theatres, Inc. v. United States, 334 U.S. 110, 68 Sup.Ct. 947, 92 L.Ed. 1245 (1948); United States v. Crescent Amusement Co., 323 U.S. 173, 65 Sup.Ct. 254, 89 L.Ed. 160 (1944).

of the remedial action is to break up or render impotent the monopoly power violating the Act.[579]

The propriety of divorcement is dependent upon the relationship of the monopolistic practices or unreasonable restraints to defendant's status in the market.[580] The court must look to the future as well as the present, and appraise present power potentials, keeping in mind their propensities under reasonably foreseeable market conditions.[581] However, in dealing with integrated companies, the court cannot blindly order divorcement without constructively applying the yardstick of effective competition to the resultant units in the market.[582] In other words, the remedy is designed to restore (or create) effective or workable competition in the market, and where divorcement will not aid in achieving this end, it will not be ordered.

In determining the extent of power in an industry which will be consistent with the antitrust laws, the following factors are relevant: (1) the number and strength of the firms in the market; (2) their effective size from the standpoint of technological development, and measured by competition with substitute materials and foreign trade; (3) national security interests in the preservation of strong productive facilities, and maximum scientific research and development; and (4) the public interest in lowered costs and uninterrupted production.[583]

D. *The Petroleum Industry*

In any pipe line regulation study, there are three general problems which require treatment. The first of these, specific evils identifiable with pipe lines, has been discussed at some length in the earlier sections of this book. The second issue relates to the behavior of the petroleum industry as a whole. Pipe lines may be adversely affected by extra-legal practices in other phases of the industry. That is to say, due to the doctrines evolved

---

[578] Schine Chain Theatres, Inc. v. United States, 334 U.S. 110, 68 Sup.Ct. 947, 92 L.Ed. 1245 (1948).

[579] *Id.* at 128–129; 68 Sup.Ct. at 957, 92 L.Ed. at 1258.

[580] United States v. Paramount Pictures, Inc., 334 U.S. 131, 172, 68 Sup.Ct. 915, 936, 92 L.Ed. 1260, 1300 (1948); United States v. Aluminum Company of America, 91 F.Supp. 333, 334 (S.D.N.Y. 1950).

[581] United States v. Aluminum Company of America, 91 F.Supp. 333, 346 (S.D.N.Y. 1950).

[582] *Ibid.* The purpose of the Act is not to reduce an industry to isolated units of the lowest degree. United States v. Winslow, 227 U.S. 202, 33 Sup.Ct. 253, 57 L.Ed. 481 (1913). *A fortiori*, the court will not break up integrated defendants where effective competition is present. See text at note 497 *supra;* see also United States v. Aluminum Company of America, 91 F.Supp. 333 (S.D.N.Y. 1950).

[583] United States v. Aluminum Company of America, 91 F.Supp. 333, 347 (S.D.N.Y. 1950).

in the recent remedy cases, a violation of the Sherman Act by an integrated oil company could result in a court order to divorce pipe lines even though no specific wrongdoing was attributable to the lines.

From the previous discussion of Section Two violations, it would seem that the logical corridor of attack against the major oil companies is under the "conspiracy to monopolize" clause (accompanied of course, by a count charging a conspiracy in restraint of trade).[584] Any determination of the existence of such a conspiracy would necessitate an examination, *inter alia*, of conservation or proration practices, patent arrangements, price leadership mechanisms, effect of crude oil and gasoline exchange agreements, trade association activities, marketing devices and the influence of foreign oil production, all of which are beyond the scope of this thesis. Professor Rostow attempted such a survey in his book, *A National Policy for the Oil Industry*. Without criticism of the author, it is obvious that his choice of a broad coverage necessarily limited incisive treatment of the component parts.

In 1940 the Department of Justice brought a nation-wide industry suit in *United States v. American Petroleum Institute*,[585] known as the *Mother Hubbard* case.[586] The case was suspended during the war due to the deleterious effect on the war effort, but was returned to the docket in 1946. It was suspended again in December, 1946, in favor of separate regional actions such as *Standard Oil Company of California v. United States*,[587] *United States v. Standard Oil Company of California*,[588] and others.[589] One can only surmise that the underlying reason for this shift in emphasis was a realization that *the means of accurately measuring the petroleum industry as a national entity presently are not at hand*. Notwithstanding Professor Rostow's criticism that this treatment of the problem is "symptomatic,"[590] it appears to be a wise move. For one thing, regional suits take cognizance of the relative competitive market concept. The 22 majors do not market their products in every state. Their number in certain areas is as few as six, while in other localities as many as sixteen are

---

[584] The Complaint in United States v. Standard Oil Company of California, Civil No. 11584—C, S.D. Cal., May 12, 1950, is pregnant with "conspiracy."

[585] Civil No. 8524, D. D.C., Sept. 30, 1940.

[586] The reader will recall the old nursery rhyme about the bare content of Mother Hubbard's closet.

[587] 377 U.S. 293, 69 Sup.Ct. 1051, 93 L.Ed. 1371 (1949).

[588] Civil No. 11584–C, S.D. Cal., May 12, 1950.

[589] *E.g.*, United States v. Sun Oil Co., Civil No. 10483, E.D. Pa., Jan. 12, 1950; United States v. Richfield Oil Corp., Civil No. 6896–PH, S.D. Cal., April 30, 1947.

[590] Rostow, A National Policy for the Oil Industry (1948) *passim*.

locked in a competitive struggle for consumer patronage.[591] In his out-standing work on the Pacific Coast petroleum industry, Professor Bain has shown that a delimitation of the relative competitive market can be accomplished successfully in a petroleum industry study.[592] Another advantage of the regional approach is that it narrows the scope of the examination to manageable limits. Moreover, it permits the Justice Department to pass over areas where active competition obviously is flourishing and to concentrate on regions where market conditions seem inimical to the public interest.

In his charge against the oil industry, Professor Rostow has alleged that the major oil companies are oligopsonists in the crude purchasing market and oligopolists in the sale of refined products.[593] His allegation is supported by commonly accepted economic definitions.[594] But to call the majors oligopolists (and oligopsonists) is merely to begin an appraisal of the industry, not to end it.[595] Oligopoly has not yet been outlawed,[596] so there remains the consideration of the majors' business behavior and performance in the market. The final determination of the adequacy of business performance essentially is a value judgment.[597] Because of this, one of the greatest needs in concentration cases is for tests which can be applied by a court or administrative agency.

The third problem is one of remedy. Previous discussion has shown that even if an integrated oil company (or companies) would be found guilty of violating the Sherman Act, it does not necessarily follow that divorcement will be ordered. The court will appraise the effect of divorcement of each stage on present competitive conditions in the industry and on conditions in the foreseeable future.[598] This book will be limited to those effects expected from pipe line divorcement. Of necessity, any esti-

---

[591] See FARISH & PEW, REVIEW AND CRITICISM ON BEHALF OF STANDARD OIL CO. (N.J.) AND SUN OIL CO. OF MONOGRAPH NO. 39 WITH REJOINDER BY MONOGRAPH AUTHOR 69 (TNEC Monograph 39-A, 1941).

[592] 1 BAIN, THE ECONOMICS OF THE PACIFIC COAST PETROLEUM INDUSTRY c. 2 (1944).

[593] See text at note 341 *supra.*

[594] See definition of oligopoly and oligopsony in Section III B 11 *supra.* See also text at note 407 *supra.*

[595] Adelman, *Integration and Antitrust Policy,* 63 HARV. L. REV. 27, 62 (1949); see Meriam, *Bigness and the Economic Analysis of Competition,* 28 HARV. BUS. REV. 109, 120 (No. 2, 1950); Mason, *The Current Status of the Monopoly Problem in the United States,* 62 HARV. L. REV. 1265, 1281 (1949).

[596] See Section III C (2-a) *supra.*

[597] See Mason, *The Current Status of the Monopoly Problem in the United States,* 62 HARV. L. REV. 1265, 1281 (1949).

[598] See Section III C 3 *supra.*

mate of probable results must use *a priori* methods. Two separate problems must be considered: (1) the effect of divorcement on existing lines; and (2) the effect of divorcement on future lines.

1. EFFECT OF DIVORCEMENT ON EXISTING LINES. The first observation which presents itself is that divorcement would not change the physical location of existing lines. It has already been observed that this location is such that extensive use of pipe lines by independent refiners is not practical from a physical standpoint.[599] Changing the ownership of these lines would not alter the situation. Nor would divorcement greatly affect the fortunes of those independent refiners whose physical location permits access to the lines. There is no reason to suspect that the new owners would be less eager to conduct a profitable enterprise than are the present shipper-owners. In fact, a pipe line entrepreneur whose sole interest is making a profit is apt to seek higher rates than the refiner-owner whose primary object is to obtain a continuous supply of crude or a steady outlet for his refined products.[600] Moreover, change in ownership of the lines would neither increase nor diminish the power or effectiveness of the regulatory measures of the Interstate Commerce Commission and the state regulatory agncies. What could a change in ownership accomplish?

The chief advocate of pipe line divorcement has been the independent jobber.[601] His greatest worry is the trend toward a shrinking[602] price margin[603] caused by the action of integrated companies in passing on distribu-

---

[599] See Section I D *supra.*

[600] FRANCIS, DIVORCEMENT OF PIPE LINES 14 (1935). This is amply substantiated by the present "make-it-while-it's-hot" tactics of independent (intrastate) pipe line owners in Michigan and Wyoming. See also MILLS, THE PIPE LINE'S PLACE IN THE OIL INDUSTRY 87–88 (1935).

[601] The jobber's complaint is that the lack of competition by independent refiners has caused them to be dependent on the majors for their supply of gasoline. They believe that an increase in independent refiner competition would enable them to purchase their supply at lower tank-car prices, which would give them more freedom to compete with the majors in the tank-wagon market.

[602] *TNEC Hearings* 8872–8876.

[603] The jobbers' extreme interest in a large price margin is due to more than a desire for excessive profits. The majors have established a substantial consumer preference for their products through national advertising. This advantage is limited to a small price differential which varies with general conditions. In prosperous times, it may be able to support a three to five cents per gallon difference, while during a depression, a one-half cent differential will cause customers to shift their patronage. The "normal" difference is from one and a half to two and a half cents per gallon. Thus, an independent jobber, selling unbranded gasoline, must overcome this handicap by selling at a lower price. Given a wide margin, an independent jobber can profitably sell below the differential price and take gallonage away from the majors. Such a margin can only be obtained through the ability to purchase gasoline from refineries at very low tank-car prices. When "hot oil" was abundant, independent refiners were able to buy large quantities of the illegally produced crude oil at extremely low prices, and in turn, sold the gasoline produced therefrom to the jobbers at greatly reduced prices. Also, in periods of business depression or oversupply, independent refiners frequently were forced to sell "dis-

tion economies to the public in the form of reduced prices.[604] However, the independent jobber's prospects are hinged to the position of the independent refiner.[605] Since independent refiners would not benefit from divorcement of present lines, it follows that the jobber's lot would not be improved. It has been argued that divorcement of pipe lines would deprive the major oil companies of the revenue presently derived from pipe line ownership, and that the independent jobber would have an easier time competing with a marketing organization no longer "subsidized" by pipe line "profits." The fallacy of this argument is apparent. The capital formerly invested in pipe lines would be invested in gilt edge securities or in expanded refinery facilities and the income derived therefrom would still be available to "subsidize" the marketing operation of the majors. Unless the majors are atomized to a single accounting unit enterprise, the "profits" of one unit will "subsidize" the others.[606]

The independent producer actually would be harmed by pipe line divorcement. Under the present set-up, most producers sell at the well,[607] and the gathering lines (laid at pipe line expense) extend up to their producing leases.[608] If the lines were divorced, the producer would have to bear the burden of taking his oil to the market, instead of the present situation where the market is brought to him.[609] No doubt at first the major refiners would continue to purchase oil from their present "connections." But as more favorable sources became available, these companies, not being committed to the area through investment in the pipe line, would shift their purchases to the more advantageous localities.[610] Especially is this true of stripper-well areas, where majors owning pipe lines have continued to purchase their production, even absorbing a loss on the gathering charges to do so.[611] For this reason, independent producers, particularly the stripper-well operators, vigorously have opposed pipe line divorcement.[612]

tress" gasoline at low prices. Under such circumstances, the jobbers were able to maintain a wide margin, but proration and the Connally "Hot Oil" Act, 49 STAT. 30 (1935), 15 U.S.C. § 715 (1946), have greatly restricted this source of cheap gasoline.

[604] *TNEC Hearings* 7271, 8162–8163, 8453, 8499, 8548, 8706.

[605] See note 603 *supra.*

[606] Adelman, *Integration and Antitrust Policy*, 63 HARV. L. REV. 27, 43 (1949).

[607] See note 264 *supra;* see also *TNEC Hearings* 8247.

[608] *TNEC Hearings* 8339.

[609] *Id.* at 7309, 8281; MILLS, THE PIPE LINE'S PLACE IN THE OIL INDUSTRY 90–91 (1935).

[610] *TNEC Hearings* at 8281; see also REPORT OF SPECIAL STUDY COMMITTEE OF THE INDEPENDENT PETROLEUM ASSOCIATION OF AMERICA, June 6, 1939.

[611] See note 102 *supra;* see also CONWAY, PIPE LINE DIVORCEMENT 40 (unpublished thesis in University of Oklahoma Law School Library, 1950); BEARD, REGULATION OF PIPE LINES AS COMMON CARRIERS 123 (1941); Dow, THE ISSUE OF PIPE LINE DIVORCEMENT 22–23 (1939); MILLS, THE PIPE LINE'S PLACE IN THE OIL INDUSTRY 92 (1935).

[612] *TNEC Hearings* 7176, 7309, 7566, 8281; *Hearings before Subcommittee of Com-*

It is pertinent to ask how the pipe lines would fare as independent units. The only precedents available are the experiences of the Crusader Pipe Line Company (an independently financed line) and the Prairie Pipe Line Company after its divorcement from the Standard Oil Company (N. J.) in 1911. The Crusader Pipe Line project was financed by stock sold directly to the public. It was constructed to transport crude from the Smackover, Arkansas, field to the Mississippi River at Vidalia, Louisiana. Lacking an assured outlet, the line never carried a barrel of oil, and eventually was sold for use as a natural gas line.[613] Subsequent to divorcement from Standard, the Prairie Pipe Line Company voluntarily was separated from the Prairie Oil and Gas Company in order to conduct an independent common carrier business. The line prospered at first due to the large volume of business tendered by its former owner, the major purchaser in the Mid-continent field. Later, the Oil and Gas Company, having lost its outlets, was forced to withdraw from the field as a purchaser. This left the pipe line company without sufficient business to meet the costs of operation. As a result, it had to turn back its connections, leaving the operators without an outlet and facing abandonment of the stripper wells due to the enforced shutdown.[614] The dismal record of these two enterprises, together with the acknowledged reliance of pipe lines on assured, continuous demand for transportation, has caused observers to predict that independent pipe line operation would result in less efficient service, higher rates, and frequent bankruptcies.[615]

2. Effect of Divorcement on Future Lines. The interdependence of pipe lines and refineries has already been mentioned. Its relevance at this point lies in its effect on the determination of the physical location of new (independent) lines. Assume that an independent pipe line company has been formed for the purpose of conducting a common carrier business. A small independent refiner (or group of refiners) approaches the pipe line company with a request for the construction of a pipe line. At the same

---

mittee on Interstate and Foreign Commerce on H.R. 290 & H. R. 7372, 76th Cong., 3d Sess., Part 4, 1881 (1940); Dow, The Issue of Pipe Line Divorcement 21–23 (1939); Francis, Divorcement of Pipe Lines 12 (1935); Mills, The Pipe Line's Place in the Oil Industry 96 (1935).

[613] A.P.I., Survey 64 (1935); Mills, The Pipe Line's Place in the Oil Industry 86–87 (1935); *cf. TNEC Hearings* 8593; Dow, The Issue of Pipe Line Divorcement 4 (1939).

[614] Mills, The Pipe Line's Place in the Oil Industry 93–95 (1935); *cf.* Beard, Regulation of Pipe Lines as Common Carriers 123 (1941).

[615] Dow, The Issue of Pipe Line Divorcement 17–18, 23 (1939); Mills, The Pipe Line's Place in the Oil Industry 99–102 (1935); Francis, Divorcement of Pipe Lines 14 (1935); *cf.* Beard, Regulation of Pipe Lines as Common Carriers 122 (1941); Pogue, Economics of Pipe-Line Transportation in the Petroleum Industry (1932).

time, a major oil company also is interested in having a pipe line laid to a different location. The pipe line company naturally will be influenced by the volume and continuity of the business offered. Under the circumstances, the major oil company represents far greater assurance of future traffic, and, consequently, will get the line.[616] Multiply this incident by the number of major refiners, and the result will be very similar to the present location of long distance pipe lines.

Another aspect of the problem is the extension of existing lines. The first effect to be expected would be a delay on the part of an independent pipe line in making extensions to new fields. A company engaged solely in transportation, being uncertain of the extent and probable productivity of the new pool, would hesitate longer before extending into the field than would an integrated company which was seeking more oil reserves.[617] This would appreciably diminish "wildcatting" activity, because the operators would have to "prove out" a large acreage, and erect a substantial amount of tankage before the independent pipe line company would feel justified in coming into the field.[618] The independent producer of limited resources (and who isn't?) would be severely handicapped. Not being able to free his assets in order to drill more wells, the small operator would have to wait until the pipe line came to the field, while at the same time the independent pipe line would be reluctant to build its line to the field until it had been drilled.[619] The outcome of this impasse might well be the sale of the independent's acreage to a major oil company that could afford to drill enough test wells to satisfy the pipe line company before selling any of its production.[620] Obviously, this would be exactly the opposite of the result sought to be achieved.

The most persuasive argument in favor of divorcement is that it would create more competition between refiners for crude oil purchases and in the refinery gasoline market. However, it is contrary to common experience to believe that the mere divorcement of pipe lines would counteract the effect of large buying power. The independent producer would rather sell his oil to a steady, large volume buyer than to a fly-by-night who might give a premium today but shift his purchase the next day and never buy

[616] See *TNEC Hearings* 8288–8289.

[617] *TNEC Hearings* 7176; BEARD, REGULATION OF PIPE LINES AS COMMON CARRIERS 122–123 (1941); Dow, THE ISSUE OF PIPE LINE DIVORCEMENT 18–19 (1939); MILLS, THE PIPE LINE'S PLACE IN THE OIL INDUSTRY 97–98 (1935).

[618] BEARD, REGULATION OF PIPE LINES AS COMMON CARRIERS 122 (1941); MILLS, THE PIPE LINE'S PLACE IN THE OIL INDUSTRY 97 (1935).

[619] See *TNEC Hearings* 7176; CONWAY, PIPE LINE DIVORCEMENT 41 (unpublished thesis in University of Oklahoma Law School Library, 1950).

[620] Dow, THE ISSUE OF PIPE LINE DIVORCEMENT 19 (1939).

the producer's oil again. The independent pipe line owners would be just as inclined to favor their large customers, the major refiners, as would present pipe line management. In fact, due to their "open target" position, present pipe line companies frequently lean over backwards to avoid discrimination against the smaller shippers. Even assuming *arguendo* that divorcement of pipe lines would cause independent refiners to spring up in the populated market centers, the effect of this would only be to foreclose the present independent refiners in the field, with the majors acquiring some of the field location business in the process.

3. SUMMARY OF THE EFFECTS OF PIPE LINE DIVORCEMENT. Viewing divorcement of pipe lines by itself, the results to be expected appear unfavorable. There would seem to be little, if any, competitive gain on the part of independent refiners and jobbers, and detriment to independent producers and "wildcatters." The stability of independently operated pipe lines seems questionable. In all probability, rates would be higher than the present level due to overhead costs, uncertainty of continuous, high capacity operation, and the loss of co-ordination economies present in integrated operation. The consumer would be the ultimate recipient of these disadvantages which would be transmitted to him in the form of higher retail prices.

IV. INCONSISTENCIES OF ANTITRUST ENFORCEMENT

In 1935, the NRA[621] died at the hands of the Supreme Court in the *Schechter* case,[622] but its philosophy of "soft" competition has survived and vastly increased its strength. Within two years after the *Schechter* decision, the Robinson-Patman Act[623] and the Miller-Tydings Amendment to the Sherman Act had been enacted.[624] The former was reputedly drafted by counsel of the United States Wholesale Grocers Association,[625] and the latter implemented the state "Fair Trade" Acts which, by and large, had adopted the retail druggists' code.[626] Both Acts were designed to protect small wholesalers and retailers from their large competitors.

The philosophy of protecting individual competitors is inconsistent

[621] 48 STAT. 195 (1933).

[622] Schechter Poultry Corp. v. United States, 295 U.S. 495, 55 Sup.Ct. 837, 79 L.Ed. 1570 (1935).

[623] 49 STAT. 1526 (1936) as amended, 15 U.S.C. § 13 (1946).

[624] 50 STAT. 693 (1937), 15 U.S.C. § 1 (1946).

[625] Keeton, *Price Discrimination and the Robinson-Patman Act* in SOUTHWESTERN LEGAL FOUNDATION 1950 INSTITUTE ON ANTITRUST LAWS AND PRICE REGULATIONS 117, 118 (1950).

[626] Fleming, *Is Regulation Superseding Competition in State and National Policy?* in SOUTHWESTERN LEGAL FOUNDATION 1950 INSTITUTE ON ANTITRUST LAWS AND PRICE REGULATIONS 225, 230 (1950).

with the basic antitrust premise of safeguarding competition.[627] Unfortunately, recognition of this inconsistency has been conspicuously lacking. The fact is that the proponents of individual competitor protection have successfully assumed the disguise of seeking to preserve competition. In the *Morton Salt* case,[628] the Supreme Court held that a showing that one buyer was forced to pay a higher price than his competitor was *per se* proof of injury to competition. Through a process of "intellectual osmosis,"[629] the notion that injury to a competitor is injury to competition has been carried over into the Sherman Act.[630] Despite criticism of this equasion by economists,[631] Congressmen,[632] The Council of Economic Advisers,[633] and even

[627] See, *e.g.*, Keeton, *supra* note 625, at 118; Sunderland, *Save the Sherman Act from its "Friends"* in SOUTHWESTERN LEGAL FOUNDATION 1950 INSTITUTE ON ANTITRUST LAWS AND PRICE REGULATIONS 211, 213–215 (1950); Adelman, *Effective Competition and the Antitrust Laws*, 61 HARV. L. REV. 1289, 1334–1350 (1949); Berger & Goldstein, *Meeting Competition under the Robinson-Patman Act*, 44 ILL. L. REV. 315, 316 (1949); Burns, *The Anti-Trust Laws and the Regulation of Price Competition*, 4 LAW & CONTEMP. PROB. 301, 308–320 (1937); McAllister, *Price Control by Law in the United States: A Survey*, 4 LAW & CONTEMP. PROB. 273, 289–296 (1937); Note, 59 YALE L. J. 158, 159 (1949).

[628] Federal Trade Commission v. Morton Salt Co., 334 U.S. 37, 68 Sup.Ct. 822, 92 L.Ed. 1196 (1948). "The committee reports on the Robinson-Patman Act emphasized a belief that § 2 of the Clayton Act had 'been too restrictive, in requiring a showing of general injury to competitive conditions. . . .' The new provision, here controlling, *was intended to justify a finding of injury to competition by a showing of 'injury to the competitor. . . .'*" *Id.* at 49, 68 Sup.Ct. at 830, 92 L.Ed. at 1206 (Emphasis supplied).

[629] *Cf.* Standard Brands, Inc. v. Smidler, 151 F.2d 34, 41 (2d Cir. 1945).

[630] Meriam, *The Sherman Antitrust Act and Business Economics* in N. Y. BAR ASS'N ANTITRUST LAW SYMPOSIUM 93, 99 (1950); Adelman, *Integration and Antitrust Policy*, 63 HARV. L. REV. 27, 56 (1949); Note, 58 YALE L. J. 969, 981 (1949); *cf.* Kaysen, *Basing Point Pricing and Public Policy*, 63 Q. J. ECON. 289, 314 (1949). In support of this proposition, Professor Meriam cites the language of the district judge in *United States v. New York Great Atlantic & Pacific Tea Co.*, 67 F.Supp. 626, 676 (E.D.Ill. 1946): "Sometimes I doubt whether we ever needed the Robinson-Patman law, with all its elusive uncertainty. I have thought that the Sherman Act, properly interpreted and administered, would have remedied all the ills meant to be cured." See Fleming, *Is Regulation Superseding Competition in State and National Policy?* in SOUTHWESTERN LEGAL FOUNDATION 1950 INSTITUTE ON ANTITRUST LAWS AND PRICE REGULATIONS 225, 233 (1950); Adelman, *Antitrust Upside-Down Cake and Eat It Too*, FORTUNE, March, 1950, p. 57.

[631] *E.g.*, EDWARDS, MAINTAINING COMPETITION 168 (1949); LEARNED, INTEGRATION IN AMERICAN INDUSTRY 5 (1949); Meriam, *supra* note 630, at 98–101; Adelman, *The A & P Case: A Study in Applied Economic Theory*, 63 Q. J. ECON. 238, 256 (1949); *cf.* Mason, *The Current Status of the Monopoly Problem in the United States*, 62 HARV. L. REV. 1265 (1949).

[632] Compare the following language of the Conference Committee in their report on S. 1008, 81st Cong., 1st Sess. (1949): "We must always distinguish between injury to competition and injury to a competitor. To promote and protect competition is the primary function of the antitrust laws. However, we cannot guarantee competitors against all injury. This can only be accomplished by prohibiting competition." H.R. REP. No. 1422, 81st Cong., 1st Sess. 6 (1949).

[633] *Hearings before Subcommittee on Study of Monopoly Power of the Committee on the Judiciary*, 81st Cong., 1st Sess., Part 1, 113 (Dr. John D. Clark).

a member of the Federal Trade Commission,[634] it has spread like wildfire, saturating decisions under the Federal Trade Commission Act.[635]

The state of confusion created by the failure to recognize and deal with present inconsistencies in antitrust enforcement has furnished grounds for the belief held by businessmen that "they will be damned if they do and damned if they don't." Businessmen are attacked for maintaining a rigid price policy, but at the same time they cannot safely give quantity[636] or functional discounts,[637] nor direct[638] or indirect allowances to buyers for brokerage services.[639] They are charged with seeking "monopolistic" profits by restricting output and keeping up prices,[640] but if they lower their gross profit rate in order to induce greater volume, they risk prosecution by the government for selling below cost and unfairly burdening competition.[641]

It may be desirable to underwrite a program of shielding certain areas of business from competition. However, before such a program is adopted, it must be recognized as an exception to the antitrust laws, and not be treated as a part of them. It must be an exception "worth more to society than it costs."[642] Moreover, there is grave danger in permitting the pro-

[634] Commissioner Mason speaking: "We must not confuse 'injury to competition' with the normal effect resulting from the clash between two businessmen, both endeavoring to obtain the patronage of the consumer by making a better product for less. As I said in my Standard Oil dissent, 'We mouth the phrase "injury to competition" so often that we confuse it with "injury to a competitor." When you meet your competitor's lower price so as to keep a customer he sought to take away from you, he feels that he has been injured. Of course he has, *but that does not mean that competition has been injured.* On the contrary, it may have been improved.'" Minneapolis-Honneywell Regulator Co., 44 F.T.C. 351, 403 (1948) (Emphasis supplied).

[635] 38 Stat. 717 (1914), as amended, 15 U.S.C. §§ 41–58 (1946).

[636] "The law of this case, in a nutshell, is that no quantity discount is valid if the [Federal Trade] Commission chooses to say it is not." Mr. Justice Jackson, dissenting in Federal Trade Commission v. Morton Salt Co., 334 U.S. 37, 58, 68 Sup.Ct. 822, 834, 92 L.Ed. 1196, 1210 (1948); see Note, 1 Okla. L. Rev. 320 (1948). See also Minneapolis-Honneywell Regulator Co., 44 F.T.C. 351 (1948).

[637] Standard Oil Company v. Federal Trade Commission, 173 F.2d 210 (7th Cir. 1949), now pending a rehearing before the Supreme Court.

[638] Great Atlantic & Pacific Tea Co. v. Federal Trade Commission, 106 F.2d 667 (3d Cir. 1939); *cert. denied,* 308 U.S. 625, 60 Sup.Ct. 380, 84 L.Ed. 521 (1940); *cf.* United States v. New York Great Atlantic & Pacific Tea Co., 173 F.2d 79 (7th Cir. 1949).

[639] Oliver Brothers, Inc. v. Federal Trade Commission, 102 F.2d 763 (4th Cir. 1939); Biddle Purchasing Co. v. Federal Trade Commission, 96 F.2d 687 (2d Cir. 1938).

[640] Rostow, A National Policy for the Oil Industry (1948) *passim; cf.* Chamberlin, The Theory of Monopolistic Competition 88 (6th ed. 1948).

[641] United States v. New York Great Atlantic & Pacific Tea Co., 173 F.2d 79 (7th Cir. 1949); see Adelman, *The A & P Case: A Study in Applied Economic Theory,* 63 Q. J. Econ. 238, 241 (1949).

[642] Vegelahn v. Guntner, 167 Mass. 92, 106, 44 N.E. 1077, 1080 (1896).

gram to go too far. Failure to realize this may result in the destruction of the competitive system.[643]

V. CONCLUSIONS

In the ancient Roman Empire, all roads led to Rome. In similar fashion, the problems of modern industry regulation converge on a single policy issue, namely, what kind of competition is desired and in what areas is this standard to be applied. Vacillation between the idea of "hard" competition as embodied in the Sherman Act and the concept of "soft" competition contained in the Robinson-Patman Act has resulted in an extremely inconsistent program. Failure of the FTC and the Justice Department to co-ordinate their activities[644] has placed businessmen in the undesirable position of being lashed on the back to compete and slapped in the face when they do.[645] Obviously, this state of affairs is not conducive to successful law enforcement nor to constructive co-operation on the part of industry.

Assuming that a choice is made in favor of "hard" competition in the petroleum industry, a question of standard arises. Is the industry to be gauged by its structure or by its behavior and performance? It is submitted that a three-fold test of structure, behavior and performance will furnish the best yardstick.[646]

Largely due to the failure to resolve the basic issue stated above, means of adequate measurement of [the petroleum] industry in the public interest are not presently available. There is a large field of service awaiting economists and lawyers interested in industry regulation problems.

In the absence of industry-wide regulation, the maintenance of com-

[643] H.R. Rep. No. 1422, 81st Cong., 1st Sess. 6 (1949); Simon, *Meeting Price Competition* in N. Y. Bar Ass'n Antitrust Law Symposium 53, 62 (1950); Sunderland, *supra* note 627, at 212–215; Adelman, *Integration and Antitrust Policy*, 63 Harv. L. Rev. 27, 77 (1949).

[644] As Commissioner Lowell B. Mason himself says: "It's about time we had a suit to quiet title between the position of the Department of Justice and the Federal Trade Commission." Mason, *The Federal Trade Commission with a New Look* in N. Y. Bar Ass'n Antitrust Law Symposium 23, 26 (1950).

[645] See Mr. Justice Jackson's dissent in Standard Oil Company of California v. United States, 337 U.S. 293, 324, 69 Sup.Ct. 1051, 1064, 93 L.Ed. 1371, 1391 (1949). See also Meriam, *The Sherman Antitrust Act and Business Economics* in N. Y. Bar Ass'n Antitrust Law Symposium 93, 100 (1950).

[646] For specific criteria under the three-fold test, see *e.g.*, United States v. Aluminum Company of America, 91 F.Supp. 333, 347 (S.D.N.Y. 1950); *TNEC Hearings*, 8712; Farish & Pew, *op. cit. supra* note 91, at 64; Arnold, The Bottlenecks of Business (1940); Kreps & Wright, Measurement of Social Performance of Business (TNEC Monograph 7, 1940); Oppenheim, *A New Look at Antitrust Enforcement Trends* in N. Y. Bar Ass'n Antitrust Law Symposium 69, 76 (1950); and literature cited in note 357 *supra*.

petitive conditions in the petroleum industry can best be accomplished by regional suits designed to prevent abusive restraints of trade or any undue use of leverage made possible by large aggregations of economic power. Divorcement of pipe lines, *per se,* apparently would not aid this program. On the contrary, it would render a disservice to several of the independent groups presently operating in the industry.

The specific problems raised by pipe line rates and service requirements should be handled by the Interstate Commerce Commission, which has been given jurisdiction over them by law.[647]

[647] The succeeding chapter of this book will contain a survey of the regulation of pipe lines by the Interstate Commerce Commission.

SECTION TWO

REMEDIAL DEVICES

INTRODUCTION

Section I of this book contained a survey of the problems raised by major company pipe line ownership. The specific issues relating to pipe line rates and service requirements were isolated and examined in detail. Briefly summarized, these consisted of alleged excessive rates and unduly restrictive service requirements, which in turn, have been asserted to be part of a program designed by the major oil companies to restrict the operations of independent refiners and marketers. Upon analysis, this question was divided into two subordinate issues, *i.e.*, (1) are the rates and service requirements *reasonable*, and (2) does the alleged restrictive program exist in fact? The latter issue obviously would require an industry-wide study and, consequently, was deemed beyond the scope of this study. The discussion of the former question necessarily anticipated the content of the present section to the extent that the decisions of the Interstate Commerce Commission have affected rates and service requirements. The actual influence on rates and service requirements exerted by the Commission, and the fact that regulation of these matters has been vested by law in the Commission, led to the conclusion that they should be handled by the Commission. It is fitting, therefore, that our examination now be directed to pipe line regulation by the Commission.

I. REGULATION UNDER THE INTERSTATE COMMERCE ACT

A. Plant Facility or Common Carrier?

Because pipe lines are transportation facilities, and especially because practically all lines have been made statutory common carriers by state or federal enactments, it is perhaps natural to assume that they were constructed primarily for the purpose of transporting petroleum for profit. However, nothing could be further from the actual fact. Only one interstate pipe line has ever been constructed by interests unconnected with production or refining and for carrier purposes only. This line, the Crusader Pipe Line, was built with independent capital for the purpose of pumping crude from the Smackover, Arkansas, field to Vidalia, Louisiana, on the Mississippi River. Because it lacked an established outlet, the line never carried a barrel of oil and finally was sold for use as a natural gas line.[1] Actually, from the beginning, it has been the refiners, seeking means of securing a supply of crude oil, who have constructed the crude oil lines.[2] The reasons for this fact mainly lie in the inherent nature of pipe lines. There is a tremendous initial capital investment required,[3] the venture is extremely hazardous,[4] and successful operation requires continuous movement of traffic at near-capacity levels.[5] The refiner is faced with a need for a steady supply of crude oil, and the pipeliner requires an assured, continuous volume of traffic. Ever since the early days of the petroleum industry, this community of interest has wed the pipe line to the refinery.[6]

As old fields declined, lines were extended to new fields, and gradually, extensive pipe line systems developed. The large Standard Companies pioneered long-distance pipe lines, seeking to connect the producing fields with their huge refineries, conveniently located near heavily populated market areas. This tactic was adopted quickly by Standard's competitors, Texas, Shell, Gulf, Pure, and Sun, who found it a means of preventing Standard from squeezing them out of business. Later, aggressive independents, whose refineries were contiguous to the producing fields, sought to reach out and place their products on distant markets at competitive prices. To accomplish this, they built their own products lines or joined with other independents in constructing joint products lines. This foresight proved to be so provident that they became major integrated com-

---

[1] *Hearings before Temporary National Economic Committee, pursuant to Pub. Res. 113* (75th Cong.), 76th Cong., 2d & 3d Sess., Parts 14-17A (hereinafter cited *TNEC Hearings*) 8593 (1939-1941); Dow, THE ISSUE OF PIPE LINE DIVORCEMENT 4 (1939) (mimeographed); A.P.I., A SURVEY OF THE PRESENT POSITION OF THE PETROLEUM INDUSTRY AND ITS OUTLOOK TOWARD THE FUTURE (hereinafter cited as SURVEY) 64 (1935); MILLS, THE PIPE LINE'S PLACE IN THE OIL INDUSTRY 86-87 (1935).

[2] *TNEC Hearings* 8593; Dow, THE ISSUE OF PIPE LINE DIVORCEMENT 4 (1939); A.P.I., SURVEY 55 (1935); MILLS, THE PIPE LINE'S PLACE IN THE OIL INDUSTRY 19 (1935).

[3] Prairie Oil & Gas Co. v. United States, 204 Fed. 798, 801 (Comm.Ct. 1913); WEP, BIG INCH AND LITTLE BIG INCH 16 (1946); ASS'N OF AMERICAN RAILROADS, REPORT BY SUBCOMMITTEE ON PIPE LINE TRANSPORT 14 (1944); Hill, *Engineering Economics of Long Petroleum Pipe Lines* in PETROLEUM DEVELOPMENT & TECHNOLOGY 231, 233-234 (1942); see Emerson, *Salient Characterstics of Petroleum Pipe Line Transportation*, 26 LAND ECON. 27, 31 (No. 1, 1950).

[4] Reduced Pipe Line Rates and Gathering Charges, 243 I.C.C. 115, 142 (1940); Brundred Brothers v. Prairie Pipe Line Co., 68 I.C.C. 458, 461 (1922); *TNEC Hearings* 7184, 7253, 8302, 9731, 9761.

[5] *TNEC Hearings* 7203, 8302, 9936; SHUMAN, THE PETROLEUM INDUSTRY 95, 114 (1940); Hill, *supra* note 3, at 243. The "break-even" figure is apparently between 70 to 75 percent line capacity. *Ibid.* See Emerson, *supra* note 3, at 31-32.

[6] It was estimated in 1939 that 80-90 percent of American refiners owned some pipe line facilities. *TNEC Hearings* 8332.

panies themselves.[7] Thus, the refiner has been primarily responsible for the development of both crude and products pipe line systems, and the impetus of development has been the constant need for pipe lines as functional utilities of refineries rather than as purveyors of a transportation service engaged in for profit.[8] This fact was high-lighted by the famous "Splawn Report" to the 72d Congress in 1933, wherein it is stated: "Oil pipe lines are found as a result of this investigation to be plant facilities in an integrated industry."[9] Despite this fact, policy considerations have caused our lawmakers, both legislative and judicial, to fasten the legal mantle of common carriers on most pipe lines.

The section immediately following this discussion is devoted to an examination of the growth of the common carrier concept, but in order to appreciate it fully, it will be helpful, at this point, to recognize the fundamental inconsistency[10] of pipe line status as plant facility by nature,[11] common carrier by law,[12] and a combination of the two in fact.[13] Consideration of the legal concept of common carrier status for pipe lines conveniently

---

[7] Petroleum Rail Shippers' Ass'n v. Alton & Southern R.R., 243 I.C.C. 589, 669-670 (1941). Perhaps the two leading examples of aggressive independents achieving major status in the period 1920-1936 are Phillips Petroleum Co. and Sun Oil Co.

[8] *TNEC Hearings* 8593; Dow, THE ISSUE OF PIPE LINE DIVORCEMENT 5 (1939); A.P.I., SURVEY 54, 58 (1935); MILLS, THE PIPE LINE'S PLACE IN THE OIL INDUSTRY 21 (1935); 2 SHARFMAN, THE INTERSTATE COMMERCE COMMISSION 58 (1931).

[9] H.R. REP. No. 2192, 73d Cong., 2d Sess. LXXVIII (1933).

[10] For an excellent discussion of the inconsistent views, see BEARD, REGULATION OF PIPE LINES AS COMMON CARRIERS 149-173 (1941). Also see Emerson, *Salient Characteristics of Petroleum Pipe Line Transportation*, 26 LAND ECON. 27, 36 (1950); Whitesel, *Recent Federal Regulation of the Petroleum Pipe Line as a Common Carrier*, 32 CORN. L. Q. 337, 338-339 (1947).

[11] H.R. REP. No. 2192, 72d Cong., 2d Sess. LXXVIII (1933); BURKE, THE PIPE LINE'S PLACE IN TRANSPORTATION 3 (1949) (mimeographed); ROSTOW, A NATIONAL POLICY FOR THE OIL INDUSTRY 62 (1948); A.P.I., SURVEY 58 (1935); FRANCIS, DIVORCEMENT OF PIPE LINES 11 (paper presented before the Mineral Law Section, American Bar Ass'n on July 16, 1935); Emerson, *supra* note 10, at 36.

[12] Champlin Refining Co. v. United States, 329 U. S. 29, 67 Sup.Ct. 1, 91 L.Ed. 22 (1946); Valvoline Oil Co. v. United States, 308 U. S. 141, 60 Sup.Ct. 160, 84 L.Ed. 151 (1939); The Pipe Line Cases, 234 U. S. 548, 34 Sup.Ct. 956, 58 L.Ed. 1459 (1914); Schmitt v. War Emergency Pipelines, Inc., 175 F.2d 335 (8th Cir. 1949).

[13] *Compare* BURKE, THE VIEWS OF THE TRANSPORTATION AGENCIES: PIPE LINE TRANSPORT 6 (1949) (mimeographed); BURKE, THE PIPE LINE'S PLACE IN TRANSPORTATION 3-4 (1949) (mimeographed); FARISH & PEW, REVIEW AND CRITICISM ON BEHALF OF STANDARD OIL CO. (N.J.) AND SUN OIL CO. OF MONOGRAPH No. 39 WITH REJOINDER BY MONOGRAPH AUTHOR 31-33 (TNEC Monograph 39-A, 1941), *with* SEN. REP. No. 25, 81st Cong., 1st Sess. 20 (1949); COOK, CONTROL OF THE PETROLEUM INDUSTRY BY MAJOR OIL COMPANIES 23 (TNEC Monograph 39, 1941).

may be divided into the following topics: voluntary devotion to public use, public grants, eminent domain, and general business legislation.[14]

1. VOLUNTARY DEVOTION TO PUBLIC USE. In the early days of the industry, the pipe lines which connected the producing fields to nearby refineries or railroads were strictly service facilities. They ran everybody's oil, evidencing the shipper's ownership thereof by issuing "pipe line certificates" which were sold to refiners or the pipe line company at current market prices.[15] When controversies arose from the use of these lines and found their way into court, the resemblance to the old common carriers at common law quickly was recognized.[16] The basis of these decisions was the "holding out" or actual undertaking to carry everyone's oil indifferently.[17] State statutes were quick to codify the "voluntary devotion" concept as making pipe lines common carriers.[18] Under these statutes whether the business conducted by a pipe line company is that of a common carrier is a question of fact to be decided by an appropriate tribunal.[19] Where an

[14] The organization of this sub-section and portions of the material therein have been derived from BEARD, REGULATION OF PIPE LINES AS COMMON CARRIERS 29-55 (1941).

[15] SEN. DOC. No. 61, 70th Cong., 1st Sess. 34 (1928) ; CONWAY, PIPE LINE DIVORCEMENT 3 (unpublished thesis in University of Oklahoma Law School Library, 1950).

[16] Hall v. Cumberland Pipe Line Co., 193 Ky. 728, 237 S.W. 405 (1922) ; Giffin v. South West Pennsylvania Pipe Lines, 172 Pa. 580, 33 Atl. 578 (1896) ; National Transit Co. v. Weston, 121 Pa. 485, 15 Atl. 569 (1888) ; West Virginia Transportation Co. v. The Volcanic Oil & Coal Co., 5 W.Va. 382 (1872).

[17] Producers Transportation Co. v. Railroad Commission 251 U. S. 228, 40 Sup.Ct. 131, 64 L.Ed. 239 (1920) ; 2 CALIF. L. REV. 494 (1914), 14 COL. L. REV. 662 (1914) ; *cf.* Brass v. Stoeser, 153 U.S. 391, 14 Sup.Ct. 857, 38 L.Ed. 757 (1894) ; Budd v. New York, 143 U.S. 517, 12 Sup.Ct. 468, 36 L.Ed. 247 (1892) ; Munn v. Illinois, 94 U.S. 113, 24 L.Ed. 77 (1876) ; Interstate Natural Gas Co. v. Louisiana Public Service Commission, 34 F.Supp. 980 (E.D.La. 1940) ; Producers Pipe Line Co. v. Martin, 22 F.Supp. 44 (W.D.Ky. 1938).

[18] *E.g.*, CAL. GEN. LAWS., act 5633, § 1 (Deering 1944), Producers Transportation Co. v. Railroad Commission, 176 Cal. 499, 169 Pac. 59 (1917), *aff'd*, 251 U.S. 228, 40 Sup.Ct. 131, 64 L.Ed. 239 (1920) ; 52 OKLA. STAT. § 56 (1941), *In re* Assessment of Champlin Refining Co., 129 Okla. 166, 264 Pac. 160 (1928) ; TEX. CIV. STAT. ANN., art. 6018 § 1 (Vern. 1949), Atlas Pipe Line Co. v. Sterling, 4 F.Supp. 441 (E.D.Tex. 1933) ; Standard Oil Company of Louisiana v. Louisiana Public Service Commission, 154 La. 557, 97 So. 859 (1923). For a compilation of common carrier statutes, see BEARD, REGULATION OF PIPE LINES AS COMMON CARRIERS 45-48 (1941).

[19] *See e.g.*, Producers Transportation Co. v. Railroad Commission, 176 Cal. 499, 169 Pac. 59 (1917), *aff'd*, 251 U.S. 228, 40 Sup.Ct. 131, 64 L.Ed. 239 (1920) ; Interstate Natural Gas Co. v. Louisiana Public Service Commission, 34 F.Supp. 980 (E.D.La. 1940) ; Associated Pipe Line Co. v. Railroad Commission, 176 Cal. 518, 169 Pac. 62, L.R.A. 1918 C, 849 (1917) ; Standard Oil Company of Louisiana v. Louisiana Public Service Commission, 154 La. 557, 97 So. 859 (1923) ; Michigan Consolidated Gas Co. v. Sohio Petroleum Co., 321 Mich. 102, 32 N.W. 2d 353 (1948).

otherwise private line has carried outside oil for another refiner[20] or producer,[21] such conduct has been held to impress the pipe line with common
carrier status.[22] This result cannot be subverted by the formation of an
agency to pool the production of many independent operators.[23]

2. PUBLIC GRANTS. The federal government, under its constitutional
authority to dispose of public lands,[24] requires pipe line recipients of rights-
of-way to assume the burdens of common carriage.[25] Lessees of public oil
lands, if they are owners, operators, or holders of a controlling interest in
any pipe line accessible to the oil derived from the leases, must agree to
carry oil for other lessees of public lands who do not have pipe line facilities.[26] A substantial number of states have similar enactments on their
books, particularly with reference to ways across public streams and highways.[27]

3. EMINENT DOMAIN. It often is necessary for pipe line companies
to obtain rights-of-way by condemnation proceedings. Many state statutes
grant pipe line companies the right of eminent domain and simultaneously
impress them with common carrier status.[28] The exercise of condemnation
rights by a pipe line company under such a statute is deemed conclusive

[20] Pierce Oil Corp. v. Phoenix Refining Co., 79 Okla. 36, 190 Pac. 857 (1920), *aff'd,* 259
U.S. 125, 42 Sup.Ct. 440, 66 L.Ed. 855 (1922).

[21] Producers Transportation Co. v. Railroad Commission, 176 Cal. 499, 169 Pac. 59
(1917), *aff'd,* 251 U.S. 228, 40 Sup.Ct. 131, 64 L.Ed. 239 (1920) ; *In re* Assessment of Champlin
Refining Co., 129 Okla. 166, 264 Pac. 160 (1928).

[22] See notes 20 & 21 *supra;* BEARD, REGULATION OF PIPE LINES AS COMMON CARRIERS
31-33 (1941) ; *but cf.* Associated Pipe Line Co. v. Railroad Commission, 176 Cal. 518, 169 Pac.
62, L.R.A. 1918 C, 849 (1917) ; Tidewater Pipe Co. v. Board of Review, 311 Ill. 375, 143 N.E.
87 (1924).

[23] Producers Transportation Co. v. Railroad Commission, 176 Cal. 499, 169 Pac. 59
(1917), *aff'd,* 251 U.S. 228, 40 Sup.Ct. 131, 64 L.Ed. 239 (1920).

[24] U.S. CONST. Art. IV, § 3(2).

[25] 41 STAT. 449 (1920), as amended, 49 STAT 678 (1935), 30 U.S.C. § 185 (1946) ; see
Montana-Dakota Utilities Co. v. Federal Power Commission, 169 F.2d 392 (8th Cir. 1948),
cert. denied, 335 U.S. 853, 69 Sup.Ct. 82, 93 L.Ed. 401 (1948) ; Montana Eastern Pipe Line
Co. v. Montana Dakota Utilities Co., 26 F.Supp. 284 (D.Mont. 1938).

[26] 41 STAT. 449 (1920), as amended, 49 STAT. 678 (1935), 30 U.S.C. § 185 (1946).

[27] BEARD, REGULATION OF PIPE LINES AS COMMON CARRIERS 37-39 (1941). At one time
Oklahoma flatly forbade leasing public lands to pipe line or affiliated companies. 64 OKLA.
STAT. § 286 (1941). However, it was discovered in 1947 that this provision had been repealed
by S. 181 of the 6th Legislature, Laws 1917, p. 462, but had been re-enacted by mistake in
compiling the statutes. Accordingly, 64 OKLA. STAT. § 286 (1941) was repealed by Laws 1947,
p. 412, § 1.

[28] *E.g.,* CAL. GEN. LAWS, act. 5633 (Deering 1944) ; 52 OKLA. STAT. §§ 56, 60 (1941) ;
TEX. CIV. STAT. ANN., arts. 6018 and 6022 (Vern. 1949). For compilation of other states, See
BEARD, *op. cit. supra* note 27, at 39-42.

evidence of a dedication of its lines to public use.[29] However, exercise of condemnation rights is not necessarily a condition precedent to common carrier status. It is enough that the statute has granted the extraordinary right to pipe lines constructed after the passage of the act.[30]

4.GENERAL BUSINESS LEGISLATION. Although limited by the doctrine of unconstitutional conditions[31] and the federal power over interstate commerce,[32] a state may prescribe the conditions under which it will grant a foreign corporation the right to conduct an intrastate business within its borders.[33] The application of this principle to impose common carrier status on foreign corporations was tested in *Pierce Oil Corporation v. Phoenix Refining Company*.[34] Oklahoma's laws provide that pipe lines transporting crude petroleum within Oklahoma "for hire or otherwise" shall be deemed common carriers as at common law,[35] simultaneously giving them the right of eminent domain and the right to use public highways.[36] These statutes were in effect when Pierce (a Virginia Corporation) built its line. Later, Pierce attempted to avoid carrying Phoenix Refining Company's oil by asserting it was not a common carrier in fact, but the Oklahoma Supreme Court rejected this contention on the basis that Pierce had constructed its line in accordance with, and accepted the benefits of, the very law it now sought to attack.[37] This position was approved by the

[29] Producers Transportation Co. v. Railroad Commission, 176 Cal. 499, 169 Pac. 59 (1917), *aff'd,* 251 U.S. 228, 40 Sup.Ct. 131, 64 L.Ed. 239 (1920); *cf.* State v. Consumers Gas Trust Co., 157 Ind. 345, 61 N.E. 674 (1901); State v. American & European Commercial News Co., 43 N.J.L. 381 (Sup.Ct. 1881); 2 CALIF. L. REV. 494-495 (1914); *see* Associated Pipe Line Co. v. Railroad Commission, 176 Cal. 518, 169 Pac. 62, L.R.A. 1918 C, 849 (1917).

[30] Martin v. Producers Pipe Line Co., 113 F.2d 817, 820 (6th Cir. 1940); Producers Pipe Line Co. v Martin, 22 F.Supp. 44, 47 (W.D.Ky. 1938); Texas Co. v. Commonwealth, 303 Ky. 590, 593, 198 S.W.2d 316, 318 (1946); *cf.* Pierce Oil Corp. v. Phoenix Refining Co., 79 Okla. 36, 190 Pac. 857 (1920), *aff'd,* 259 U.S. 125, 42 Sup.Ct. 440, 66 L.Ed., 855 (1922).

[31] See Merrill, *Unconstitutional Conditions,* 77 U. OF PA. L. REV. 879 (1929).

[32] International Paper Co. v. Mass., 246 U.S. 135, 38 Sup.Ct. 292, 62 L.Ed. 624 (1918); Sioux Remedy Co. v. Cope, 235 U.S. 197, 35 Sup.Ct. 57, 59 L.Ed. 193 (1914); Western Union Telegraph Co. v. Kansas, 216 U.S. 1, 30 Sup.Ct. 190, 54 L.Ed. 355 (1910); State v. Stanolind Pipe Line Co., 216 Iowa 436, 249 N.W. 366 (1933).

[33] Kansas City, Memphis & Birmingham R.R. v. Stiles, 242 U.S. 111, 37 Sup.Ct. 58, 61 L.Ed. 176 (1916); Baltic Mining Co. v. Mass., 231 U.S. 68, 34 Sup.Ct. 15, 58 L.Ed. 127 (1913); Horn Silver Mining Co. v. New York, 143 U.S. 305, 12 Sup.Ct. 403, 36 L.Ed. 164 (1892); Paul v. Virginia, 8 Wall. 168, 19 L.Ed. 357 (U.S. 1869).

[34] 79 Okla. 36, 190 Pac. 857 (1920), *aff'd,* 259 U.S. 125, 42 Sup.Ct. 440, 66 L.Ed. 855 (1922).

[35] 52 OKLA. STAT. § 56 (1941).

[36] 52 OKLA. STAT. § 52 (1941).

[37] Pierce Oil Corp. v. Phoenix Refining Co., 79 Okla. 36, 38, 190 Pac. 857, 859 (1920).

United States Supreme Court which labelled defendent's contention of deprivation of property without due process of law as "futile to the point almost of being frivolous."[38]

B. *Interstate Commerce Commission Jurisdiction Over Pipe Lines*

The abuses of the Standard Oil monopoly over pipe lines in the early days of the industry led to the adoption of the "oil amendment" of the Hepburn Act of 1906[39] which was designed to regulate interstate pipe lines as common carriers.[40] At first the large pipe line companies attempted to avoid the impact of the statute by privately purchasing rights-of-way, refusing to run any oil except their own production or that which they had purchased at the wellhead, and incorporating separate companies in each state through which oil moved by pipe line and transferring title to the oil at state borders.

The effectiveness of these maneuvers was considered by the Interstate Commerce Commission in a 1911 hearing entitled *In the Matter of Pipe Lines*.[41] Declining to consider the constitutional question of the alleged "taking" of property for public use without just compensation, the Commission examined the legislative history of the Hepburn Act and found that Senator Lodge had anticipated the device of refusing to carry for the public by causing the enactment to be phrased in such a manner as to include *all* interstate oil pipe lines.[42] The action of the Senate in accepting Senator Lodge's phrasing, supported by subsequent floor debates and the flood of opposition to the "oil amendment" offered by the petroleum industry, convinced the Commission that all interstate oil pipe lines were included within the scope of the Act.[43] Moreover, the Commission brushed aside the technical devices of using different corporations in each state and of transferring title at state boundaries, remarking that the interruption

---

[38] *Idem.*, 259 U.S. 125, 128, 42 Sup. Ct. 440, 441, 66 L.Ed. 855, 857 (1922).

[39] 34 Stat. 584 (1906), as amended, 49 U.S.C. § 1 (1946).

[40] Valvoline Oil Co. v. United States, 308 U.S. 141, 144, 60 Sup.Ct. 160, 162, 84 L.Ed. 151, 154 (1939) ; The Pipe Line Cases, 234 U.S. 548, 558, 34 Sup.Ct. 956, 957-958, 58 L.Ed. 1459, 1469 (1914) ; Champlin Refining Co. v. United States, 95 F.Supp. 170, 173, (W.D.Okla. 1950) ; 40 Cong. Rec. 6365-6366 (1906) ; Beard, Regulation of Pipe Lines as Common Carriers 16-18 (1941) ; 2 Sharfman, The Interstate Commerce Commission 59, 96 (1931) ; Whitesel, *Recent Federal Regulation of the Petroleum Pipe Line as a Common Carrier*, 32 Corn. L. Q. 337, 341 (1947) ; Prewitt, *The Operation and Regulation of Crude Oil and Gasoline Pipe Lines*, 56 Q. J. Econ. 177, 201 n.9 (1942).

[41] 24 I.C.C. 1 (1912).

[42] *Id.* at 4-5.

[43] *Id.* at 6. See 40 Cong. Rec. 6361, 6365-6366, 6999-7009, 9254-9256 (1906).

was not "made in good faith for some necessary purpose," and, therefore, could not divest the traffic of its interstate character.[44]

In accordance with these conclusions, the Commission entered orders to the interstate pipe lines directing them to file tariffs.[45] Several of the respondent companies promptly instituted proceedings in *Prairie Oil and Gas Company v. United States*,[46] asking the Commerce Court to set aside and annul the Commission's order. They based their action on two propositions: first, that the Amendment of 1906 applied only to such pipe line companies as were common carriers at the date of enactment, or thereafter should become such by voluntary action or judicial proceeding; and, second, that if the Amendment were construed to apply to all interstate pipe lines transporting oil, including private pipe lines used solely for moving the owner's oil, it would be unconstitutional, because it would deprive the pipe line owners of their property without due process of law and take property for public use without just compensation. The Commerce Court upheld the Commission's construction of the Act,[47] but also held that Congress' action in opening up all private interstate pipe lines to public use was a deprivation of private property without just compensation.[48] Concluding, therefore, that the enactment of the pipe line amendment exceeded the powers of Congress, the court granted a preliminary injunction against the enforcement of the Commission's order to file tariffs.[49] A commentator was impressed by the force of the argument that the existing pipe line companies held a virtual monopoly of crude oil transportation, which in turn, gave them control over the crude market.[50]

[44] *Id.* at 6-7. "It shall be unlawful for any common carrier subject to the provisions of this chapter to enter into any combination, contract, or agreement, expressed or implied, to prevent, by change of time schedule, carriage in different cars, or by other means or devices, the carriage of freights from being continuous from the place of shipment to the place of destination; and no break of bulk, stoppage, or interruption made by such common carrier shall prevent the carriage of freights from being and being treated as one continuous carriage from the place of shipment to the place of destination, *unless such* break, stoppage, or *interruption was made in good faith for some necessary purpose,* and without any intent to avoid or unnecessarily interrupt such continuous carriage or to evade any of the provisions of this chapter." 24 STAT. 382 (1887), as amended, 49 U.S.C. § 7 (1946) (emphasis supplied).

[45] In the Matter of Pipe Lines, 24 I.C.C. 1, 11 (1912).

[46] 204 Fed. 798 (Comm.Ct. 1913).

[47] *Id.* at 805-806.

[48] *Id.* at 817.

[49] *Id.* at 821.

[50] 26 HARV. L. REV. 631 (1913). The writer approved the statutory remedy making legal common carriers out of those already common carriers in a physical sense. But the statute apparently included the Uncle Sam Oil Company and others who merely transported, for their own use, oil produced from their own wells, an activity hardly contrary to public policy. Since the Act did not seem divisible, he concluded that the inclusion of all pipe line carriers rendered it unconstitutional.

The government appealed to the Supreme Court, where Mr. Justice Holmes, speaking for the court in *The Pipe Line Line Cases*,[51] approved the inclusion of all interstate pipe lines engaged in the business of transporting oil. Noting that ". . . the Standard Oil Company had made itself master of the only practicable oil transportation between the oil fields east of California and the Atlantic Ocean and carried much the greater part of the oil between those points,"[52] and "[i]n this way it made itself master of the fields without the necessity of owning them and carried across half the continent a great subject of international commerce coming from many owners but, by the duress of which the Standard Oil Company was master, carrying it all as its own,"[53] Justice Holmes held that the plain meaning[54] of the Amendment showed an evident purpose to include within its scope pipe lines that, although not technically common carriers, yet were carrying all oil offered at a price acceptable to the carriers.[55] He felt that the carriage to the seaboard of "nearly all the oil east of California" was transportation within the meaning of the Act, and that this fact was not changed by the technicality of a forced sale to the carrier.[56]

The concept of interstate commerce was deemed to be a practical one, not wholly dependent upon technical questions of title, but determined by the essential character of the carriage.[57] The same considerations[58] which made the carriage transportation within the meaning of the Act also made it "commerce."[59] Having found that the transcontinental carriers were common carriers in substance, Justice Holmes reasoned that Congress constitutionally could require them to become common carriers in form.[60] He was careful to point out that the Amendment did not compel the carriers to continue in operation, nor did it require them to carry every-

[51] 234 U.S. 548, 34 Sup.Ct. 956, 58 L.Ed. 1459 (1914).

[52] *Id.* at 559, 34 Sup.Ct. at 958, 58 L.Ed. at 1470.

[53] *Ibid.*

[54] *Cf.* Caminetti v. United States, 242 U.S. 470, 37 Sup.Ct. 192, 61 L.Ed. 442 (1917); United States v. First National Bank, 234 U.S. 245, 34 Sup.Ct. 846, 58 L.Ed. 1298 (1914).

[55] The Pipe Line Cases, 234 U.S. 548, 560, 34 Sup.Ct. 956, 958, 58 L.Ed. 1459, 1470 (1914).

[56] *Ibid.*

[57] *Ibid.* See also Valvoline Oil Co. v. United States, 308 U.S. 141, 145, 60 Sup.Ct. 160, 162, 84 L.Ed. 151, 154 (1939); Atlantic Coast Line R.R. v. Standard Oil Company of Kentucky, 275 U.S. 257, 268, 48 Sup.Ct. 107, 110, 72 L.Ed. 270, 274 (1927); Public Utilities Commission v. Landon, 249 U.S. 236, 245, 39 Sup.Ct. 268, 269, 63 L.Ed. 577, 586 (1919); Rearick v. Pennsylvania, 203 U.S. 507, 512, 27 Sup.Ct. 159, 160, 51 L.Ed. 295, 297 (1906); Champlin Refining Company, Valuation of Pipe Line, 49 Val.Rep. 463, 470 (1942).

[58] Carriage to the seaboard of nearly all the oil east of California, "beginning in purchase and ending in sale."

[59] The Pipe Line Cases, 234 U.S. 548, 560, 34 Sup.Ct. 956, 958, 58 L.Ed. 1459, 1470 (1914).

[60] *Id.* at 561, 34 Sup.Ct. at 958, 58, L. Ed. at 1470. For a case where this technique was reversed to make a common carrier in form become one in substance, see Minnelusa Oil Corp. v. Continental Pipe Line Co., 258 I.C.C. 41 (1944).

one's oil, but simply that they must give up requiring a sale to themselves before carrying the oil they did receive.[61] In considering the constitutionality of the Act, Justice Holmes distinguished between pipe lines engaged in transportation at the time of enactment and lines constructed thereafter, saying there could be no doubt concerning the validity of its application to the latter.[62]

The case of the Uncle Sam Oil Company was distinguished on the ground that the movement of its own oil from its own wells to its own refinery for its own use was not *transportation within the meaning of the Act,* being only an incident to use at the end.[63] Accordingly, the decree of the Commerce Court in favor of the Uncle Sam Oil Company was affirmed, while the decrees in favor of the other respondents were reversed.

The commentators approved the result of the case, remarking that it represented a triumph of economic necessity over logic, and that the end justified the means.[64] There was a general agreement that the factor governing the outcome of the case was the economic duress practiced by the [monopsonistic] Standard pipe lines.[65] They perceived the distinction between the Standard lines and Uncle Sam's line to be the purchase by the

---

[61] The Pipe Line Cases, 234 U.S. 548, 561, 34 Sup.Ct. 956, 959, 58 L.Ed. 1459, 1471 (1914).

[62] "So far as the statute contemplates future pipe lines and prescribes the conditions upon which they may be established there can be no doubt that it is valid." *Id.* at 561, 34 Sup.Ct. at 958, 58 L.Ed. at 1470. See also Pierce Oil Corp. v. Phoenix Refining Co., 259 U.S. 125, 128, 42 Sup.Ct. 440, 442, 66 L.Ed. 855, 858 (1922); Champlin Refining Co. v. United States, 59 F.Supp. 978, 982 (W.D.Okla. 1945); Valvoline Oil Co. v. United States, 25 F.Supp. 460, 464 (W.D.Pa. 1938); Associated Pipe Line Co. v. Railroad Commission, 176 Cal. 518, 530, 169 Pac. 62, 66, L.R.A. 1918 C, 849, 855 (1917); Pierce Oil Corp. v. Phoenix Refining Co., 79 Okla. 36, 38, 190 Pac. 857, 858 (1920); Champlin Refining Company Accounts and Reports, 274 I.C.C. 409, 414 (1949); Champlin Refining Company, Valuation of Pipe Line, 49 Val.Rep. 542, 548 (1944).

[63] The Pipe Line Cases, 234 U.S. 548, 562, 34 Sup.Ct. 956, 959, 58 L.Ed. 1459, 1471 (1914). Chief Justice White, in a concurring opinion, felt that the Uncle Sam Oil Company was engaged in transportation within the meaning of the Act but that the application of the statute to it would be a taking of private property without just compensation. His distinction was that Uncle Sam was a private carrier whereas the Standard Companies were actually common carriers in the first place. *Id.* at 563, 34 Sup.Ct. at 959, 58 L.Ed. at 1471. The view that the Uncle Sam Oil Company also was engaged in transportation of oil in interstate commerce finds support in two earlier State decisions: Prairie Oil & Gas Co. v. Ehrhardt, 244 Ill. 634, 91 N.E. 680 (1910) and Columbia Conduit Co. v. Commonwealth, 90 Pa. 307 (1879) (transportation).

In his dissenting opinion, Mr. Justice McKenna also rejected the majority's distinction between the Uncle Sam Oil Company and the other carriers. However, unlike the Chief Justice, he objected to making any of the pipe lines common carriers.

[64] 2 CALIF. L. REV. 494 (1914); 79 CENT. L. J. 19 (1914); 14 COL. L. REV. 662 (1914).

[65] Because of this, one writer felt that the majority's reasoning unjustifiably omitted any consideration of whether the large pipe lines were aggressively endeavoring to purchase outside oil, or were simply accepting oil that was offered for sale since they were able to transport it. 79 CENT. L. J. 19 (1914).

former of "everybody's" oil by a pipe line company having the power to dictate the purchase price.[66]

The California Supreme Court drew the same distinction in *Associated Pipe Line Company v. Railroad Commission of California*.[67] In this case the Associated Pipe Line Company and Kern Oil & Trading Company[68] had joined in the construction of two pipe lines of 38,000 barrels daily capacity. Under their agreement, no charge was made for the transportation of oil other than the actual cost of operation and maintenance of the lines, and each company had been allotted one-half of the daily capacity since commencement of operations. The Kern Oil & Trading Company produced sufficient crude to utilize its allotted 19,000 barrels per day line capacity, and the Associated Oil Company, parent of the defendant pipe line company, produced 16,500 barrels per day and purchased about 30,-000 barrels per day. To move its 46,500 barrels to its refineries, the Associated Oil Company used its 19,000 barrels share of the pipe lines in question and two other 15,000 barrels per day lines. The California Supreme Court distinguished the instant case from *The Pipe Line Cases* by saying the latter holding rested on the fact that the monopoly of the means of transportation had made the Standard Companies masters of all the oil fields east of California. Subject to the conditions of sale to the carriers on their own terms, they *carried everybody's oil to market*, whereas in the case at bar the pipe line owners produced most of the oil transported through the lines and purchased the rest in *competition* with a number of other pipe lines running from the field.

The Illinois Supreme Court, in *Tidewater Pipe Company v. Board of Review*,[69] greatly enlarged the private carrier concept created for the Uncle Sam Oil Company in the earlier case. Tidewater purchased oil from many producers in Crawford County, Illinois, which it transported through its gathering system to a tank farm near Stoy. From Stoy, it pumped this oil into a trunk line running to its refinery in Bayonne, New Jersey. The Illinois court held that no distinction arose merely because Tidewater had purchased oil in Crawford County instead of producing the oil itself, and therefore, like the Uncle Sam Oil Company, the Tidewater line was not a common carrier engaged in interstate commerce under the Act.[70] This

---

[66] 79 Cent. L. J. 19 (1914); *cf.* Mr. Justice McKenna's analysis of the majority's distinction in The Pipe Line Cases, 234 U.S. 548, 573, 34 Sup.Ct. 956, 963, 58 L.Ed. 1459, 1475 (1914).

[67] 176 Cal. 518, 169 Pac. 62, L.R.A. 1918 C, 849 (1917).

[68] The oil subsidiary of the Southern Pacific Co.

[69] 311 Ill. 375, 143 N.E. 87 (1924).

[70] *Id.* at 377, 143 N.E. at 88.

decision seems questionable,[71] especially in the light of a previous contrary decision by the same court.[72] Perhaps the case may be explained by the fact that state taxation was involved. Interestingly enough, the Tidewater Pipe Company, which had vigorously resisted its denomination as interstate common carrier in *The Pipe Line Cases,* now based its defense on the fact that it *was* an interstate common carrier, only to have the Illinois Supreme Court decide it was not.

The jurisdiction of the Commission over petroleum pipe lines again was involved in *Valvoline Oil Company v. United States.*[73] Valvoline specialized in refining a very high grade lubricating oil and was not a crude producer. It purchased its oil from the operators of some 9020 stripper wells[74] in Pennsylvania, West Virginia and Ohio. In 1932 the company was forced to shut down its refinery at Warren, Pennsylvania, but instead of limiting its purchases to the quantity of oil required by its refinery at East Butler, it continued to purchase all proffered oil of suitable grade with the result that its pipe line carried oil in excess of its refinery requirements. Disposition of this excess was effectuated by contractual arrangements with a Pennsylvania refiner and a West Virginia refiner. However, all the oil sold to the Pennsylvania refiner originated in Pennsylvania and its movement through Valvoline's lines was intrastate, and likewise as to the West Virginia refiner. Based on these facts, the Valvoline Oil Company resisted the Interstate Commerce Commission's Valuation Order[75] requiring maps, charts and schedules of company property, by proceedings in the federal district court to enjoin the Commission's order, alleging that it was a private carrier and, like the Uncle Sam Oil Company in *The Pipe Line Cases,* beyond the scope of the amended Interstate Commerce Act.

In its consideration of the case, the district court first examined Section 400 of the 1920 Transportation Act.[76] The court held that this rephrasing of the language of the Hepburn Act worked no change in its meaning.[77]

---

[71] Valvoline Oil Company Petition in Valuation of Pipe Lines, 47 Val. Rep. 534, 539-540 (1937).

[72] Prairie Oil & Gas Co. v. Ehrhardt, 244 Ill. 634, 91 N.E. 680 (1910).

[73] 25 F.Supp. 460 (W.D.Pa. 1938), *aff'd,* 308 U.S. 141, 60 Sup.Ct. 160, 84 L.Ed. 151 (1939). See 47 Val.Rep. 534 (1937) for hearing before the Interstate Commerce Commission.

[74] The daily average production of the Pennsylvania wells was 0.20 barrel, West Virginia—0.56, Ohio—0.25 barrel.

[75] See note 71 *supra.*

[76] 41 STAT. 474 (1920), as amended, 49 U.S.C. § 1 (1946).

[77] Valvoline Oil Co. v. United States, 25 F.Supp. 460, 463 (W.D.Pa. 1938). The Supreme Court concurred in this interpretation, saying: "In the present Act there is a change of language but we perceive none in meaning." *Idem.,* 308 U.S. 141, 145, 60 Sup.Ct. 160, 162, 84 L.Ed. 151, 154 (1939) ; see H.R. REP. No. 456, 66th Cong., 1st Sess. 27 (1919) ; see also Champlin Refining Company, Valuation of Pipe Line, 49 Val.Rep. 463, 468 (1942).

Applying this construction, the district court found Valvoline to be an interstate common carrier within the meaning of the amended Interstate Commerce Act.[78] After pointing out that the decision was limited to the question of whether the Interstate Commerce Commission could order a valuation under Section 19(a) of the Act,[79] and that the smallness of the operation was immaterial,[80] the court upheld the right of the Commission to order the valuation, and dismissed Valvoline's petition for injunction. On appeal, the Supreme Court held that Valvoline was obviously an interstate pipe line company,[81] and that the phrase "engaged in such transportation . . . as common carriers for hire"[82] was a conjunctive clause, and did not modify the general application of the first clause defining common carriers as used in the Act to include (*inter alia*) *all* pipe line companies engaged in interstate transportation of oil within the meaning of the Act.[83] The court held that Valvoline was engaged in "transportation" within the meaning of the Act, distinguishing it from the Uncle Sam Oil Company on the grounds that Valvoline purchased crude from many sources and represented the sole means of transporting to market the oil of many thousands

[78] Valvoline Oil Co. v. United States, 25 F.Supp. 460, 463 (W.D.Pa. 1938). The court rejected Valvoline's contention of taking property without just compensation, saying: "It is equally clear that the imposition upon the Valvoline of the status of a common carrier subject to the provisions of the Act as a condition of its engaging in interstate transportation did not amount to the taking of its property without just compensation in violation of the fifth amendment." *Id*. at 464. The Supreme Court avoided this issue by stressing the separate significance of the valuation order. See note 79 *infra*.

[79] *Id*. at 464. The Supreme Court also took the position that the valuation provisions were separate from the regulatory provisions, thereby making premature the constitutional issue of taking. *Idem*., 308 U.S. 141, 146, 60 Sup.Ct. 160, 163, 84 L.Ed. 151, 155 (1939).

[80] Valvoline Oil Co. v. United States, 25 F.Supp. 460, 464 (W.D.Pa. 1938). This holding also was affirmed by the Supreme Court. *Idem*., 308 U.S. 141, 147, 60 Sup.Ct. 160, 163, 84 L.Ed. 151, 155 (1939). See National Labor Relations Board v. Fainblatt, 306 U.S. 601, 59 Sup.Ct. 668, 83 L.Ed. 1014 (1939) ; Brass v. Stoeser, 153 U.S. 391, 14 Sup.Ct. 857, 38 L.Ed. 757 (1894).

[81] Valvoline Oil Co. v. United States, 308 U.S. 141, 144, 60 Sup.Ct. 160, 162, 84 L.Ed. 151, 154 (1939) ; see also Schmitt v. War Emergency Pipelines, Inc., 175 F.2d 335, 337 (8th Cir. 1949) ; Champlin Refining Co. v. United States, 59 F.Supp. 978, 982 (W.D.Okla. 1945) ; Champlin Refining Company, Valuation of Pipe Line, 49 Val.Rep. 463, 469 (1942).

[82] Sec. 1(3)(a). "The term 'common carrier' as used in this chapter shall include all pipe-line companies; express companies; sleeping-car companies; and all persons, natural or artificial, engaged in such transportation as aforesaid as common carriers for hire." 49 U.S.C. § 1(3)(a) (1946).

[83] Valvoline Oil Co. v. United States, 308 U.S. 141, 146, 60 Sup.Ct. 160, 162, 84 L.Ed. 151, 154 (1939) ; see also Schmitt v. War Emergency Pipelines, Inc., 175 F.2d 335, 336 (8th Cir. 1949) ; H.R. REP. No. 456, 66th Cong., 1st Sess. 27 (1919) ; 40 CONG. REC. 6361-6366, 6999-7009, 9254-9256 (1906).

of producers,[84] whereas Uncle Sam's line was used for the sole purpose of conducting oil from its own wells to its own refinery [for its own use]. Accordingly, the Supreme Court affirmed the district court's dismissal of Valvoline's bill for injunction.[85]

In 1941, the Commission turned its attention to products pipe lines which were operated as private carriers. It decided to bring a test case against either the Champlin Refining Company or the Standard Oil Company (Ind.)[86] in such a manner as to raise the question of jurisdiction under Section 19(a).[87] Accordingly, after a hearing on the question, the Commission issued an order to Champlin[88] requiring the filing of certain maps and information necessary for valuation of Champlin's line.[89] Champlin instituted proceedings in a three-judge federal district court sitting in Oklahoma City for an injunction to restrain the enforcement of the Commission's order.[90] From a dismissal by the district court, Champ-

---

[84] The lower court had found that if Valvoline refused to accept the oil it presently carried, the producers would have to tender five barrels per day in order to justify a connection to the common carrier pipe lines in the area. Due to the extremely limited production of most of the wells, this requirement would deprive many of the producers of an outlet. Valvoline Oil Co. v. United States, 25 F.Supp. 460, 461-462 (W.D.Pa. 1938). Whitesel, *Recent Federal Regulation of the Petroleum Pipe Line as a Common Carrier*, 32 Corn. L. Q. 337 (1937) says the essence of the case was the presence of a monopoly situation that needed public regulation. *Id.* at 343.

[85] As a result, Valvoline [now the Freedom-Valvoline Oil Company] has filed valuation data and *tariffs* with the Commission since the date of the decision. However, the company has never transported oil for anyone else, nor will it accept shipment of outside oil due to the fact that the *Valvoline* case merely decided the question of the Commission's power to require valuation data. During the course of the argument before the Supreme Court, the late Chief Justice Hughes assured counsel for Valvoline that the court would reconsider the situation if outside shipments were tendered to the line. Letter from J. Campbell Brandon, Brandon & Brandon, attorneys for Valvoline, dated June 14, 1950, to author.

[86] *Hearings before Special Committee to Study Problems of American Small Business pursuant to S. Res. 20,* 80th Cong., 1st Sess., Part 19, 2111 (1947), citing Transcript of Record, pp.3-4, Champlin Refining Co. v. United States, 329 U.S. 29, 67 Sup.Ct. 1, 91 L.Ed. 22 (1946).

[87] "The Commission shall, as hereinafter provided, investigate, ascertain, and report the value of all the property owned or used by every common carrier subject to the provisions of this chapter . . . ." 37 Stat. 701 (1913), as amended, 49 U.S.C. § 19(a) (1946). Section 19(e) provides: "Every common carrier subject to the provisions of this chapter shall furnish to the commission or its agents from time to time and as the commission may require maps, profiles, contracts, reports of engineers, and any other documents, records, and papers, or copies of any or all of the same, in aid of such investigation and determination of the value of the property of said common carrier . . . ." 37 Stat. 702 (1913), as amended, 49 U.S.C. § 19(e) (1946).

[88] Champlin Refining Company, Valuation of Pipe Line, 49 Val.Rep. 463 (1942).

[89] The question arises as to why Champlin, rather than "big" Standard Oil (Ind.) was selected. The answer possibly lies in the vulnerability of Champlin's line due to the pricing system, described *infra*, which was not present in the case of the Standard line.

[90] Champlin Refining Co. v. United States, 59 F.Supp. 978 (W.D.Okla. 1945).

lin lodged an appeal with the Supreme Court in *Champlin Refining Company v. United States.*[91]

The case involved Champlin's six-inch products line running from Enid, Oklahoma, to Rock Rapids, Iowa. The line was 516 miles long, cost $3,198,028.66, and was constructed entirely over right-of-way purchased without the use of eminent domain. Champlin had never held itself out as a public carrier, had never published tariffs, and had never been asked by any other person to transport its products. In fact there were no connections to the line except the intake at Champlin's refinery in Enid, and at three bulk terminals belonging to Champlin at Hutchinson, Kansas, Superior, Nebraska, and Rock Rapids, Iowa. Delivery to customers at these three terminals was not made from the pipe line but from truck and railcar loading racks manifolded to Champlin's storage tanks.

Mr. Justice Jackson, speaking for the five-judge majority, accepted the construction of "common carrier" by the court in the *Valvoline* case to the effect that it included "all pipe line companies"[92] and therefore addressed his attention to Champlin's contention that the "transportation" mentioned in the Act did not refer to the carriage of one's own goods. He admitted that Champlin was "not a common carrier in the sense of the common law carrier for hire,"[93] but said the Act did not stop at this but included all pipe lines. In refusing to apply the Uncle Sam Oil Company exception to Champlin, he assumed the controlling fact under the statute to be the transporting of commodities from state to state by pipe line. The pricing methods used by Champlin[94] and the fact that the product was not being transported for Champlin's *own use* [apparently distinguishing sale from refinery consumption], but that interstate facilities were utilized to place Champlin's finished products in the *market* led him to hold that Champlin's operation was transportation within the meaning of the Act.[95]

[91] 329 U.S. 29, 67 Sup.Ct. 1, 91 L.Ed. 22 (1946).

[92] *Id.* at 32, 67 Sup.Ct. at 2, 91 L.Ed. at 25.

[93] *Id.* at 33, 67 Sup.Ct. at 3, 91 L.Ed. at 25-26.

[94] Champlin sold its products by "spot-market" or "contract" sales whereby the purchaser paid an amount equal to refinery net at Enid plus a differential roughly equivalent to the through rail rate from Enid to destination, less an allowance for charges incurred in movement from Champlin's terminals to destination. There were some local modifications due to competition from other refiners. Champlin Refining Co. v. United States, 59 F.Supp. 978, 980 (W.D.Okla. 1945).

[95] Champlin Refining Co. v. United States, 329 U.S. 29, 34, 67 Sup.Ct. 1, 3, 91 L.Ed. 22, 26 (1946). Another case in which pricing methods played a large part is Reagan County Purchasing Co. v. State, 110 S.W.2d 1194, 1199 (Tex.Civ.App. 1937). In this case, the defendent crude purchasing company was held to be a common carrier under TEX. CIV. STAT. ANN., art. 6018 (Vern. 1949) largely because it operated under a sales contract calling for a delivery price equal to the current posted crude price plus a fixed 20c differential. The rationale of these decisions appears to be that the pipe line companies were in fact furnishing a *transportation service* for the consumers, thus becoming common carriers in substance.

Champlin's contention was that Congress had violated the due process clause of the Fifth Amendment by converting a private line into a public utility, thereby taking property without just compensation. Mr. Justice Jackson held that Congress has the power to regulate a private carrier engaged in interstate commerce; that the action at bar did not seek to open up Champlin's line to all comers in the sense of the common-law common carrier but only required Champlin to furnish information as to facilities being used in interstate marketing of its products; *ergo,* the due process contention was "... too premature and hypothetical to warrant consideration on this record."[96]

Mr. Justice Reed, speaking for the four dissenting judges, noted that the *Pipe Line* and *Valvoline* cases did *not* bring within the scope of the Act *all* pipe lines which carried oil interstate but only those which were found to be common carriers in substance because they purchased and carried all oil offered. In his opinion, the evil sought to be remedied was the mastery of oil through control of the gathering facilities, and "[i]f a line does not carry oil of others, it is not transporting within the contemplation of the act."[97] Since the applicable statutes had not been changed appreciably since *The Pipe Line Cases*, he could see no distinction between the Uncle Sam Company and Champlin. To him, the incidental pipe line use was alike, *i.e.,* each carried its own oil for the same ultimate purpose of reaching the market. Nor did he see any significant distinction between the cases because of Champlin's modified basing-point pricing practice. He reasoned that the delivered price must include some transportation cost. The method used to calculate this cost did not seem germane to the question of whether Champlin was a "common carrier engaged in the transportation of oil" within the meaning of the Act. Moreover, he disagreed with the majority's analysis of the valuation section of the Act. As he was careful to point out, Section 19 does not require valuation reports from *all* owners of pipe lines carrying oil in interstate commerce, *but only* from "every common carrier subject to the provisions" of the Act.[98] He contended that the determination of the case at bar must turn on the construction of Section 1 defining which enterprises were "subject to the provisions" of the Act. In deciding whether Champlin's pipe line came within Section 1, he would consider the fact that the definition of Section 1 flows not only into Section 19 but also into various other sections. He felt that once found to be included in Section 1, an enterprise is subjected to other provisions of the Act, such as

[96] Champlin Refining Co. v. United States, 329 U.S. 29, 35, 67 Sup.Ct. 1, 4, 91 L.Ed. 22, 26 (1946).

[97] *Id.* at 38, 67 Sup.Ct. at 5, 91 L.Ed. at 28.

[98] See note 87 *supra;* 20 Temp. L. Q. 592, 594 (1947); 33 Va. L. Rev. 212,213 (1947).

filing tariffs[99] and providing equal and reasonable transportation to all comers.[100] Under this construction, Champlin's contention of taking property without just compensation was pertinent.[101]

The majority's holding that the valuation provisions of the Act are separate from the rest of the Act seems clearly in error.[102] The least unfavorable result flowing from this misconstruction was the position in which Champlin was placed, *i.e.*, a private carrier forced to file "common carrier" valuation reports and to maintain a "common carrier" Uniform System of Accounts. The more drastic implication suggested by the minority opinion to the effect that once brought under the Act for valuation purposes, other common carrier incidents will follow, promptly proved prophetic. Within a year's time, the Interstate Commerce Commission had requested Champlin to file annual reports and to institute and maintain the Uniform System of Accounts required of *common carriers* by Section 20 of the Act. Four months later, the Commission requested Champlin to file tariffs as required of *common carriers* by Section 6.

Champlin's refusal to comply with these requests resulted in a hearing before the Commission. Champlin's position rested on two basic propositions: (1) its pipe line operation was not that of a common carrier engaged in transportation within the meaning of the Act; and (2) it would be a taking of property without just compensation, and hence violative of the Fifth Amendment, for the Commission to order Champlin to publish tariffs.[103] The Commission ruled adversely on the first contention, citing the *Champlin Refining Company* case.[104] It refused to pass on the constitutional question, remarking that the determination of that issue was for

---

[99] Section 6(1).

[100] Section 1(4).

[101] Significantly, the legal commentators agreed with the minority's opinion. 35 GEO. L. J. 404 (1947) ; 20 TEMP. L. Q. 592 (1947) ; 33 VA. L. REV. 212 (1947). However, an economist felt that it did not recognize the economic realities of the case, *i.e.*, Champlin's operations affected the public the same way the operations of the old Standard Companies in *The Pipe Line Cases* did. He felt that control over the "only effective means" of transporting gasoline into certain areas gave Champlin the power to control retail gasoline prices and to compel the public to deal with it. Whitesel, *Recent Federal Regulation of the Petroleum Pipe Line as a Common Carrier,* 32 CORN. L. Q. 337, 348-349 (1947). Unfortunately, Professor Whitesel's analysis did not recognize the *factual* realities of the case, *i.e.*, Champlin's line furnished only 1.98 percent of the total gasoline consumed in the area served by the line, and gasoline prices were determined by local competition, not by Champlin. See Champlin Refining Co. v. United States, 95 F.Supp. 170, 172, 175 (W.D.Okla. 1950).

[102] Whitesel, *Recent Federal Regulation of the Petroleum Pipe Line as a Common Carrier,* 32 CORN. L. Q. 337, 347-348 (1948) ; 20 TEMP. L. Q. 592, 594 (1947) ; 33 VA. L. REV. 212, 213-214 (1947).

[103] Brief for Respondent, pp. 1-2, Champlin Refining Company Accounts and Reports, 274 I.C.C. 409 (1949).

[104] Champlin Refining Company Accounts and Reports, 274 I.C.C. 409, 412 (1949).

the courts.[105] Accordingly, it issued an order requiring Champlin to comply with its earlier requests.[106] After a vain attempt to obtain a reconsideration, Champlin initiated proceedings in a federal district court for an injunction against enforcement of the Commission's order. On the identical argument that was presented before the Commission, the three-judge district court found that Champlin was not a common carrier engaged in transportation within the meaning of the Act, and enjoined the enforcement of the Commission's order.[107]

Pending the final outcome of the *Champlin* case which recently was argued before the Supreme Court, a tentative recapitulation of the cases may be made.* Under its very language, the Act applies to *all pipe line companies* engaged in *transportation* within the meaning of the Act.[108] Moreover, any oil company which operates a pipe line to move petroleum and its products across state lines probably is a "pipe-line company" as that term is employed by the Act.[109] There remains the statutory construction question of what constitutes "transportation" within the meaning of the Act and the constitutional issue of taking private property without just compensation.

[105] *Id*. at 415-416.

[106] *Id*. at 416.

[107] Champlin Refining Co. v. United States, 95 F.Supp. 170 (W.D.Okla. 1950).

* Since this section was written, the Supreme Court handed down its decision in Champlin Refining Company v. United States. 71 Sup.Ct. 715 (1951). The plurality (JJ. Clark, Jackson, Minton & C. J. Vinson) upheld the *Champlin I* doctrine of severable sections. Under this view, they supported the Commission's order to file annual and special reports and to maintain a Uniform System of Accounts as required by § 20, but held that Congress did not intend for § 6 [imposing the duty of serving the public at regulated rates] to apply to private lines "whose services were unused, unsought after, and unneeded by independent producers."

Mr. Justice Douglas (JJ. Reed and Burton concurring) disclaimed the severable section doctrine, holding that the term "common carrier" had but one meaning in the Act—that given it in § 1. This does not include prrivate carriers who are not common carriers in substance or who have not dedicated their line to public use. As indicated later in the text of this section, this renders unnecessary a consideration of the constitutional issue of taking private property without just compensation. Under this view, neither § 6 nor § 20 applies to Champlin.

Mr. Justice Frankfurter joined the Court's opinion but would overrule *Champlin I* on the ground set forth in the dissent in that case. The author reads this to mean that the sections are not severable and that application of the Act to Champlin would be unconstitutional as a taking of private property without due process.

Mr. Justice Black dissented on the ground that the sections are not severable, that the Act in its entirety applies to *all* interstate pipe line companies, and the constitutional issue was "frivolous," having been settled long ago as to future pipe lines by Mr. Justice Holmes' dictum in *The Pipe Line Cases*.

It is interesting to note that the preponderance of the Court (JJ. Black, Douglas, Reed, Burton and Frankfurter) rejected the several section theory; *notwithstanding which fact* it remains the "opinion of the Court."

[108] See text at notes 42, 43, 47, 55, 83 and 92 *supra*.

[109] See note 81 *supra*.

Insofar as the latter issue is concerned, the only decision passing directly on the point is *The Pipe Line Cases,* wherein it was held that the Act constitutionally could be applied to pipe line companies already common carriers in substance. Justice Holmes' dictum in that case has been cited frequently for the proposition that under the Commerce Clause, Congress had the power to impose common carrier status upon all future pipe lines desiring to engage in interstate transportation of oil.[110] Despite the pronounced tendency of oft repeated dictum to crystallize into a rule of law, the "future pipe line" doctrine has been challenged by the recent decision of the three-judge district court in the second *Champlin* case.[111]

[110] See note 62 *supra*. It should be noted that the references in these cases to Holmes' statement are dicta themselves. The *Pierce Oil* case rested on the ground that a person cannot attack the constitutionality of a statute after having acceped its benefits; the first *Champlin* and *Valvoline* cases decided only that valuation reports may be required of *all* interstate carriers, including private carriers; and the *Associated Pipe Line* case held invalid the application of a similar statute to a private carrier in existence at the time of enactment.

[111] Champlin Refining Co. v. United States, 95 F.Supp. 170 (W.D.Okla. 1950). "We conclude that Champlin is not in substance a common carrier of petroleum products and may not be required to construct receiving facilities and delivery facilities and carry the petroleum products of others as a common carrier for hire, or cease operation of its pipe line, and that to hold otherwise would be to take its property without due process of law, in violation of the Fifth Amendment." *Id.* at 175.

In *Frost & Frost Trucking Company v. Railroad Commission*, 271 U.S. 583, 46 Sup.Ct. 605, 70 L.Ed. 1101 (1926), the question arose whether California constitutionally could require a "future" contract carrier to cease transportation by auto truck over a certain route until it had obtained a certificate of public convenience and necessity. The California Supreme Court held that it could, relying on the power of a state to impose reasonable conditions on the use of its highways. Frost v. Railroad Commission, 197 Cal. 230, 240 Pac. 26 (1925). The United States Supreme Court reversed the California court, holding that the Due Process Clause of the Fourteenth Amendment prevented a state from compelling a private carrier to assume against its will the duties and burdens of common carriage, and that this unconstitutional result could not be accomplished by the indirect device of requiring a surrender [voluntary only in form]. See Merrill, *Unconstitutional Conditions*, 77 U. OF PA. L. REV. 879 (1929). Although this case was decided under the Fourteenth Amendment it is applicable here since the restraints imposed on Congress by the Due Process Clause of the Fifth Amendment generally are the same as those imposed on the states by the Due Process Clause of the Fourteenth Amendment. Bowles v. Willingham, 321 U.S. 503, 518, 64 Sup.Ct. 641, 649, 88 L.Ed. 892, 905 (1944) ; Curry v. McCanless, 307 U.S. 357, 370, 59 Sup.Ct. 900, 907, 83 L.Ed. 1339, 1349 (1939) ; Heiner v. Donnan, 285 U.S. 312, 326, 52 Sup.Ct. 358, 361, 76 L.Ed. 772, 779 (1932) ; Coolidge v. Long, 282 U.S. 582, 596, 51 Sup.Ct. 306, 308-309, 75 L.Ed. 562, 566 (1931).

Under the view of the district court in the second *Champlin* case and the Supreme Court in the *Frost* case the distinction between future pipe lines and those in existence at the time of the questioned regulation would appear to be more fancied than real. Following this line of reasoning, the apposite rule of law is that a state [or the federal government] cannot "by mere legislative fiat or by any regulating order of a commission convert [a pipe line never devoted by its owner to public use] into a public utility or make its owner a common carrier." Producers Transportation Co. v. Railroad Commission, 251 U.S. 228, 230, 40 Sup.Ct. 131, 132, 64 L.Ed. 239, 242 (1920) ; The Pipe Line Cases, 234 U.S. 548, 563, 34 Sup.Ct. 956, 959, 58 L.Ed. 1459, 1471 (1914) ; Prairie Oil & Gas Co. v. United States, 204 Fed. 798 (Comm.Ct.

It would appear that the time is at hand when the Supreme Court must either (1) decide that "transportation" as used in the Act includes common carriers in form and in substance but *excludes* purely private carriers which have never transported for others nor in any other manner dedicated their lines to public use, or (2) pass on the constitutionality of the Act as applied to a "future" private pipe line.[112] If the Supreme Court should decide that a purely private carrier such as Champlin is engaged in "transportation" within the pale of the Act, then it must squarely face the "future pipe line" question. In order to uphold the validity of the Act as applied to Champlin, the Court necessarily must hold that Congress *has* the power

---

1913); Texoma Natural Gas Co. v. Railroad Commission, 59 F.2d 750, 753 (W.D.Tex. 1932); Associated Pipe Line Co. v. Railroad Commission, 176 Cal. 518, 169 Pac. 62, L.R.A. 1918 C, 849 (1917); *cf.* Frost & Frost Trucking Co. v. Railroad Commission, 271 U.S. 583, 592, 46 Sup.Ct. 605, 607, 70 L.Ed. 1101, 1104 (1926); Michigan Public Utilities Commission v. Duke, 266 U.S. 570, 577-578, 45 Sup.Ct. 191, 193, 69 L.Ed. 445, 450 (1925).

112 Both parties presently before the Supreme Court recognize this fact. "It is submitted therefore that it is appropriate for the Court to pass upon the question whether the due process limitations of the Fifth Amendment are violated if Champlin may be required, under any circumstance, to transport goods other than its own." Brief for Appellants, p. 39, United States v. Champlin Refining Co., Civil No. 433, Sup.Ct., March, 1951; *cf.* Brief for Appellees, pp. 16-17, 21, *Idem.*

Previous decisions have turned on the fact that Congress may require valuation reports from private carriers. In the present case the issue is whether the Interstate Commerce Commission may require Champlin to file *tariffs*. It is well settled that the filing of tariffs is an undertaking to perform the transportation service specified therein; *ergo,* an order to file tariffs raises the constitutional question of "taking" property without just compensation. The Pipe Line Cases, 234 U.S. 548, 34 Sup.Ct. 956, 58 L.Ed. 1459 (1914); Prairie Oil & Gas Co. v. United States, 204 Fed. 798 (Comm.Ct. 1913); Champlin Refining Co. v. United States, 95 F.Supp. 170, 174 (W.D.Okla. 1950); *cf.* Producers Transportation Co. v. Railroad Commission, 251 U.S. 228, 40 Sup.Ct. 131, 64 L.Ed. 239 (1920); Champlin Refining Company Accounts and Reports, 274 I.C.C. 409, 417 (1949) (Splawn, Commissioner, dissenting); *Id.* at 418 (Mitchell, Commissioner, dissenting); *but cf. Id.* at 415 (majority opinion).

"The power to regulate a private carrier in interstate commerce is one thing, but the power to compel a private carrier either to cease its operations as such, or to become a common carrier and to carry the goods of others for hire is quite a different thing." Champlin Refining Co. v. United States, 95 F.Supp. 170, 175 (W.D.Okla. 1950); *cf.* Frost & Frost Trucking Co. v. Railroad Commission, 271 U.S. 583, 593, 46 Sup.Ct. 605, 607, 70 L.Ed. 1101, 1104 (1926); Champlin Refining Company Accounts and Reports, 274 I.C.C. 409, 417 (1949).

The argument that "just compensation" will be paid for such taking by means of "compensatory" tariffs completely ignores the obvious distinction between remuneration for *use* and payment for property. There are elements of damage due to the subjection of the property to public use which are not covered by charges for services performed. In Champlin's case, opening its line to use by its large competitors is likely to deprive Champlin of its markets and force it out of business. Transcript of Record, pp. 30, 39-42, 94-96, Champlin Refining Company Accounts and Reports, 274 I.C.C. 409 (1949); *cf.* Champlin Refining Company Accounts and Reports, 274 I.C.C. 409, 417-418 (1949). That this constitutes a taking of Champlin's property without just compensation, admits of no controversy. Associated Pipe Line Co. v. Railroad Commission, 176 Cal. 518, 169 Pac. 62, L.R.A. 1918 C, 849 (1917); *cf.* Prairie Oil & Gas Co. v. United States, 204 Fed. 798, 808, 817 (Comm.Ct. 1913).

to legislate a private carrier into a common carrier. However, if the Court perceives the meaning of "transportation" to be the dividing line between strictly private carriers and those engaged in public transportation in form or otherwise, the constitutional issue will be moot. It has already been decided by *The Pipe Line Cases* that pipe lines which were common carriers in substance at the time of the regulation could be made statutory common carriers. *A fortiori*, "future" carriers of *that* type are amenable to such regulation.[113] Therefore, if the carrier is held to be engaged in furnishing a public transportation service, the imposition of statutory common carriage is a foregone conclusion, whereas if the facts disclose that the carrier in question is a strictly private carrier, the Act by its terms does not apply.

The government contends that the *Uncle Sam* exception should be limited to carriage, *for the carrier's own use,* of a product produced and owned by it.[114] However, it is submitted that this construction is too narrow and mechanical. The private carrier concept is well established in both the motor carrier and water carrier fields. There seems to be no valid reason why it should be excluded from the pipe line area. This is true especially in view of the fact that the *Uncle Sam Company* case is the basis for that concept in the other fields. Moreover, the dissenting opinions of both Chief Justice White and Mr. Justice McKenna in *The Pipe Line Cases* clearly recognize its validity.

The economic issue of monopoly power which constantly has lurked in the background like a "brooding omnipresence in the sky" will con-

---

[113] This would seem to be the true meaning of Mr. Justice Holmes' enigmatic dictum in *The Pipe Line Cases*. Read thus in its context, the validity of the statement is axiomatic. But taken from its setting and quoted for an independent proposition, it raises grave questions as to its constitutional validity. See note 111 *supra*.

[114] See Champlin Refining Company Accounts and Reports, 274 I.C.C. 409, 413-414 (1949); Champlin Refining Company, Valuation of Pipe Line, 49 Val.Rep. 542, 545-546 (1944); *Idem,* 49 Val.Rep. 463, 469-470 (1942); Valvoline Oil Company Petition in Valuation of Pipe Lines, 47 Val.Rep. 534, 537-538 (1937). In determining the status of carriers under the Motor Vehicle Act, the Commission consistently has used the test whether a carrier's transportation services are "incidental to its principal business" and whether such services "are engaged in as a separate and distinct undertaking." Woitishek Common Carrier Application, 42 M.C.C. 193, 196-199 (1943); Swanson Contract Carrier Application, 12 M.C.C. 516, 520 (1939); see Marcellus Contract Carrier Application, 43 M.C.C. 128 (1944); Dull Contract Carrier Application, 32 M.C.C. 158 (1942); Thornburgh Sales Company Contract Carrier Application, 20 M.C.C. 39 (1939); see also Interstate Commerce Commission v. Clayton, 127 F.2d 967 (10th Cir. 1942). Had the Commission employed this test to determine Champlin's status, the result would have been different. Champlin's line obviously is incidental to its principal business as a refiner, and it is not engaged in a "separate and distinct undertaking" in operating its products line. Not only has there never been a holding out to serve the public, but the full use of the pipe line is vitally necessary to Champlin's existence as a refiner. Transcript of Record, pp. 17, 25-30, 35, 51, 53, Champlin Refining Company Accounts and Reports, 274 I.C.C. 409 (1949).

tinue to be present as an inarticulated major premise in deciding whether a carrier in question is a wholly private carrier. Thus in *The Pipe Line Cases,* the controlling factor was the [monopsonistic] duress practiced by the Standard Lines. In the *Associated Pipe Line* case, defendant's crude oil purchases were very limited, and the competition from several pipe lines connected to the field so negated the existence of coercive buying practices that the court refused to permit the conversion of defendant's private line into a common carrier. The turning point of the *Valvoline* case was the fact that Valvoline's line represented the *only* practicable means of transporting the stripper-well production involved. In the first *Champlin Refining Company* opinion, the Supreme Court held that Champlin's modified basing-point pricing system constituted a significant distinction from the *Uncle Sam* case. Thus it would seem that when free competition would be enhanced by opening up seemingly private lines to common carriage, the courts are very skillful in "detecting" signs of devotion to public use.[115]

C. Results Achieved by the Commission

The accomplishments of the Interstate Commerce Commission have occurred in three areas of activity: rate reduction, lowering minimum tender requirements, and valuation and systematizing accounts. After the Supreme Court had confirmed the Commission's jurisdiction in *The Pipe Line Cases,* a long period of inactivity in pipe line regulation ensued. The first complaint against pipe line transportation was brought before the

---

[115] BEARD, REGULATION OF PIPE LINES AS COMMON CARRIERS 28 (1941) ; 35 GEO. L. J. 404, 406 (1947) ; *cf.* FRANCIS, DIVORCEMENT OF PIPE LINES 6 (1935).

In Champlin's particular case, it seems that the overall effect of opening up its products line would have exactly the opposite result. Champlin abandoned its "differential" pricing system on May 10, 1948. It posts prices at its terminals which are competitive with local conditions (for example, it posts a lower price at its Rock Rapids, Iowa, terminal rather than at its Superior, Nebraska, terminal which is 260 miles closer to the Enid refinery). By opening the line to outsiders (the "majors" are peculiarly in a position to take advantage of this), Champlin would be deprived *pro tanto* of the use of its line which it is using presently on a 21-24 hour basis to compete in the North Central market. The net result would be that Champlin's business would flee its premises and the area would lose one of its strongest independent competitors. Nor can Champlin properly be termed a monopolist and likened to the Standard lines of *The Pipe Line Cases.* It supplies only 1.98% of the gasoline consumed in the area, and *meets* the local prices rather than setting them. Moreover, its line cannot be considered an important means (let alone the sole means) of reaching the marketing territory. It has only 9800 barrels out of the 234,100 barrels daily pipe line capacity (of which 172,800 is common carrier) available to Kansas and Oklahoma refineries. A line carrying less than 4.2% of the gasoline transported by pipe line into an area where common carrier [pipe line] transportation is available to all, can hardly be found "affected with a public interest" as was "the sole means of transporting thousands of producers' oil" in the *Valvoline* case. See Champlin Refining Co. v. United States, 95 F.Supp. 170, 172 (W.D.Okla. 1950) ; Champlin Refining Company Accounts and Reports, 274 I.C.C. 409, 412-413 (1949).

Commission in 1920. A prospective shipper protested a proposed cancellation of a joint rate set by the Prairie Pipe Line Company and the National Transit Company on movements of crude oil from the Midcontinent field to Lacy Station, Pennsylvania. The Commission suspended the cancellation, and at the hearing before the Commission, the companies agreed to continue the rate subject to certain blanket increases made subsequent to the suspension.[116] In *Brundred Brothers v. Prairie Pipe Line Company*,[117] the Commission approved the rates from points in Kansas, Oklahoma, and Texas to Franklin and Lacy Station, Pennsylvania, but ordered respondent crude pipe lines to reduce their minimum tender requirement to 10,000 barrels.

Investigation of rates and gathering charges of interstate pipe lines was commenced by the Commission, acting on its own motion, in June, 1934. After considerable delay, probably occasioned by a desire to have the completed valuation figures available,[118] the proceedings culminated in a 1940 decision termed *Reduced Pipe Line Rates and Gathering Charges*,[119] wherein the Commission ordered 37 crude pipe lines to show cause within 60 days why an order should not be entered reducing minimum tenders so as not to exceed 10,000 barrels and requiring adjustment of rates in such a way that earnings would not exceed eight percent on the Commission's valuation of investment.

The increasing importance of product pipe line shipments was recognized by the Commission in *Petroleum Rail Shippers' Ass'n v. Alton & Southern R.R.*[120] In this case, certain independent Midcontinent refiners claimed they were being crowded out of the Midwestern and North Central gasoline market. They alleged that both railroads and pipe lines were exacting high and discriminatory rates, which "held an umbrella" over the area, permitting the pipe line shipper-owners to realize a large profit by matching the rail rates while operating at a greatly lowered cost. This profit was allegedly "rebated" back to the shipper-owners in the form of dividends, and in turn, used to subsidize price concessions to jobbers and retailers in the marketing area, thereby diverting outlets from complainants and driving them out of business. The Commission found complainants' decrease in sales to be substantially due to a 63 percent increase in refinery

[116] Crude Petroleum Oil from Kansas & Oklahoma to Lacy Station, Pa., 59 I.C.C. 483 (1920).

[117] 68 I.C.C. 458 (1922).

[118] Prewitt, *The Operation and Regulation of Crude Oil and Gasoline Pipe Lines*, 56 Q. J. Econ. 177, 207 (1942).

[119] 243 I.C.C. 115 (1940).

[120] 243 I.C.C. 589 (1941).

capacity in the marketing area.[121] Nevertheless, the Commission ordered rail and pipe line rates lowered[122] and the minimum tenders adjusted to 5000 barrels of the same specifications from one shipper to one consignee, subject to delay until the carrier had accumulated 25,000 barrels of the same specifications.[123]

Several other important issues were raised in the *Petroleum Rail Shippers' Ass'n* case, and their disposition by the Commission is worth noting. *First,* the complainants contended that the rail defendants should be required to lower rates in order to equalize the cost of rail transportation with the cost of pipe line transportation ultimately incurred by the integrated oil companies after dividends from subsidiary pipe line companies had been considered. The Commission rejected this argument, saying the cost of pipe line transportation does not afford a measure of reasonable rates for rail transportation, for although rail rates may be reduced to meet changing competitive conditions, they will not be *forced* below the cost of operation and a reasonable profit.[124] *Second,* the complainants sought a multiple-car-shipment rate based on estimated savings in handling expenses.[125] Judging from the evidence presented on this point, it appears that 25-carload shipments moving in *preferred* service would not yield lower operating expenses, and restricted service would require greater shipper investment in storage and tankcars. However, the majority opinion recommended that the rail carriers should study carefully the possibilities of establishing such rates and service.[126] *Third,* it was alleged that the integrated companies were engaged in certain "unfair trade practices," one of which was trading gasoline on a barter basis. For example, Phillips' pipe line serves East St. Louis but not Minneapolis while Great Lakes Pipe Line serves Minneapolis and not East St. Louis. Suppose Continental Oil Com-

---

[121] *Id.* at 593.

[122] *Id.* at 664-665. The maximum pipe line rates were based on 10% return on investment. *Id.* at 663. The rates prescribed for Phillips Petroleum Company were still in effect at the time of this writing. *Compare Id.* at 665 *with* Phillips Petroleum Company, I.C.C. Tariff No. 88, Dec. 1, 1949, Item No. 95.

[123] *Id.* at 665. These are being complied with. See Phillips Petroleum Company, I.C.C. Tariff No. 88, Dec. 1, 1949, Item No .15.

[124] Petroleum Rail Shippers' Ass'n v. Alton & Southern R.R., 243 I.C.C. 589, 639, 665 (1941). See also Whitesel, *supra* note 102, at 362.

[125] Whitesel, *supra* note 102, at 362, suggests the following economies: less car-handling in terminals, fewer stops and less time in transit, one bill of lading, one collection of freight charges, and one entry on the way bill. See Spal, *Oil Pipe Lines,* 15 ICC Pract. J. 563, 569-572 (1948) for an account of multiple-car rates successfully competing with pipe lines in West Texas.

[126] Petroleum Rail Shippers' Ass'n v. Alton & Southern R.R., 243 I.C.C. 589, 655 (1941); *but see Id.* at 668-669 (dissenting opinion). See Molasses from New Orleans, La., to Peoria and Pekin, Ill., 235 I.C.C. 485 (1939).

pany (one of Great Lakes' eight owners) needs 20,000 barrels of gasoline in East St. Louis and Phillips desires the same quantity in Minneapolis. Instead of each actually shipping over the other's line, the companies "swap out" gasoline at one point for gasoline at another. This sounds like good, common horse sense, but the independent's complaint is that the practice is discriminatory inasmuch as the practical effect is to deliver to the trading parties gasoline transported at *cost* whereas independents seeking to reach the same markets over the same lines must pay tariff *rates*, with a resultant unfair competitive advantage. There was no charge that the majors refused to trade with independents but it is obvious that most independent refiners are unable to participate in such exchanges. Other alleged "unfair practices" consisted of local price cutting, "concessions" to retailers in the form of reduced rentals on service-station property, leasing stations at high rentals from the owners and then sub-leasing them back to the owners at low rentals, and valuable free advertising.[127] The Commission decided that these issues were beyond its jurisdiction which was limited to deciding whether the rates and regulations of defendants were unreasonable or discriminatory. Accordingly, it refused to pass on the question, presumably leaving it to the Federal Trade Commission.

In the case of *Minnelusa Oil Corporation v. Continental Pipe Line Company*,[128] the Commission clarified some of the questions raised by earlier decisions. It approved the 8 percent return on crude line valuation established by its earlier decision in *Reduced Pipe Line Rates and Gathering Charges*. The distinction between the 10 percent return allowed for products lines and 8 percent permitted on crude lines was attributed to the greater hazards and risks involved in products line service.[129] Observing the shipper-owner status of defendant pipe line companies, the Commission remarked that the reasonableness of *their* pipe line charges would bear additional scrutiny. Judicial notice was taken of defendants' part in the consent decree in *United States v. Atlantic Refining Company*,[130] prescribing a seven percent (on valuation) limit on the dividends paid by pipe lines to their shipper-owners. The Commission concluded that rates based on cost of the service, taxes,[131] and a fair [8%] return on value would re-

---

[127] For description of these practices, see Petroleum Rail Shippers' Ass'n v. Alton & Southern R.R., 243 I.C.C. 589, 623, 628-629 (1941).

[128] 258 I.C.C. 41 (1944).

[129] *Id.* at 56.

[130] Civil No. 14060, D. D.C., Dec. 23, 1941.

[131] Income taxes were allowed by the Commission due to the Supreme Court's decisions in Georgia Ry. & Power Co. v. Railroad Commission, 262 U.S. 625, 43 Sup.Ct. 680, 67 L.Ed. 1144 (1923) and Galveston Electric Co. v. Galveston, 258 U.S. 388, 42 Sup.Ct. 351, 66 L.Ed. 678 (1922), but excess profit taxes were excluded as "abnormal and temporary." Minnelusa Oil Corp. v. Continental Pipe Line Co., 258 I.C.C. 41, 49 (1944).

move any unjust discrimination and undue prejudice,[132] and entered an order to that effect.[133]

It is interesting to note the development of the theory of rate regulation deemed applicable to pipe lines. In the beginning, the Commission accepted the tariffs filed by pipe line companies as presumptively fair.[134] There was little occasion for rate complaints to arise, because the lines were utilized principally by the shipper-owners.[135] The early rates were maintained at levels comparable to competitive rail rates, which suggests that the theory employed was that of the "value of the service."[136] In 1934, the Commission embarked on an investigation of rates and gathering charges which was hindered by the absence of information from independent shippers concerning the value of the service to them. The Commission finally decided that pipe line rates should not exceed eight percent[137] on their valuation,[138] and required respondents to show cause within 60 days why

[132] Minnelusa Oil Corp. v. Continental Pipe Line Co., 258 I.C.C. 41, 58 (1944).

[133] *Id.* at 61. The Commission awarded damages to Wasatch Oil Refining Company to compensate for the discrimination in rates from the filing of the complaint to the date of the order. Wasatch was "estopped" from recovering damages for prior discriminatory rates because it had participated in joint tariffs and division of rates covering its 0.56 mile 6-inch line connecting its refinery to defendants' pipe line.

[134] There are several reasons for this. First, the Commission had little or no experience with pipe lines, but a respectable background of railroad regulation. In the latter field, competition was such that rival roads or interested [prospectively injured] shippers inevitably would attack the rates filed with the Commission. Thus, the Commission safely could rely on adversary proceedings to develop a complete picture of the prospective rate and its effect. Naturally, the Commission carried over this idea into the pipe line field. Second, the Commission had no basis on which to judge the reasonableness of pipe line rates. Valuation of pipe lines had not been accomplished at this time. Third, it is only natural for an administrative agency or court, unfamiliar with the operation of a business, to give considerable weight to the business judgment of those engaged in the business.

[135] This fact perhaps is the most significant reason why only two complaints were filed with the Commission prior to 1939. However, on numerous occasions, a charge has been leveled that the cost of presenting a complaint to the Commission is prohibitive. See *TNEC Hearings* 7338 ($20,000 to $30,000 to dispute the reasonableness of a rate); but see *Id.* at 8283-8284 (anyone can intervene in Commission proceedings without cost, and an individual protest can be presented for $3000-$5000).

[136] Another way of expressing this, is "all that the traffic can bear." See Edgerton, *Value of the Service as a Factor in Rate Making*, 32 HARV. L. REV. 516 (1919).

[137] The Commission recognized that the hazards and uncertain future of pipe line common-carrier business justified a somewhat larger rate of return than would be reasonable to expect in a more stable industry. It noted that 14 of the respondents earned less than the 8 percent figure, deemed "ample" by the Commission. Reduced Pipe Line Rates and Gathering Charges, 243 I.C.C. 115, 142 (1940). Products lines were considered even more hazardous a venture, thus warranting a 10 percent return. Petroleum Rail Shippers' Ass'n v. Alton & Southern R.R., 243 I.C.C. 589, 663 (1941).

[138] For a statement of the Commission's method of valuation, see Atlantic Pipe Line Co., 47 Val.Rep. 541, 584 (1937).

an order should not issue to that effect.[139] This approach clearly reflects the traditional "fair rate on a fair value" concept enunciated in *Smyth v. Ames*.[140] It has been criticized as involving circular reasoning[141] due to the fact that earnings under the accepted rate determine the value of a going enterprise.[142] The Commission's decision presupposed a lack of competition between similarly located pipe lines, and analogized pipe lines to public-service company monopolies.[143]

Commissioner Mahaffie dissented from this decision on the ground that the pipe lines involved were competitive and that, therefore, this approach was not practicable. He cited the case of the four large lines from the Midcontinent field to Chicago, each of which at the time of the decision was charging 38.5 cents per barrel for transportation. Under the majority's rule, they should have charged 33.5, 30.5, 29.5, and 17.5 cents respectively. He reasoned that unless the other three companies met the 17.5 cent rate, the business of the line having the lowest rate would be increased to such an extent that a further reduction would be necessary. At this point, it is helpful to realize that the Commission's problem was not one of setting a *minimum* rate which would be compensatory, but rather was that of setting a *maximum* rate which would not represent an unreasonable charge to outside shippers. If the lines were strictly plant facilities as assumed by the majority, the difference in rates would not divert traffic from the higher-rate lines to the lower because those shipper-owners would be merely charging themselves a higher "book" rate. On the other hand, if there truly was a competitive situation, the other lines would not be *forced* to post higher rates but could meet competition by lowering their rates beneath the upper limit established by the Commission's order. The actual result of the decision has been to lower the rates of these lines to 25 cents.[144] Succeeding cases before the Commission have followed the rate-making technique of the *Reduced Pipe Line Rates and Gathering Charges* case.[145]

[139] Reduced Pipe Line Rates and Gathering Charges, 243 I.C.C. 115, 144 (1940).

[140] 169 U.S. 466, 18 Sup.Ct. 418, 42 L.Ed. 819 (1898).

[141] See Rostow, A National Policy for the Oil Industry 59–62 (1948).

[142] Federal Power Commission v. Hope Natural Gas Co., 320 U.S. 591, 601, 64 Sup.Ct. 281, 287, 88 L.Ed. 333, 344 (1944).

[143] Mahaffie, Commissioner, dissenting in Reduced Pipe Line Rates and Gathering Charges, 243 I.C.C. 115, 145 (1940) ; see Whitesel, *Recent Federal Regulation of the Petroleum Pipe Line as a Common Carrier*, 32 Corn. L. Q. 337, 360, (1947) ; Prewitt, *The Operation and Regulation of Crude Oil and Gasoline Pipe Lines*, 56 Q. J. Econ. 117, 210-211 (1942).

[144] Reduced Pipe Lines Rates and Gathering Charges, 272 I.C.C. 375, 381 (1948).

[145] Petroleum Rail Shippers' Ass'n v. Alton & Southern R.R., 243 I.C.C. 589 (1941); Minnelusa Oil Corp. v. Continental Pipe Line Co., 258 I.C.C. 41 (1944) ; Reduced Pipe Line Rates and Gathering Charges, 272 I.C.C. 375 (1948). The constitutional requirement is fulfilled if the approved rate enables the company to operate successfully, to maintain its financial integrity, to attract capital, and to compensate its investors for the risks assumed. Federal

One of the control mechanisms in rate regulation is statistical information on the regulated carrier's operations. In order to determine the earnings of carriers and adequately to compare one carrier's operations with another's, it becomes imperative that a common accounting system be adopted. Section 20 of the Interstate Commerce Act vested power in the Commission to prescribe a Uniform System of Accounts for the carriers under its jurisdiction. The Commission circularized letters among the pipe line companies seeking information and recommendations relative to the establishment of a common system of accounts for pipe lines.[146] The first step was a classification of operating expenses,[147] then revenues, and somewhat later, a form was adopted for general balance sheet statements.[148] These items comprised the body of a special report which became effective on January 1, 1911.[149] This report proved unsatisfactory due to divergent interpretations of the Commission's definitions by the various pipe line company accountants.[150] Moreover, improvement was not promptly forthcoming, as the Commission adopted a "wait-and-see" attitude pending the outcome of the *Prairie Oil and Gas Company* case.[151] After the Supreme Court had upheld the Commission's jurisdiction over interstate pipe lines in *The Pipe Line Cases*,[152] improvements on the reports were resumed. The 1915 accounting order included carrier investments,[153] and by 1919 an annual report form had been prescribed, commencing with the calendar year 1918.[154] The Transportation Act of 1920[155] required the Commission to prescribe, "as soon as practicable," a system of depreciation accounting.[156] The Commission sought the aid of the American Petroleum Institute which appointed a "pipe-line depreciation committee" to act on behalf of the pipe line companies represented. The committee submitted a memorandum and conferred with the Commission; this resulted in a questionnaire

Power Commission v. Hope Natural Gas Co., 320 U.S. 591, 605, 64 Sup.Ct. 281, 289, 83 L.Ed. 333, 346 (1944). So long as the rate fulfills the foregoing requirements, the theory or method of rate-making employed by the Commission is immaterial and will not be a subject of inquiry by the courts. *Id.* at 603, 64 Sup.Ct. at 288, 88 L.Ed. at 345.

[146] 20 ICC Ann. Rep. 62 (1906).

[147] *Id.* at 60.

[148] 23 ICC Ann. Rep. 57-58 (1909).

[149] 24 ICC Ann. Rep. 31 (1910).

[150] FTC, Report on Pipe-Line Transportation of Petroleum 70 (1916); Beard, Regulation of Pipe Lines as Common Carriers 58 (1941).

[151] 26 ICC Ann. Rep. 35 (1912).

[152] See text at notes 51-63 *supra*.

[153] Beard, Regulation of Pipe Lines as Common Carriers 59 (1941); Mills, The Pipe Line's Place in the Oil Industry 48 (1935).

[154] 33 ICC Ann. Rep. 37 (1919).

[155] 41 Stat. 493-494 (1920), as amended, 49 U.S.C. § 20(4) (1946).

[156] 34 ICC Ann. Rep. 34 (1920).

requiring certain information to be furnished by the pipe line companies reporting to the Commission.

In the meantime, the Commission had conducted an investigation on the subject of depreciation in the telephone and steam-railroad field, the result of which appeared in *Telephone and Railroad Depreciation Charges.*[157] The Commission's Bureau of Accounts proposed that pipe line depreciation charges apply substantially the same standards as those of the steam railroads.[158] The pipe line companies protested this action on the basis that the uncertainties of oil pool service life precluded the analogy.[159] The controversy was resolved by a 1934 decision termed *Depreciation Charges of Carriers by Pipe Lines,*[160] in which the Commission prescribed a system of depreciation accounting for pipe lines to become effective on January 1, 1936.

The "First Revised Issue of the Uniform System of Accounts" for pipe lines was issued by the Commission in 1934, becoming effective on January 1, 1935.[161] Since that time, revisions have been made in 1943[162] and 1948.[163] In addition, modification orders have been issued from time to time in order to keep the system abreast of current developments.[164] In view of the fact that the Commission was impeded by initial doubt as to its jurisdiction, unfamiliarity with pipe line operation, and overloads of other items[165] requiring the greater amount of the time and personnel available to the Bureau of Accounts,[166] the formulation of a comprehensive Uniform System of Accounts for pipe lines was achieved in a satisfactory manner.

In regard to the valuation of pipe lines, it appears that largely due to

---

[157] 118 I.C.C. 295 (1926); subsequent hearing, 177 I.C.C. 351 (1931).

[158] Depreciation Charges of Carriers by Pipe Lines, 205 I.C.C. 33, 34-35 (1934).

[159] BEARD, REGULATION OF PIPE LINES AS COMMON CARRIERS 59 (1941).

[160] 205 I.C.C. 33 (1934).

[161] BEARD, REGULATION OF PIPE LINES AS COMMON CARRIERS 59 (1941); see 49 ICC ANN. REP. 41 (1935). This also was the product of joint endeavor on the part of the Commission and pipe line representatives. MILLS, THE PIPE LINE'S PLACE IN THE OIL INDUSTRY 49 (1935).

[162] 57 ICC ANN. REP. 68 (1943).

[163] See UNIFORM SYSTEM OF ACCOUNTS FOR PIPE LINES (American Petroleum Institute, revised to May 1, 1948).

[164] See, *e.g.*, 63 ICC ANN. REP. 72 (1949).

[165] For example, more than half of the Bureau's accountants were assigned to assist an investigation of railroad financial practices conducted by the Senate Committee on Interstate Commerce from 1935 to 1939. 50 ICC ANN. REP. 34 (1936); 51 ICC ANN. REP. 30 (1937); 52 ICC ANN. REP. 48 (1938); 53 ICC ANN. REP. 50 (1939). The special accounting investigations of carriers required by Section 77 of the Bankruptcy Act proved to be another man-hour consumer. *Ibid.* See also 46 ICC ANN. REP. 40-41 (1932); 45 ICC ANN. REP. 1 (1931).

[166] The official title is now the Bureau of Accounts and Cost Finding.

the lack of sufficient funds[167] and to the press of other matters,[168] the Commission's Bureau of Valuations did not begin the valuation of pipe lines until 1934.[169] The actual field work of inventory, land valuation, audit, and compilation of reports commenced on May 1, 1935.[170] This was completed within a year, whereupon the task of pricing inventories and preparing underlying reports and tentative valuations was initiated.[171] The program called for service of tentative valuations on the carrier involved, a thirty day period was to be allowed for protest by the carrier, States, or other interested parties, and in default of protest, the tentative valuation was to become final. In the event of a protest, a hearing would be held to determine the proper figure.[172] Valuations once determined were to be kept current by means of reports made by the companies.[173] Due to the pressing need for the completed valuation figures occasioned by the Commission's own investigation in *Reduced Pipe Lines Rates and Gathering Charges,*[174] the pipe line valuation program was accelerated despite a lack of funds appropriated for that purpose.[175] Eight tentative valuations were served on carriers during 1937,[176] twenty-five in 1938,[177] and thirteen in 1939.[178] During this period, protest hearings were scheduled, and the number of final valuations began to mount.[179] The basic program of pipe line valuation was completed in 1940.[180] Also in the same year, there was instituted a supplemental program of valuing pipe lines brought under the Commission's jurisdiction after the commencement of the original valuation pro-

[167] 47 ICC ANN. REP. 76 (1933) ; 46 ICC ANN. REP. 92 (1932).

[168] 46 ICC ANN. REP. 92-93 (1932) ; 45 ICC ANN. REP. 67 (1931) ; 44 ICC ANN. REP. 59 (1930) (activities concentrated on recapture cases).

[169] 48 ICC ANN. REP. 78-79 (1934) ; BEARD, REGULATION OF PIPE LINES AS COMMON CARRIERS 60-61 (1941) ; Prewitt, *The Operation and Regulation of Crude Oil and Gasoline Pipe Lines,* 56 Q. J. ECON. 177, 204 (1942).

[170] 49 ICC ANN. REP. 93 (1935).

[171] 50 ICC ANN. REP. 104 (1936).

[172] *Ibid.*

[173] *Id.* at 105; BEARD, REGULATION OF PIPE LINES AS COMMON CARRIERS 61 (1941) ; see also 54 ICC ANN. REP. 133 (1940).

[174] 50 ICC ANN. REP. 104 (1936).

[175] 53 ICC ANN. REP. 135 (1939) ; 52 ICC ANN. REP. 118 (1938) ; 51 ICC ANN. REP. 102 (1937) ; Prewitt, *The Operation and Regulation of Crude Oil and Gasoline Pipe Lines,* 56 Q. J. ECON. 177, 205 (1942).

[176] 51 ICC ANN. REP. 102 (1937).

[177] 52 ICC ANN. REP. 118 (1938).

[178] 53 ICC ANN. REP. 135 (1939).

[179] BEARD, REGULATION OF PIPE LINES AS COMMON CARRIERS 62 (1941).

[180] 54 ICC ANN. REP. 133 (1940). Under this program, the properties of 52 operating companies and 1 lessor were valued as of Dec. 31, 1934.

gram.[181] During the war years the Commission's Bureau of Valuation was extensively engaged in making appraisals and performing other similar work for the Army, Navy, Maritime Commission, and other government agencies concerned with war activities.[182] The task of bringing valuations down to date [Dec. 31, 1947] began in 1947.[183] Although hampered by limited funds for this work,[184] steady progress has been made and the new valuations should be completed shortly.

One other service performed by the Commission warrants comment. The Bureau of Transport Economics and Statistics prepares statistical summaries of pipe line operations. Formerly, only annual summaries were published, but the publishing of a quarterly statistical series was commenced in 1939 because of the increasing interest in this type of information.[185] Since then, the Bureau has continued to furnish valuable summaries of financial and operating data on the reporting pipe lines.[186]

Finally, before leaving the subject of pipe line regulation by the Commission, a few specific suggestions seem in order.[187] It is obvious that the Commission's work has been handicapped by lack of sufficient funds. Therefore, the following proposals must be considered on the assumption that sufficient appropriations will be made to carry them out. *First,* the system of relying on adversary proceedings to develop the complete picture in a pipe line rate or minimum tender case is not practicable as a general rule. It has been recommended that the specific problems raised by pipe line rates and service requirements should be handled by the Commission, which has been given jurisdiction over them by law.[188] For the Commission adequately to discharge this responsibility, it is suggested that proceedings to determine the reasonableness of rates and service requirements be initiated by the Commission, on its own motion, at regular intervals not exceeding five years.[189] *Second,* a particular division of the Com-

---

[181] 54 ICC Ann. Rep. 133 (1940).

[182] 57 ICC Ann. Rep. 125-126 (1943).

[183] 62 ICC Ann. Rep. 129 (1948).

[184] 63 ICC Ann. Rep. 128 (1949).

[185] 53 ICC Ann. Rep. 130 (1939).

[186] See, for example, Statement No. 4944, Oct. 1949.

[187] For some excellent general suggestions, see Oppenheim, The National Transportation Policy and Inter-Carrier Competitive Rates, c. 5 (1945); Williams, *The ICC and the Regulation of Intercarrier Competition,* 63 Harv. L. Rev. 1349 (1950).

[188] See Part 1, text at note 647.

[189] The Commission already has conducted such an investigation in the *Reduced Pipe Line Rates and Gathering Charges* case. In many states, the regulatory bodies are required to conduct annual hearings to determine whether pipe line rates yield only a fair return on the investment. Francis, Divorcement of Pipe Lines 7 (1935).

mission should be selected to hear disputes in pipe line cases and to conduct the investigations suggested above.[190] It is probable that the full time of this division would not be occupied by pipe line matters. However, the remainder of its time could be devoted to railroad and other carrier cases. The important thing is to develop an operational background and familiarity with previous pipe line regulation which will make possible a regulatory program which has continuity and which is in accord with the realities of pipe line operation in the field. It is believed that this may be accomplished more successfully by channeling pipe line cases before a certain group of Commissioners rather than by having the disputes settled by a group which has only infrequently dealt with pipe line problems.

II. THE ELKINS ACT CONSENT DECREE

A. *The Background of the Decree*

Earlier in this book the competitive advantages of pipe line ownership were discussed.[191] Inasmuch as this subject provides the background for the Elkins Act Consent Decree, a brief recapitulation seems necessary. The great distances separating the areas of greatest crude oil production from the areas of greatest gasoline consumption give transportation facilities a strategic position in the oil industry.[192] Moreover, due to the land-locked location of many retail centers, additional emphasis is placed on overland transportation.

It was demonstrated early in the history of petroleum-industry development that pipe lines were the most efficient and economical method of transporting petroleum over long land distances. Since that time, the disparity between pipe line costs and rail rates continuously has increased to the extent that long distance pipe line and rail transportation can not even be considered competitive.[193] Largely because of this fact, and the ruthless competition formerly waged in the oil industry, the large oil companies either constructed or purchased their own lines.[194] Certain of the more aggressive smaller companies also built their own lines, and became "major" companies themselves through the increased volume of business

---

[190] This, too, has a precedent. See 49 ICC Ann. Rep. 38 (1935) (Division 5 assigned Motor Carrier cases).

[191] See Part I, Section II, Inequalities of Competition Engendered by Major Company Pipe-Line Ownership.

[192] See Part I, text at notes 274–277.

[193] *Id.* at note 282.

[194] See text at note 7 *supra*.

obtained thereby.[195] The end result of this has been an industrial structure wherein pipe line ownership is mainly concentrated in the hands of twenty [now twenty-two] "major" oil companies.[196] This has raised some serious problems. Due to the strategic position occupied by pipe lines, it is imperative that free and *equal* access to the lines be maintained.[197] The Interstate Commerce Act prescribes that all pipe line companies engaged in transportation within the meaning of the Act[198] shall furnish equal and reasonable transportation to all comers, and that tariffs listing the charges for this service shall be filed with the Interstate Commerce Commission.[199] In 1914 a skirmish over the scope of the Act between the major company shipper-owners and the Commission was settled in favor of the Commission by the Supreme Court in *The Pipe Line Cases*.[200] Since then, the major lines have filed tariffs with the Commission and have transported, *under the terms of those tariffs*, the traffic tendered by outside shippers. To the extent that a pipe line company handles the shipments of both outside shippers and of its shipper-owner on the basis of the published rates, the principle of equal treatment would appear satisfied. The problem arises from the fact that the profits earned by the pipe line company from this carriage are passed on to the parent shipper-owner in the form of dividends declared on its stock ownership. For example, assume the cost to the pipe line company of moving crude from East Texas to the Gulf Coast to be five cents per barrel and the posted tariff rate to be seventeen and one-half cents per barrel.[201] The outside shipper and the shipper-owner would both pay seventeen and one-half cents per barrel to the pipe line company, but the shipper-owner would receive a return dividend of twelve and one-half cents per barrel not only on its own traffic but on that of its competitor. The wider the spread between pipe line costs and rates, the greater this advantage becomes. Obviously, with no limit to this cost-rate disparity, a shipper-owner could drive a non-integrated competitor out of business. One practical factor establishing an upper limit to this spread is the rate charged by other means of transportation. Thus, in the years immediately preceding and subsequent to the enactment of the Hepburn Act in 1906, the pipe line rates tended to match the rail rates.[202] Later, a more competitive situation

195 *Ibid.*

196 See Part I, text at notes 37–39, 286.

197 *Id.* at note 285.

198 See Part II, Section I B—Interstate Commerce Commission Jurisdiction over Pipe Lines.

199 See notes 99 & 100 *supra.*

200 234 U.S. 548, 34 Sup.Ct. 956, 58 L.Ed. 1459 (1914).

201 See *TNEC Hearings* 7582.

202 Reduced Pipe Line Rates and Gathering Charges, 243 I.C.C. 115, 124 (1940).

arose in the industry and rates gradually were reduced.[203] However, the spread was still so large in 1939 that numerous complaints were voiced during the *TNEC Hearings*.[204] During the course of the *Hearings*, members of the Federal Trade Commission[205] and the Department of Justice expressed their opinion that payment by a pipe line company to its shipper-owner of any part of the difference between cost and tariff rate constituted an illegal rebate.[206] In view of this fact, it is not surprising that the Department of Justice instituted suits on September 30, 1940, against the Great Lakes Pipe Line Company,[207] Phillips Petroleum Company and Phillips Pipe Line Company,[208] and Standard Oil Company (Indiana),[209] alleging that the shipper-owner oil companies were receiving rebates from their pipe line subsidiaries (or departments) contrary to the provision of the Interstate Commerce Act,[210] and the Elkins Act.[211] The Department demanded that the defendant pipe lines and shippers be enjoined from granting and receiving the alleged rebates and that the defendant shippers be required to pay the United States the authorized forfeiture[212] of three times the total amount of money and other valuable considerations found by the Court to have been illegally received since January 1, 1939.[213]

The Department's contention in the original suits that the payment of dividends to the shipper-owner amounted to an illegal rebate under the Elkins Act represented a novel,[214] and somewhat debatable theory. On the one hand, it is supported by the principle of equality among shippers embodied in the Interstate Commerce Act.[215] Also, there have been several

[203] *Ibid.*

[204] See Part I, text at notes 75–76.

[205] *TNEC Hearings* 7233–7234, 7256–7257, 7261–7262, 8166–8168.

[206] *TNEC Hearings* 7203–7204, 7235–7236, 7251–7252, 7256–7257.

[207] United States v. Great Lakes Pipe Line Company, Civil No. 183, D. Del., Sept. 30, 1940.

[208] United States v. Phillips Petroleum Company and Phillips Pipe Line Company, Civil No. 182, D. Del., Sept. 30, 1940.

[209] United States v. Standard Oil Company (Indiana), Civil No. 201, N.D. Ind., Sept. 30, 1940.

[210] 24 STAT. 379, 381 (1887), as amended, 49 U.S.C. §§ 2, 6(7) (1946).

[211] 32 STAT. 847–848 (1903), as amended, 34 STAT. 587–589 (1906), 49 U.S.C. §§ 41–43 (1946).

[212] Section 1(3) of the Elkins Act, *supra* note 211.

[213] See note 207–209 *supra;* 9 U. OF CHI. L. REV. 503 (1942).

[214] *Cf.* 9 U. OF CHI. L. REV. 503, 508 n.37 (1942).

[215] New York, New Haven & Hartford R.R. v. Interstate Commerce Commission, 200 U.S. 361, 26 Sup.Ct. 272, 50 L.Ed. 515 (1906); *cf.* Louisville & Nashville R.R. v. Mottley, 219 U.S. 467, 31 Sup.Ct. 265, 55 L.Ed. 297 (1911); Armour Packing Co. v. United States, 209 U.S. 56, 28 Sup.Ct. 428, 52 L.Ed. 681 (1908); 3-B SHARFMAN, THE INTERSTATE COMMERCE COMMISSION 359–370 (1931); Black, *Oil Pipe Line Divorcement by Litigation and Legislation*, 25 CORN. L. Q. 510, 514–519 (1940); 9 U. OF CHI. L. REV. 503, 505 (1942).

dicta indicating that the Elkins Act was designed to strengthen the anti-rebate provisions of the Interstate Commerce Act by reaching *all* devices by which transportation was furnished for less than the published rate.[216] On the other hand, rebates and dividends are entirely different concepts,[217] and the "plain meaning" rule of statutory construction renders difficult the

[216] *E.g.,* Union Pacific R.R. v. United States, 313 U.S. 450, 461–462, 61 Sup.Ct. 1064, 1071, 85 L.Ed. 1453, 1463–1464 (1941) ; United States v. Koenig Coal Co., 270 U.S. 512, 519, 46 Sup.Ct. 392, 394, 70 L.Ed. 709, 712 (1926) ; United States v. Union Stockyard & Transit Co., 226 U.S. 286, 309, 33 Sup.Ct. 83, 90, 57 L.Ed. 226, 235 (1912) ; Armour Packing Co. v. United States, 209 U.S. 56, 72, 28 Sup.Ct. 428, 432, 52 L.Ed. 681, 691 (1908) ; see Black, *supra* note 215, at 519–523.

[217] The essence of a rebate is a payment [by a carrier to a shipper] unsupported by any consideration. In effect, it is a gratuity. The carrier is obliged to furnish transportation at the published tariff rate and the shipper is required to pay the posted rate. The payment of a rebate to the shipper for his business amounts to giving the shipper something for nothing since he was already obliged to pay the full rate. Thus, in *Armour Packing Company v. United States,* 209 U.S. 56, 28 Sup.Ct. 428, 52 L.Ed. 681 (1908), Armour paid a rate of twenty-three cents per pound despite a published tariff rate of thirty-five cents per pound. The difference of twelve cents per pound, unsupported by any consideration, clearly was a gratuity. The same result follows *pro tanto* where the carrier's payment is supported by an inadequate consideration. For example, where a railroad borrowed money at four percent [the current rate of interest] and loaned it to a shipper at two percent, the difference was held to be a rebate. Vandalia R.R. v. United States, 226 Fed. 713 (7th Cir. 1915), *cert. denied,* 239 U.S. 642, 36 Sup.Ct. 163, 60 L.Ed. 482 (1915). The payment of a rebate need not take the form of money. It may consist of furnishing services at no expense or inadequate compensation. See Baltimore & Ohio R.R. v. United States, 305 U.S. 507, 59 Sup.Ct. 284, 83 L.Ed. 318 (1939) (warehousing services furnished at non-compensatory rates). Every case applying the relevant provisions of the Interstate Commerce Act and the Elkins Act has turned on the fact that a purveyor of transportation service covered by a tariff has remitted a part of the tariff charge, or has rendered a free service, or a service below cost to some shippers and not others. Union Pacific R.R. v. United States, 313 U.S. 450, 481, 61 Sup.Ct. 1064, 1080, 85 L.Ed. 1453, 1474 (1941).

The essence of a dividend is a division of gains, profits or assets, which is supported by an independent consideration. "Dividends are the appropriate fruit of stock ownership, are commonly reckoned as income, . . . the tangible and recurrent returns upon . . . stock, analogous to the interest and rent received upon other forms of invested capital." Lynch v. Hornby, 247 U.S. 339, 344–345, 38 Sup.Ct. 543, 545, 62 L.Ed. 1149, 1151 (1918) ; *cf.* Hellmich v. Hellman, 276 U.S. 233, 236–237, 48 Sup.Ct. 244, 245, 72 L.Ed. 544, 546 (1928).

Certainly, neither rebates nor offsets are analogous to "interest and rent received from other forms of invested capital." Moreover, the difference between rebates and dividends is made clear by the effects produced by each. Since the essence of a rebate is a gratuity made without independent consideration therefor, the amount of the rebate does not constitute income either to the carrier or to the shipper. It only reduces the transportation expense of the shipper, just as if the amount thereof had never passed. *Cf.* Uniform Printing & Supply Co. v. Commissioner, 88 F.2d 75 (7th Cir. 1937). In the case of dividends, however, the carrier realizes income, and when declared as a dividend and appropriated to the stockholder use, it results in income to him.

application of the Elkins and Interstate Commerce Acts to dividends.[218] Lacking the support of the statutory language, the government was forced to fashion a "mosaic of significance out of the innuendoes of disjointed bits" of the statutes in question.[219] The long period of acquiescence by the Interstate Commerce Commission in the payment of dividends to shipper-owners by common carrier pipe lines[220] and the tenuous nature of the government's theory might well have caused the Court to construe the statutes against the United States.[221] However, the question became moot when, after a preliminary joust over a venue issue,[222] a "consent" decree was entered into by the United States and twenty major companies and fifty-nine pipe line companies in a new action filed by the government on December 23, 1941, for that purpose.[223]

The particular facts surrounding the negotiations between the Justice Department and the defendant oil companies are rather obscure, but the threat of damages amounting to three times the dividends paid over a two year period, together with the agitation raised by certain legislators for pipe line divorcement, caused the oil companies to look favorably on the opportunity to dispose of a troublesome question.[224] Apparently to avoid long drawn out discussions in the midst of preparations for war, a hastily drawn decree was accepted by both sides in full recognition of the fact that it was satisfactory to neither. The Department relinquished its position that *all* dividends were illegal rebates, settling for the proposition that any payment above seven percent [on the carrier's valuation] was illegal. The theory behind this action presumably was that the "freezing" of all income over the permitted seven percent would bring about rate reductions, thereby

---

218 "[T]he plain, obvious and rational meaning of a statute is always to be preferred to any curious, narrow, hidden sense that nothing but the exigency of a hard case and the ingenuity and study of an acute and powerful intellect would discover." Lynch v. Alworth-Stephens Co., 267 U.S. 364, 370, 45 Sup.Ct. 274, 276, 69 L.Ed. 660, 662 (1925) ; *cf.* Old Colony R.R. v. Commissioner, 284 U.S. 552, 560, 52 Sup.Ct. 211, 213, 76 L.Ed. 484, 489 (1932); Caminetti v. United States, 242 U.S. 470, 485, 37 Sup.Ct. 192, 194, 61 L.Ed. 442, 452–453 (1917).

219 *Cf.* Palmer v. Massachusetts, 308 U.S. 79, 83, 60 Sup.Ct. 34, 36, 84 L.Ed. 93, 97, (1939).

220 Not only would the inaction of the Commission tend to make the Court reluctant to disturb the situation, but the Commission's acquiescence might be evidence that the shipper-owners did not *knowingly* take rebates. Lehigh Coal & Navigation Co. v. United States, 250 U.S. 556, 565, 40 Sup.Ct. 24, 26, 63 L.Ed. 1138, 1142 (1919) ; 9 U. OF CHI. L. REV. 503, 508 n.37 (1942) ; *cf.* Whitesel, *Recent Federal Regulation of the Petroleum Pipe Line as a Common Carrier*, 32 CORN. L. Q. 337, 372 (1947).

221 9 U. OF CHI L. REV. 503, 508 (1942). See United States v. Cooper Corp., 312 U.S. 600, 613–614, 61 Sup.Ct. 742, 748, 85 L.Ed. 1071, 1079 (1941).

222 United States v. Phillips Petroleum Co., 36 F.Supp. 480 (D.Del. 1941) ; United States v. Great Lakes Pipe Line Co., 36 F.Supp. 486 (D.Del. 1941).

223 United States v. Atlantic Refining Co., Civil No. 14060, D. D. C., Dec. 23, 1941.

224 The consent decree waived all past claims for damage.

reducing the competitive advantages held by shipper-owners over non-integrated firms to the seven percent figure deemed a reasonable return on the capital invested in the lines.[225] Accordingly, the government filed a new complaint, upon which a "final judgment" was entered on December 23, 1941.[226]

B. Ambiguities of the Decree

It has already been noted that the decree was drafted rather hastily. In addition, the decree is short and rather general, which makes for uncertainty and ambiguity. The present discussion is not intended to exhaust all the possible conflicts but merely to illustrate the unworkable character of the decree as it now exists. The main problems arise from the interpretation of paragraphs III,[227] and V of the decree.[228]

1. Sums of Money or Other Valuable Considerations. Paragraph III provides for a seven percent [on valuation of carrier's property] per annum limit on payments of any "earnings, dividends, sums of money or other valuable considerations" made by defendant common carriers to their shipper-owners.[229] The looseness of this wording presents several problems, the most common of which are among the following:

[225] *Cf.* Rostow, A National Policy for the Oil Industry 64–65 (1948).

[226] See note 223 *supra*.

[227] "III. No defendant common carrier shall credit, give, grant, or pay, directly or indirectly, through or by any means or device whatsoever, to any shipper-owner in any calendar year, commencing as of January 1, 1942, any earnings, dividends, sums of money or other valuable considerations derived from transportation or other common carrier services which in the aggregate is in excess of its share of seven percentum (7%) of the valuation of such common carrier's property, if such common carrier shall have transported during said calendar year any crude oil, or gasoline, or other petroleum products for said shipper-owner, but shall be permitted (insofar as the Interstate Commerce and Elkins Acts are concerned) to credit, give, grant or pay said percentum. . . ."

[228] "V. Commencing January 1, 1942 each defendant common carrier shall retain (except as hereinafter provided) net earnings derived from transportation or other common carrier services in excess of the amounts permitted to be credited, granted, paid or given by paragraph III hereof and transfer such excess earnings to the surplus account within 90 days after the end of each calendar year. The said excess earnings shall be transferred to the surplus account as a separate item therein and in such a form as to be readily identifiable. The excess earnings thus transferred to the surplus account may be used by the defendant common carrier for extending existing or constructing or acquiring new common carrier facilities, for maintaining normal and reasonable working capital requirements during the current calendar year, and for retiring of any debt outstanding at the time of the entry of this judgment and decree, provided, however, that such debt or refunded debt was originally incurred for the purpose of, and the proceeds thereof expended in, constructing or acquiring common carrier property. In case of the dissolution, sale, transfer or divorcement of any defendant common carrier, any retained portion of the surplus account may be disbursed to stockholders of the corporation which owns and controls the defendant common carrier at that time."

[229] See note 227 *supra*.

(a) *Debts*. Are sums of money paid or credits made in discharge of debts to be included in the seven percent limitation or are they permitted above and beyond this amount? The Justice Department's position on this question appears to be that a distinction is to be drawn between payment of debts owed to persons dissociated with the carrier and those due the shipper-owner. In the former case, the Department appears willing to permit the payment of interest to be charged off as an expense, which automatically removes such sums from the operation of the decree. Moreover, the payment of the *principal* of any debt is deemed to be allowed under the decree. However, in the case of a debt owed by the carrier to its shipper-owner, the Department takes the position that paragraph III is to be read into paragraph V, thereby limiting the permitted payment of interest on a debt either to one not a shipper-owner or to be included in the seven percent limitation.[230] It is a well settled rule of construction that the instrument sought to be construed should be read as a whole,[231] and a specific provision will prevail over a general one unless the instrument considered in its entirety indicates a contrary intent.[232] Both the Justice Department and the oil companies agree on those abstractions, but the Department feels that paragraph III, limiting payments to shipper-owners, is the more specific clause whereas the companies' position is that the clause in paragraph V, providing for an exception in the case of a "pre-decree" debt, is more specific and therefore should prevail over the more general provision limiting payments to shipper-owners. The companies' position seems more tenable, particularly in the light of the fact that the Department's distinction between payment of interest [at the going rate] to outside concerns and to the shipper-owner is one without a difference.[233] Moreover the general words "sums of money" or "other valuable consider-

---

[230] Paragraph V provides for use of excess earnings to retire *any* debt outstanding at the time of the decree provided that it was incurred for the purpose of acquiring common carrier property. See note 228 *supra*.

[231] *E. g.,* D. Ginsberg & Sons, Inc. v. Popkin, 285 U.S. 204, 52 Sup.Ct. 322, 76 L.Ed. 704 (1932); *Ex parte* Public Bank, 278 U.S. 101, 49 Sup.Ct. 43, 73 L.Ed. 202 (1928); Baxter v. McGee, 82 F.2d 695 (8th Cir. 1936).

[232] *E. g.,* Kepner v. United States, 195 U.S. 100, 24 Sup.Ct. 797, 49 L.Ed. 114 (1904); United States v. Jackson, 143 Fed. 783 (9th Cir. 1906); *In re* Hassenbusch, 108 Fed. 35 (6th Cir. 1901).

[233] The Department's distinction would favor not only companies which had borrowed on the outside but also those which had assigned their loans to a bank prior to the entry of the decree, thus making rights dependent upon the identity of the creditor.

The qualification of "at the going rate" obviously is necessary, as a high rate of interest could be used as a subterfuge to circumvent the seven percent limitation. The criterion would appear to be an above-board, arms-length transaction on a par with the terms obtainable elsewhere. *Cf.* Kerr v. Southwestern Lumber Company of New Jersey, 78 F.2d 348 (5th Cir. 1935), *cert. denied,* 296 U.S. 611, 56 Sup.Ct. 130, 80 L.Ed. 433 (1935).

ations" immediately follow the specific enumerations "earnings" and "dividends," thus suggesting the rule of *ejusdem generis*.[234] In addition to the rule of *ejusdem generis*, the references in paragraphs III(c) and III(d) to "earnings" afford additional arguments for the companies' position. In reliance on this construction, some of the companies have made payments on debts owed to their shipper-owners which exceeded the seven percent limit. Others have avoided the issue by borrowing only from outside firms. Due to the great expansion program generally undertaken by the oil industry since World War II, this fact has not worked too great a hardship as the parent companies have not had surplus capital available. In fact, they have been forced to borrow money themselves from outside sources.

(b) *Services*. In the typical holding company organization, there are certain services such as legal, research and development, and managerial aid which are rendered by the parent organization to its subsidiaries. Are the payments for these services included in the seven percent, or are they excluded from the operation of the decree? An extremely strict and literal construction would include these payments. However, such an interpretation would prevent contractual relations between the shipper-owner and the carrier. Where a particular construction will occasion great inconvenience or injustice,[235] or will produce an absurdity, it is to be avoided if another and more reasonable interpretation is available.[236] In the present case, earnings and dividend payments logically can be distinguished from those based on *quid pro quo* transactions.[237] Thus, the preferable construction appears to be that *bona fide* payments for services rendered pursuant to an arms-length transaction, are not included in the seven percent limitation.[238] An adequate safeguard concerning the reasonableness

[234] General words or phrases following enumeration of specific things are held to refer to things of the same kind. *E.g.*, Swift & Co. v. Columbia Ry., Gas & Electric Co., 17 F.2d 46 (4th Cir. 1927) ; United States v. Certain Lands in City of Detroit, 12 F.Supp. 345 (E.D.Mich. 1935) ; Fulkerson v. Great Lakes Pipe Line Co., 335 Mo. 1058, 75 S.W.2d 844 (1934). Thus, "earnings" and "dividends" would set the pattern for interpretation.

[235] Knowlton v. Moore, 178 U.S. 41, 20 Sup.Ct. 747, 44 L.Ed. 969 (1900) ; Bate Refrigerating Co. v. Sulzberger, 157 U.S. 1, 15 Sup.Ct. 508, 39 L.Ed. 601 (1895) ; United States v. Kirby, 7 Wall. 482, 19 L.Ed. 278 (U.S. 1869).

[236] Flowers v. United States, 83 F.2d 78, 82 (8th Cir. 1936) ; United States v. Anderson, 76 F.2d 375, 378 (8th Cir. 1935) ; International Ry. v. United States, 238 Fed. 317, 321 (2d Cir. 1916).

[237] See note 217 *supra*. The same distinction is achieved by the application of the *ejusdem generis* principle. See note 234 *supra*.

[238] *Cf.* General American Tank Car Corp. v. El Dorado Terminal Co., 308 U.S. 422, 60 Sup.Ct. 325, 84 L.Ed. 361 (1940) ; United States v. Baltimore & Ohio R.R., 231 U.S. 274, 34 Sup.Ct. 75, 58 L.Ed. 218 (1913) ; Mitchell Coal & Coke Co. v. Pennsylvania R.R., 230 U.S. 247, 33 Sup.Ct. 916, 57 L.Ed. 1472 (1913) ; Interstate Commerce Commission v. Diffenbaugh, 222 U.S. 42, 32 Sup.Ct. 22, 56 L.Ed. 83 (1911). The main item worrying the Justice Department is

of the allocated charges for services supplied by the shipper-owners to their pipe line subsidiaries is furnished through their review by the Interstate Commerce Commission's Bureau of Accounts. However, some of the companies, to be on the safe side, make it a practice not to have a balance of services from the parent to the subsidiary, or if one exists, to write it off rather than to have the carrier pay for any services furnished by the parent.

(c) *Consolidations*. Another practice which is quite prevalent among holding company organizations is the consolidation of payments to outside sources in order to effect a saving. For example, group insurance plans, income taxes, etc. Are the payments made by the subsidiary to reimburse the parent to be considered within the seven percent? The same divergence of opinion appears here as was present in the last paragraph. Again, the preferable answer would seem to be that a reasonable allocation of the total payments can be made by the carrier outside the seven percent limit. For example, a reasonable formula for tax payments made by the carrier would be that part of the net company tax which the net income of the pipe line subsidiary (before taxes) bears to the net income of the company (before taxes), but not to exceed the net taxes of the company. Thus, if the net income before taxes of the carrier was $1,250,000 and that of the shipper-owner was $2,500,000, the pipe line's payment would be one-half of the net taxes of the company.

(d) *Purchase of Materials*. Many companies consolidate their purchasing operations in order to avail themselves of better discounts and terms of sale. The question arises here whether payments or credits on interdepartment (or intercompany) material transfers come within the terms of the decree. The test of reasonableness of the purchase price appears to be the best criterion. So long as there is an adequate consideration and the transaction is above board, the payments for material should not be included within the seven percent. However, many of the companies are reluctant to sell materials to their pipe line subsidiaries even at the going rate less the customary discount. They sell at actual cost, which hampers the operation of their purchasing and material departments.

(e) *Rent*. Very frequently, the offices of the pipe line subsidiary are located in the building owned by the shipper-owner. The question arises whether rental payments for these quarters are to be included in the seven

---

that payments for services could be used to mask evasions of the seven percent limitation. For example, false subsidization of a research department conceivably could be utilized to evade the dividend restriction. This concern probably underlies the position urging strict construction of the decree. However, the determination of what is a reasonable fee for research and development services should not prove unduly burdensome. The burden could be placed on the companies to justify such expenditures.

percent limit. The consensus of opinion seems to be that a fair rental is not within the scope of the decree. This problem has been obviated by some companies by moving the pipe line offices into a separate building, either renting from an outsider or purchasing their own building.

(f) *Depreciation Funds.* The companies' accounts are kept according to the uniform system of accounts for pipe lines prescribed by the Interstate Commerce Commission. Charges are made covering the depreciation of physical items which for one cause or another will go out of use. These charges are made month by month against depreciation in the operating expense accounts, and corresponding credits are entered in the depreciation reserve account. Since these charges are based on estimated service values and estimated service lives, and are computed in conformity with the group plan of depreciation accounting, it is obvious that the sums charged off do not correspond with the actual accrued physical depreciation. As a result, the depreciation reserve accounts generally show a credit balance. Could these depreciation funds be paid out in excess of the seven percent limitation? Since the shipper-owners generally are the only stockholders of the subsidiary carriers, there would be no question of shareholder objection to this action, although it is not good business practice. Moreover, an argument could be made that since depreciation funds are not "earnings," they would be outside the seven percent limitation. However, the Justice Department probably would insist that such payments were "sums of money" derived from transportation and that any attempt to disburse such funds would be a mere subterfuge to evade the terms of the decree.

(g) *Payment of Money Received from Sale of Property.* What is the status with respect to the consent decree of money received from the sale of carrier property? First, a distinction is to be drawn between profits made from such sales and returns of capital investment. The profits are "earnings." Whether they are earnings "derived from transportation" is another question, one which will be discussed in the next section. Insofar as returns of capital are concerned, the defendants' position is that they are not "earnings," and, by the *ejusdem generis* rule, not within the terms of the decree. Naturally, the government's position would be that they are "sums of money" derived from transportation and thus within the decree. The former position seems preferable except where the purchase and resale of property would be used as a device to siphon off excess earnings, thus attempting to accomplish indirectly what the decree forbids directly.

2. DERIVED FROM TRANSPORTATION OR OTHER COMMON CARRIER SERVICES. Paragraphs III and V refer to earnings "derived from transpor-

tation or other common carrier services."[239] Some questions arise from this wording. For example, pipe line companies frequently provide housing for their employees at the pump station. Is the rent received from these buildings "derived from transportation" within the meaning of the decree? Again, what is the status of income received from carrier funds invested in governmental securities? How about the money derived from sale of non-usable tank bottoms, or from the sale of accumulated "allowance oil"?[240] Suppose oil were discovered underlying land which the pipe line owned in fee, would the royalty money be "derived from transportation"? The answer to these questions appears to be to trace back and ascertain whether the business of carriage was the original source of the income. Thus, in the company housing question, the answer would be determined by whether the houses were purchased with money derived from common carriage (in which case the rents would be "derived from transportation") or if they were purchased from the original capitalization. In the cases of the accumulated "allowance oil" and the tank bottoms, it is obvious that they were derived originally from transportation, and, therefore, the income realized from their sale must be included within the seven percent limit.

3. VALUATION. The limitation imposed by the decree is seven percent of "the valuation of such common carrier's property."[241] "Valuation" is defined in paragraphs III (a)[242] and III (b) of the decree.[243] Paragraph

---

[239] See notes 227 and 228 *supra*.

[240] See Part I, note 147.

[241] See note 227 *supra*.

[242] "Valuation as hereinabove used shall mean the latest final valuation of each common carrier's property owned and used for common carrier purposes as made by the Interstate Commerce Commission. To the latest final valuation of the commission shall be added the value of additions and betterments to the common carrier property made after the date of such latest final valuation, and from this sum shall be deducted appropriate amounts for physical depreciation on, and retirements of, common carrier property, computed by the carrier as of the close of the next preceding year, in accordance with the methods used by the Interstate Commerce Commission in bringing valuations down to date, the classifications of property to conform to the uniform system of accounts for pipelines prescribed by the Interstate Commerce Commission. Such valuation shall not include the value of the common carrier facilities acquired through the investment of excess earnings transferred to and withdrawn from the surplus account as provided in paragraph V hereof."

[243] "In event the Interstate Commerce Commission has not determined the final valuation of the property owned and used for common carrier purposes by any common carrier, and until such time as the Interstate Commerce Commission has determined the final valuation of such common carrier's property, the valuation shall be determined by the common carrier and shall be based upon the records and accounts of the carrier kept in accordance with the accounting methods set forth in the Uniform System of Accounts for Pipe Lines prescribed by the Interstate Commerce Commission. To this determination of valuation by the common carrier shall be added the value of additions and betterments to the common carrier property made after the date of such determination, and from this sum shall be deducted appropriate

III (a) deals with the situation where the Interstate Commerce Commission had determined the carrier's final valuation prior to the entry of the decree. Paragraph III (b) covers those lines for which final valuation had not been made at the time of the decree. Attention is directed principally to paragraph III (a).

(a) *Latest Final Valuation.* Paragraph III (a) defines valuation as the "latest final valuation of each common carrier's property owned and used for common carrier purposes as made by the Interstate Commerce Commission."[244] One immediately asks, which final valuation? Prior to the entry of the decree, the Commission had completed a program of final valuations as of December 31, 1934.[245] Since that time, the Commission has undertaken the task of bringing valuations down to date as of December 31, 1947.[246] This promises to be completed shortly. Which final valuation should the companies use as a base for the seven percent limit? The Justice Department took the position initially that the 1934 valuation was the one designated by the decree and that all calculations should begin from that figure. It is understood that this position has been abandoned and that the 1947 valuation may be used.[247] However, this still leaves the question, what methods shall be used annually to bring the valuations down to date?

(b) *Bringing Valuations Down to Date.* Paragraph III (a) provides that "[t]o the latest final valuation of the commission shall be added the value of additions and betterments to the common carrier property made after the date of such latest final valuation, and from this sum shall be deducted appropriate amounts for physical depreciation on, and retirements of, common carrier property, computed by the carrier as of the close of the next preceding year, in accordance with the methods used by the Interstate Commerce Commission in bringing valuations down to date, . . ." Does the last phrase "in accordance with the methods used by the Interstate Commerce Commission in bringing valuations down to date" modify the whole sentence or is its operation limited to modifying the "deductions"? If it is the latter, the additions and betterments would have

---

amounts for physical depreciation on, and retirements of, common carrier property, computed as of the close of the next preceding year, in accordance with the Uniform System of Accounts for Pipe Lines prescribed by the Interstate Commerce Commission. Such determination of valuation shall not include the value of the common carrier facilities acquired through the investment of excess earnings transferred to and withdrawn from the surplus account, as provided in paragraph V hereof."

[244] See note 242 *supra*.

[245] See note 180 *supra*.

[246] See text at note 183 *supra*.

[247] This observation is based on the fact that several companies have filed returns based on the 1947 valuation which have been accepted by the Justice Department.

to be figured at original cost, whereas in the former the original cost is converted to current cost by means of a price index compiled by the Commission. Apparently, the Justice Department takes the latter view, and feels that adjustments should be made on a book basis, *i.e.*, to the latest final value are added the book costs of additions and betterments, from which sum the book depreciations and retirements are deducted. This method approaches the "historical cost" and "prudent investment" theories.[248] It has the merit of simplicity but it does not properly take account of changed conditions, *viz.*, the cost of betterments made in 1935 are not even comparable to their cost in 1948. Obviously, this would produce inequities as those lines whose additions were made during low cost years would have a much smaller base of earnings than those having later additions.

It is submitted that the foregoing construction is incorrect. For one thing, the comma between "preceding year" and "in accordance with," would be improper if the text is to be so interpreted. Moreover the only method of calculation mentioned in the text is that used by the Commission. If, as the Department contends, only the depreciation and retirements are calculated by the Commission's methods, what methods are to be used to figure additions and betterments? Under this view, the draftsmen did only half a job. The proper answer seems to lie in the construction that the whole process of bringing valuations down to date is governed by the Commission's methods.

This brings us to the next question, what are the Commission's methods? The Commission's Bureau of Valuation depreciates on an accrued physical depreciation basis and its Bureau of Accounts deals on a book basis. This represents quite a divergence. For example, suppose the 1934 valuation was $5,000,000 and the additions and betterments amount to $2,000,000. Again, suppose that the Bureau of Valuation's depreciation and retirements are $750,000, whereas those of the Bureau of Accounts are $1,500,000. Should the seven percent be based on $6,250,000 or $5,-500,000? A further complication is introduced by the argument advanced by some companies that they should be able to revaluate their properties each year, using the Commission's price index. The rationale of this argument is that the purpose of the year-to-year valuation is to arrive at substantially the same result as would have obtained had there been a Commission valuation for that year. Since the Commission would use their

---

[248] The classic exposition of the "prudent investment" theory may be found in Mr. Justice Brandeis' dissent in Missouri *ex rel.* Southwestern Bell Telephone Co. v. Public Service Commission, 262 U.S. 276, 289–312, 43 Sup.Ct. 544, 547–555, 67 L.Ed. 981, 985–995 (1923).

price index if they were revaluating, these companies suggest that they should follow the same procedure.

(c) *Restricted Funds and Valuation.* Provision is made in paragraph V of the decree for use of "excess" earnings[249] in extending existing or constructing or acquiring new common carrier facilities.[250] However, paragraph III (a) provides that the valuation used to compute the seven percent limit shall not include the value of the common carrier facilities acquired through the investment of excess earnings.[251] This provision seems clear enough, but what valuation should be used as an earnings base for properties constructed from both normal and excess [restricted] funds? Should the total value of the property, as determined by Interstate Commerce Commission elements of value, be prorated on the basis of the ratio of unrestricted funds to restricted funds in the total cost?

4. ARE ALLOWABLE EARNINGS FROZEN? Under the terms of paragraph III (c), any amounts permitted to be paid or credited by the decree [7%] if *earned*, and withheld, may be credited or paid at any time thereafter in addition to credits and payments permitted during such subsequent years, *unless*, they have been invested in common carrier facilities *and* included in the valuation mentioned above. Thus, if a pipe line earned seven percent in 1947 and withheld it in a special fund, it could pay fourteen percent in 1948 (assuming that seven percent also was earned in 1948). But suppose the seven percent was invested in common carrier facilities and included in the valuation, is it thereafter "frozen"? In regard to payment of depreciation funds accruing from the property thus purchased, the problem is the same as that discussed previously in connection with general depreciation funds except that because the original source of these funds is allowable earnings, a stronger argument could be made for permitting their payment. If the facilities purchased and included in the investment base were sold, the problem is similar to that discussed in (1-g). The return of capital would appear to be payable. This would not be avoiding the prohibition of the decree as the sale of the property would reduce the valuation to the same amount present before the investment was made and thus the allowable earnings would qualify for payment under paragraph 3 (c). Any profits made from the transaction would be "earnings," and, since, by hypothesis, their original source is transportation, they would fall under the ban of the decree.

In attempting to avoid this question, some companies are purporting

---

[249] "Excess" earnings are those earnings above and beyond the seven percent limit permitted by paragraph III to be paid to the shipper-owner.

[250] See note 228 *supra.*

[251] See note 242 *supra.*

to draw the cash required for investment purposes from the depreciation reserve account. This action presents two additional problems. *First,* there is the practical problem of proving that the investment money came from depreciation funds and not from the allowable earnings. *Second,* is there anything in the decree which forbids this action? The Justice Department probably would argue the affirmative because it results in enlarging the valuation base on which the allowable earnings are calculated. This does not seem to be a sufficient objection from the standpoint of the decree alone. But the Department [which apparently favors a "prudent investment" approach anyway] might raise the contention that since the allowable earnings are based on the valuation, the company should not be permitted to swell its valuation base where it has contributed nothing to the valuation. Their argument would be that the depreciation reserve is made up of allowances made to assure that the original investment remains as it was in the beginning, and due to the public interest in continuous adequate and proper service, the company only has a qualified title to the money which would not permit it to add depreciation funds to its capital account or pay them to shareholders as dividends.[252] However, this theory of public utility rate-making has encountered opposition and there is strong judicial authority for the proposition that, under the fair value theory, depreciation funds belong solely to the company, the public having no interest, legal or equitable, in them. The source of the money used to purchase the property is immaterial. It is enough that the property is used to render the service.[253] So it would seem to be a question for the Interstate Commerce Commission, and if they permit it (as their "fair return on a fair value" approach would seem to indicate they would), the Justice Department's objection appears ineffective.

5. DIVIDEND CARRY-BACKS. Paragraph III (d) provides that any amounts permitted to be credited or paid during any calendar year *if not earned* may be credited or paid within any one or more of the next succeeding three years, *in addition to* credits or payments permitted during each such subsequent year. Thus, if no earnings are made in 1947 or 1948 but twenty-one percent is earned in 1949, all of the twenty-one percent can be paid out in 1949. Quite obviously, this does not operate the other way, *i. e.,* if fourteen percent was earned in 1947, it could not be paid out for 1947 and 1948. All over the permitted seven percent would have to go into the surplus account under paragraph V. But suppose no earnings accrue

---

[252] Railroad Commission of Louisiana v. Cumberland Telephone & Telegraph Co., 212 U.S. 414, 29 Sup.Ct. 357, 53 L.Ed. 577 (1909).

[253] Board of Public Utility Commr's. v. New York Telephone Co., 271 U.S. 23, 46 Sup.Ct. 363, 70 L.Ed. 808 (1926).

during 1947, 1948 and 1949, and seven percent is earned in 1950. Could that seven percent be credited to 1947, thus "tolling" the three year limitation? Some of the companies urge this interpretation, arguing that the purpose of the decree is to limit the amount of dividends payable to shipper-owners to seven percent per year and it should make no difference when the payments are made, so long as the three year limitation is met. Naturally, the Justice Department will take the opposing [and preferable] view. In the first place, the text prescribes that carry-backs are to be paid "in addition" to payments permitted during the subsequent years, which would seem to indicate that the current year's dividends would have to be paid first, and the carry-backs to former years would have to come out of any surplus. Thus, in the situation posed, 1947 would be wiped off the books. This construction is in accord with the analogous situation in the income tax laws dealing with unused excess profits credit carry-backs.[254]

6. KNOWINGLY VIOLATING THE DECREE. In the event that a shipper-owner or carrier should "knowingly violate" the provisions of paragraphs III or IV,[255] it becomes liable under paragraph VI to damages equal to three times the amount of the unauthorized payments.[256] A question of vital importance involves the interpretation of the words "knowingly violate." Does this require that defendants have knowledge of the illegality of the unauthorized payments? What if a company, relying on legal advice that rental payments are not "sums of money or other valuable considerations," makes payments in excess of the seven percent limit of paragraph III? Could the Justice Department come into court five years hence and successfully demand triple damages?

Undoubtedly, the government's position on this issue will be the affirmative. It would be able to cite cases holding that violations of the commerce acts through receipt of advantages are tested by actual results, not by intentions.[257] Moreover, there are cases which hold that a honest mis-

---

[254] INT. REV. CODE § 710(c)(3)(A).

[255] "IV. No shipper-owner shall solicit, accept or receive, directly or indirectly, through or by any means or device whatsoever, from any defendant common carrier any sums of money or other valuable considerations which said defendant common carrier is prohibited from granting, crediting, paying, or giving by the provisions of paragraph III hereof."

[256] "VI. In the event a shipper-owner or defendant common carrier should knowingly violate the provisions of paragraphs III or IV hereof, then and in such event, upon proof of such violation on hearing after notice, and in lieu of any and all other remedies or proceedings for the enforcement hereof, the United States may have judgment entered in this cause against the recipient of any sums, the payment of which is prohibited by this judgment, for three times the amount by which the sum received exceeds the amount permitted by this judgment to be granted, credited, given or paid to such recipient."

[257] Union Pacific R.R. v. United States, 313 U.S. 450, 462, 61 Sup.Ct. 1064, 1071, 85 L.Ed. 1453, 1464 (1941); New York, New Haven & Hartford R.R. v. Interstate Commerce Commission, 200 U.S. 361, 398, 26 Sup.Ct. 272, 279, 50 L.Ed. 515, 524 (1906).

take, made in good faith, is not a defense to an Elkins Act violation, since wrongful intent is not an element of the offense.[258] It is also to be remembered that the purpose of the decree is to limit payments from common carriers to their shipper-owners in order to reduce the advantage held by shipper-owners over their non-integrated competitors. Thus, the gravamen of an action brought for violation of the provisions of paragraphs III and IV of the decree would be the illegality of the payments, not the *mens rea* of the defendants. For these reasons, the Justice Department would be able to present a strong case in its favor.

Notwithstanding the foregoing arguments, the companies' position also is strong. Paragraph VI of the decree is couched in the language of Section 1(3) of the Elkins Act,[259] not Section 1(1).[260] It was the latter provision which the abovementioned cases construed as not requiring a wrongful intent. On the contrary, Section 1(3), providing for triple damages, specifically requires that "sums of money or other valuable consideration" *knowingly* be received as rebates. Not only do the very words of the statute plainly require this wrongful intent but the legislative history of the enactment demonstrates beyond a reasonable doubt that such was the legislative intent.[261] Finally, the defendants file an annual report with the

---

[258] Armour Packing Co. v. United States, 209 U.S. 56, 28 Sup.Ct. 428, 52 L.Ed. 681 (1908); Chicago, St. P., M. & O. Ry. v. United States, 162 Fed. 835 (8th Cir. 1908).

[259] 34 Stat. 588 (1906), 49 U.S.C. § 41(3) (1946).

[260] 32 Stat. 847 (1903), as amended, 49 U.S.C. § 41(1) (1946).

[261] The idea of forfeiture first was suggested by President Theodore Roosevelt's message to Congress on December 5, 1905. See 40 Cong. Rec. 92 (1905). His idea was to stop what he termed "blackmail" by the large shippers, notably the Standard Oil Trust. See 40 Cong. Rec. 6358 (1906). On May 10, 1906, Senator McCumber proposed an amendment to the then pending Hepburn Bill [H.R. 12987, 59th Cong., 1st Sess. (1906)] which amendment, in its final form, emerged as the present Section 1(3) of the Elkins Act. 40 Cong. Rec. 6628 (1906). The offense described in Senator McCumber's bill was the same as in Section 1(3), *i.e.*, knowingly receiving a sum of money as a rebate. An offender was "deemed guilty of a fraud" and subject to a fine of three times the rebate. The Senator's remarks at the time he introduced the bill demonstrate conclusively that the evil attacked by the statute was the *conscious wrongful* action by the shipper in obtaining rebates from the carrier. See 40 Cong. Rec. 6628–6630 (1906); see also 40 Cong. Rec. 7021–7022 (1906). After some discussion on the matter, Senator Mc-Cumber decided that a civil action would be more efficacious than a criminal action, and he introduced, on May 17th, 1906, a substitute for his original amendment. 40 Cong. Rec. 7022 (1906). This substitute amended the Elkins Act [the original bill was to amend Section 10 of the original Interstate Commerce Act of 1887] and was word-for-word the same as the present Section 1(3) except that the phrase "knowingly and wilfully" was used instead of "knowingly" alone. 40 Cong. Rec. 7022 (1906).

The change from criminal fine to civil forfeiture was made purely for procedural and administrative reasons, such as avoiding venue questions, reducing the quantum of proof from beyond a reasonable doubt to a preponderance of the evidence, and to obviate the difficulty of shippers refusing to testify on the grounds of self-incrimination. 40 Cong. Rec. 7023 (1906). It is clear that the substituted amendment effected no change in the offense itself. *Ibid.*

Attorney-General in accordance with paragraph VIII of the decree.[262] In these reports, the companies show the total earnings available for distribution and those actually credited or distributed. Where a reasonable construction of the decree, based in good faith on the advice of counsel, has resulted in payments [such as rents] in excess of the seven percent limitation, the acceptance by the Justice Department of the reports showing these payments, and its inaction thereon, would seem to have exculpatory effect in the event that said construction later was determined to be incorrect.[263]

C. Results of the Decree

It was the hope of the Justice Department that the consent decree would result in reduced rates.[264] However, an official statement made in 1944 by the Department concerning the effectiveness of the decree seems to indicate that the object of rate reduction was not then being accomplished.[265] According to one writer, the reason for this is that the amount of restricted funds is less than the loss of profits which would follow from an increase in independent refiner competition engendered by reduction in pipe line rates.[266] The rate reductions which have taken place appear to be the result of changes in the income tax laws, the recent Interstate Commerce Commission decisions, and the modern development of competing forms of bulk petroleum transportation.[267] The decree apparently

[262] "VIII. Each defendant common carrier shall render a report to the Attorney General of the United States not later than the 15th day of April of each year, showing for the preceding calendar year: the valuation used as earnings basis; total earnings available for distribution to owners or stockholders; earnings, dividends, payments or benefits credited, paid, granted or given to all stockholders or owners; and amounts of money transferred to or withdrawn from the surplus retained pursuant to paragraph V hereof."

[263] Cf. Lehigh Coal & Navigation Co. v. United States, 250 U.S. 556, 564–565, 40 Sup.Ct. 24, 26, 63 L.Ed. 1138, 1142 (1919); Whitesel, *Recent Federal Regulation of the Petroleum Pipe Line as a Common Carrier*, 32 CORN. L. Q. 337, 374 (1942); 9 U. OF CHI. L. REV. 503, 508 n.37 (1942).

[264] ROSTOW, A NATIONAL POLICY FOR THE OIL INDUSTRY 64–65 (1948).

[265] "The Department is not in a position to inform you with regard to reduction of pipe-line tariffs resulting from the entry of the judgment without making an exhaustive study of the tariff structure of 59 pipe-line companies. The fact that 22 of the carriers placed an aggregate of $15,500,000 in the special surplus fund during 1942 would indicate that those carriers had maintained tariffs at levels which resulted in their net profits being in excess of 7 percent of valuation." Letter from Attorney-General Biddle to Senator Guy Gillette dated Feb. 22, 1944, read into the Congressional Record of March 28, 1944. 90 CONG. REC. 3163–3164 (1944).

[266] Comment, 51 YALE L. J. 1338, 1350–1351 (1942); cf. Whitesel, *Recent Federal Regulation of the Petroleum Pipe Line as a Common Carrier*, 32 CORN. L. Q. 337, 370 (1947). Also, the parent will receive the surplus if the pipe line subsidiary ever is dissolved or divorced. See paragraph V of the decree, *supra* note 228.

[267] See Part I, text at notes 71–73.

has not contributed measurably toward rate reduction and has created a host of operating problems which in themselves justify a review of the decree.[268] The threat of the triple damage penalty contained in paragraph VI and the uncertainty as to the interpretation of the decree [as illustrated by the previous discussion] have unnecessarily rendered pipe line operation extremely difficult. Nor are the antagonists of major company pipe line ownership satisfied with the decree.[269] The Justice Department is in the unfortunate position of being attacked by both sides of a controversy in which it never should have been involved. In the interest of a unified, consistent governmental regulatory policy, it would appear preferable to vacate the decree and to confine Federal regulatory authority over interstate pipe lines to a single agency, *i.e.*, to the Interstate Commerce Commission, where it belongs.

III. SUMMARY AND CONCLUSIONS

This study begins with the historical development of pipe lines. The first oil fields were discovered in sparsely populated areas yet unlinked by adequate transportation facilities to the cities which were to furnish the great markets for the products of the rising new petroleum industry. A transportation bottleneck soon was formed when the horse-and-wagon teamsters, who hauled crude oil from the producing fields to nearby railheads and refineries, began to charge excessive prices for their carriage. The necessity produced by the teamsters' monopolistic conduct was the mother of pipe line invention. At first, only small gathering lines were employed to carry crude from the fields to the railroads, but when the rail-

---

[268] In the first place the decree does not concern itself directly with rates, but rather with the distribution to shipper-owners of earnings. Of course, its operation does have an indirect bearing on rates. However, some of the impact is absorbed by the devotion of "excess" earnings under the decree to increasing the physical plant and facilities of the carriers.

Secondly, the Interstate Commerce Commission decisions in the *Reduced Pipe Line Rates* and *Petroleum Rail Shippers' Association* cases were spread of record prior to the entry of the decree on December 23, 1941, so the handwriting already was on the wall. The great reductions in overall pipe line rates took place in the period 1931–1940. There has been little change since that time. See Dep't of Commerce, Industry Report-Domestic Transportation-Petroleum Transportation 46 (1949).

Finally, the consent decree's limitation is based on over-all operations whereas the I.C.C.'s limitation applies directly to particular rates. Under the decree, particular rates earning higher than seven percent can exist along with rates earning less than seven percent so long as the composite return is below seven percent. However, particular rates may be deemed unreasonable by the I.C.C. if they exceed eight percent, and this limitation combined with the ever present rates which yield a lesser return usually result in a composite return below the consent decree's seven percent limitation. In a few instances this has not occurred, and it is here that the effect of the decree would be felt.

[269] See Comment, 51 Yale L. J. 1338, 1351 (1942).

roads established a monopoly of their own, long distance trunk lines were developed to transport crude directly from the producing fields to the refineries. The tremendous improvement in construction methods and operational techniques increased the capacity of the lines and contributed to their flexibility and efficiency of operation to such an extent that pipe lines became the dominant means of overland petroleum transportation.

Due to the tremendous initial outlay of capital required for long-distance pipe lines and the extremely hazardous nature of the venture, the lead in constructing and acquiring long distance lines was assumed by the large refining companies. They had to assure themselves of constant, large-quantity supplies of crude oil in order to realize the economies of large-scale refinery operation. At the same time, they desired to locate their plants convenient to consuming territory. The resolution of this dual need lay in ready access to pipe lines. Since successful pipe line operation depends on a constant high-level demand for carriage, and the refineries need a steady supply of crude oil, the union of pipe lines and refineries quickly was effected.

Not only were pipe lines and refineries wed by their functional interdependence, but the wild nature of the competition in the early days of the petroleum industry forced the larger companies to integrate fully in order to avoid vulnerability in one or more stages of the process from well-head to service station pump. Integration became a competitive necessity for large scale operators, and those companies who failed to realize this fact or who were unable to accomplish it, were either gobbled up by their more aggressive rivals or were relegated to a minor role in the industry. In turn, this led to concentration of control in the hands of the "major" oil companies. For example, the *TNEC Hearings* of 1939–1941 disclosed that twenty integrated majors owned or controlled 57.4 percent of the crude oil gathering line mileage, 89 percent of the crude oil trunk mileage and 96.1 percent of the products line mileage. Numerous complaints have been voiced against this concentration and the results fostered thereby. Insofar as these complaints related specifically to pipe lines, an effort was made to examine and evaluate their content. The complaints were classified into three general headings: alleged denial of independent company access to pipe lines; inequalities of competition engendered by major company pipe line ownership; and alleged creation of monopoly in the oil industry through the instrumentality of pipe line control.

The general heading of alleged denial of independent company access to pipe lines was broken down into sub-topics of rates, services requirements, ratable taking, and shippers' use of pipe lines. The examination of the rate structure disclosed that, initially, pipe line rates were set to match the comparable rail rates. Apparently, this was done in order to keep outside shippers from using the lines and quickly to repay the investment therein. Later, a more competitive situation arose and rates were somewhat reduced. Still later, the Interstate Commerce Commission initiated a program of active supervision and ordered rates reduced to a level where they would return eight percent on crude line valuations and ten percent on products lines property.

The main issues developed under service requirements were those of high minimum tenders and failure to furnish adequate storage for use by shippers. Considerable confusion has been introduced in this area by the indiscriminate use of the word "tender" to convey several different ideas. Obviating this by referring to minimum shipments, the problem proved to be essentially one of physical operation, although the device of requiring excessive minimum shipments had been employed in the period immediately subsequent to the decision in *The Pipe Line Cases* to restrict outside use of the lines. The record discloses satisfactory reductions in the minimum shipment requirements, largely occasioned by orders issued by the Commission.

The complaints against pipe lines for failure to furnish storage facilities were found to be misdirected inasmuch as the business of pipe lines is carriage, not the furnishing of storage. Above and beyond this fact, the sharp reductions in minimum shipment requirements effected by the Commission's orders have largely mooted this issue. The tariff requirements dealing with identity of products shipped, quality of product accepted, and loss in transit were found to facilitate free movement through the lines and not to be restrictions upon common carriers use of the lines.

The evidence adduced in support of alleged non-ratable taking seemed scant in quantity and insubstantial in nature. The readily available remedy at the hands of the Interstate Commerce Commission or the state regulatory bodies appears to furnish an adequate safeguard against any attempted discrimination of this nature.

Despite statistical evidence of the extremely limited use of pipe lines by outside shippers, an examination of the concomitant circumstances revealed that the principal reason for the present low level of independent use of crude lines is their physical location and not a default in performance of common carrier duties. Many of the products lines are still privately operated, and unless the Supreme Court reverses its decision in the second *Champlin* case, they will legally continue so.

Briefly summarizing the investigation of the alleged denial of independent company access to pipe lines, it may be said that in the absence of governmental intervention, the industrial pattern developed was not conducive to the maintenance of free competition, but that the regulatory authority of the Interstate Commerce Commission is sufficient to curb abuse on the part of pipe line companies. Moreover, it may be noted that the Commission already has taken effective steps to insure that the pipe lines within its jurisdiction stand ready to provide carriage to all comers at reasonable and non-discriminatory rates as provided by law.

The second general subject of complaint concerned the inequalities of competition engendered by major company pipe line ownership. The strategic position occupied by pipe lines in the oil industry has been mentioned previously. Because shipper-owners are able to transport their products at transportation *cost* and outside shippers must pay the tariff *rate,* it is obvious that a wide disparity between pipe line costs and tariff rates will produce a significant competitive inequality. If this difference is reduced to the point where it represents only a reasonable return on carrier investment, there is no discrimination, since the outside shipper is receiving transportation service at a reasonable charge and the shipper-owner is realizing the same return on his money which he would receive from any successful commercial venture.

Efforts to achieve this end have been made by the Interstate Commerce Commission in its decisions requiring rate reductions to levels which will yield reasonable returns on carrier investment, and by the Department of Justice in its suits under the Elkins Act which culminated in the *Atlantic Refining Company* Consent Decree. The consent decree was found to be riddled with ambiguities, "a potential lawsuit in every word," and apparently not to have contributed materially toward rate reduction. For these reasons, it was felt that the decree should be abolished, and that Federal regulatory authority over interstate pipe lines should be confined to the Interstate Commerce Commission.

The last major division considered was the alleged creation of monopoly in the oil industry through the instrumentality of pipe line control. After seeking definitions of monopoly in law and economics, and summarizing the teachings of the recent antitrust cases for a yardstick of industrial measurement, the conclusion was reached that means of adequate measurement of the petroleum industry in the public interest were not presently available. Approval was given to the interim device of regional antitrust suits by the Justice Department in areas where effective competition appeared to be lacking, pending the development of a comprehensive overall petroleum industry study which would permit evaluation of the industry on a more rational basis than currently is feasible.

A tentative examination of the probable consequence of pipe line divorcement was undertaken. The conclusion reached was that divorcement of pipe lines *per se* would not contribute to a program designed to prevent abusive restraints of trade and undue use of leverage made possible by large aggregations of economic power. On the contrary, it would render a disservice to many of the independent operators presently engaged in the industry.

Brief mention was made of the "crazy-quilt" patchwork of our existing laws which strive to achieve cross-purposes, thereby greatly hampering the work of the enforcement agencies, and alienate the support of businessmen. It was suggested that any program of industrial regulation should be consistent and in accord with the actualities of industrial operations.

Finally, it is obvious that although governmental regulation of pipe lines has been provided by law for almost half a century, many industry problems remain unresolved by administrative or court decision. Countless studies will have to be made and considerable experimentation must be undertaken before the desirability and scope of further regulation can be determined. It is the author's hope that some small light may have been cast upon the problem by this book.

APPENDIX

United States v. Atlantic Refining Company et al
FINAL JUDGMENT

The plaintiff, United States of America, having filed its complaint herein on December 23, 1941; all the defendants having appeared generally and severally filed their answers to such complaint denying the substantive allegations thereof; all parties hereto by their respective attorneys herein having severally consented to the entry of this final judgment herein without trial or adjudication of any issue of fact or law herein and without admission by any party in respect of any such issue and in final settlement of all claims herein in issue;

WHEREFORE IT IS ORDERED, ADJUDGED AND DECREED in compromise and in final settlement of all money claims herein in issue, including claims for penalties, damages and forfeitures, as follows:

I. That the Court has jurisdiction of this cause of action, of the subject matter hereof and of all the parties hereto.

II. For the purposes of this judgment when hereinafter used:

"Defendant common carrier" shall mean and include each and every common carrier engaged in the business of transporting crude oil or gasoline or other petroleum products in interstate commerce by pipeline which is or may be (a) a defendant, or (b) the successor of a defendant, or (c) the subsidiary of a defendant, or (d) a pipeline department of one or more defendants, or (e) a corporation, some or all of whose stock is owned by a defendant, or the successor or subsidiary of a defendant, or (f) owned or operated in such a manner that a defendant, its successor or subsidiary shall be entitled to participate in its net earnings.

"Shipper-owner" shall mean and include each defendant and its affiliates where such defendant or any of its affiliates ships crude oil or gasoline or other petroleum products by pipeline of any defendant common carrier and either the defendant or any one of its affiliates is entitled to participate in the net earnings of the defendant common carrier.

"Affiliates" shall mean and include successors and subsidiaries of any defendant, the parent of any defendant, and the subsidiaries of any such

165

parent, and such other persons, groups or corporations so related as to in effect control or to be controlled by any defendant.

"Petroleum products" shall not mean or include natural gas.

III. No defendant common carrier shall credit, give, grant, or pay, directly or indirectly, through or by any means or device whatsoever, to any shipper-owner in any calendar year, commencing as of January 1, 1942, any earnings, dividends, sums of money or other valuable considerations derived from transportation or other common carrier services which in the aggregate is in excess of its share of seven percentum (7%) of the valuation of such common carrier's property, if such common carrier shall have transported during said calendar year any crude oil, or gasoline, or other petroleum products for said shipper-owner, but shall be permitted (insofar as the Interstate Commerce and Elkins Acts are concerned) to credit, give, grant, or pay said percentum.

(a) Valuation as hereinabove used shall mean the latest final valuation of each common carrier's property owned and used for common carrier purposes as made by the Interstate Commerce Commission. To the latest final valuation of the commission shall be added the value of additions and betterments to the common carrier property made after the date of such latest final valuation, and from this sum shall be deducted appropriate amounts for physical depreciation on, and retirements of, common carrier property, computed by the carrier as of the close of the next preceding year, in accordance with the methods used by the Interstate Commerce Commission in bringing valuations down to date, the classifications of property to conform to the uniform system of accounts for pipelines prescribed by the Interstate Commerce Commission. Such valuation shall not include the value of the common carrier facilities acquired through the investment of excess earnings transferred to and withdrawn from the surplus account as provided in paragraph V hereof.

(b) In event the Interstate Commerce Commission has not determined the final valuation of the property owned and used for common carrier purposes by any common carrier, and until such time as the Interstate Commerce Commission has determined the final valuation of such common carrier's property, the valuation shall be determined by the common carrier and shall be based upon the records and accounts of the carrier kept in accordance with the accounting methods set forth in the Uniform System of Accounts for Pipe Lines prescribed by the Interstate Commerce Commission. To this determination of valuation by the common carrier shall be added the value of additions and betterments to the common carrier property made after the date of such determination, and from this sum shall be deducted appropriate amounts for physical depreciation on, and retirements of, common carrier property, computed as of the close of the next preceding year, in accordance with the Uniform System of Accounts for Pipe Lines prescribed by the Interstate Commerce Commission. Such determination of valuation shall not include the value of the common carrier facilities acquired through the investment of excess earnings transferred to and withdrawn from the surplus account, as provided in paragraph V hereof.

(c) Any amounts permitted to be credited, granted, paid or given during any calendar year as hereinabove provided, if earned and withheld, may be credited, granted, paid or given at any time thereafter in addition to credits and payments permitted during such subsequent years, unless (i) such earned and withheld sums shall have been invested in common carrier facilities and (ii) included in valuation as above defined.

(d) Any amounts permitted to be credited, granted, paid or given during any calendar year as hereinbefore provided, if not earned, may be credited, granted, paid or given within any one or more of the next succeeding three years, in addition to credits and payments permitted during each such subsequent year.

IV. No shipper-owner shall solicit, accept or receive, directly or indirectly, through or by any means or device whatsoever, from any defendant common carrier any sums of money or other valuable considerations which said defendant common carrier is prohibited from granting, crediting, paying, or giving by the provisions of paragraph III hereof.

V. Commencing January 1, 1942 each defendant common carrier shall retain (except as hereinafter provided) net earnings derived from transportation or other common carrier services in excess of the amounts permitted to be credited, granted, paid or given by paragraph III hereof and transfer such excess earnings to the surplus account within 90 days after the end of each calendar year. The said excess earnings shall be transferred to the surplus account as a separate item therein and in such a form as to be readily identifiable. The excess earnings thus transferred to the surplus account may be used by the defendant common carrier for extending existing or constructing or acquiring new common carrier facilities, for maintaining normal and reasonable working capital requirements during the current calendar year, and for retiring of any debt outstanding at the time of the entry of this judgment and decree, provided, however, that such debt or refunded debt was originally incurred for the purpose of, and the proceeds thereof expended in, constructing or acquiring common carrier property. In case of the dissolution, sale, transfer or divorcement of any defendant common carrier, any retained portion of the surplus account may be disbursed to stockholders of the corporation which owns and controls the defendant common carrier at that time.

VI. In the event a shipper-owner or defendant common carrier should knowingly violate the provisions of paragraphs III or IV hereof, then and in such event, upon proof of such violation on hearing after notice, and in lieu of any and all other remedies or proceedings for the enforcement hereof, the United States may have judgment entered in this cause against the recipient of any sums, the payment of which is prohibited by this judgment, for three times the amount by which the sum received exceeds the amount permitted by this judgment to be granted, credited, given or paid to such recipient.

VII. This judgment shall not in any manner (1) limit or qualify in any way the right of any party to introduce in the case of *United States of America v. American Petroleum Institute, et al.,* now pending in the District Court for the District of Columbia, or in any other proceeding, civil or criminal, brought under the antitrust laws, competent evidence otherwise admissible relating to the construction, operation, maintenance, use or distribution of pipelines or other means of transportation owned, operated, or controlled by the defendants herein, or with respect to the investment in, valuation of, benefits derived from ownership of or interest in, or rate of return upon, said pipelines or other methods of transportation, or (2) limit, restrict, enlarge or control in any way the right of the United States in the case of *United States of America v. American Petroleum Institute, et al.,* or in any other proceeding brought under the antitrust laws to obtain from the Court such relief, including sale, divorcement, or any other kind of rearrangement with respect to pipelines or any other means of transportation now or hereafter owned, operated or controlled by the defendants herein, as the Court deems proper.

VIII. Each defendant common carrier shall render a report to the Attorney General of the United States not later than the 15th day of April of each year, showing for the preceding calendar year: the valuation used as earnings basis; total earnings available for distribution to owners or stockholders; earnings, dividends, payments or benefits credited, paid, granted or given to all stockholders or owners; and amounts of money transferred to or withdrawn from the surplus retained pursuant to paragraph V hereof.

IX. This judgment shall not be construed to restrict, limit, or enlarge any right, privilege or exemption granted to any pipeline corporation or its stockholders (a) by the provisions of the Act of Congress approved July 30, 1941, entitled "An Act to Facilitate the Construction, Extension, or Completion of Interstate Petroleum Pipe Lines related to National Defense", or (b) by the terms of any proclamation of the President of the United States issued pursuant to said Act of July 30, 1941.

X. The jurisdiction of this case is retained for the purpose of enabling any of the parties to this judgment to apply to the Court at any time for such further orders and directions as may be necessary or appropriate in relation to the construction of or carrying out this judgment, for the modification hereof upon any ground, and for the enforcement of compliance herewith in the manner set forth above. No further modification hereof shall impose any liability upon any defendant for any act or conduct performed prior to the date of such modification, in excess of the liability imposed by paragraph VI hereof.

TABLE OF CASES

(only those mentioned in the text)

INDEX

Access to pipe lines: alleged denial of, to independent companies, 13–48
Accounting: system of depreciation, 138
Addyston case: *see* Table of Cases
Adelman, Professor M. A.: leverage defined by, 94
Aitchison, Commissioner Clyde B.: quoted, 20
Ajax Pipe Line Company: 11, 14, 44
Alcoa case: *see* Table of Cases
Allowable: *see* proration
Allowable earnings, 156; *see also* earnings
"Allowance oil": 28, 152
Aluminum Company of America (Alcoa): 75, 76, 85, 90
American Petroleum Institute: 138
American Tobacco Co.: 81, 85, 89
Antitrust enforcement: 74; inconsistencies of, 104–107; *see also* Sherman Antitrust Act
Antitrust laws: 68, 84ff; *see also* monopoly
A.P.I. gravity: 27 (n. 143), 30; *see also* gravity
Army, Navy, Maritime Commission of ICC: 141
Associated Oil Company: 121
Associated Pipe Line Company: 121
A.S.T.M. distillation specifications: 37; *see also* flow characteristics
Atlantic Refining Company: 163

Bain, J. S.: 63
Baku, U.S.S.R.: 33
Ball, Max: quoted, 5
Basic sediment and water (BS&W) of crude oil: 27 (n. 142), 37
Batching of oil: 37; *see also* contamination
"Bath-tub" conspiracy: within an integrated company, 94, 95
Batum, U.S.S.R.: 33
Bayonne, New Jersey: 121
"Behaviorists": 65; *see also* market competition
Betterments: to common carrier property, 153
"Big Inch pipe line": 8
Bigness of oil companies: 90–91; *see also* monopoly

Birge, Edwin A.: 33 (n. 169, 170, 173, 174)
Borger, Texas: 17
Brundred Brothers: 24, 133; *see also* Table of Cases
"Buffer batches" of petroleum: 34 (n. 179)
Bureau of Accounts of ICC: 139, 154
Bureau of Transport Economics and Statistics of ICC: 141
Bureau of Valuations: 140, 154
Buyers of crude oil: 59–68

Caffey, Judge F. G.: 76
California Supreme Court: 121
Cement Manufacturers Protective Association: 19 (n. 92); *see also* Table of Cases
Chamberlin, Edward: 72
Champlin Refining Company: 20, 48, 124–32
Cimarron Valley Pipe Line Company: 20
Clark, J. M.: quoted, 64
Collusion: under monopoly, 89
Columbia Steel Company: 93
Columbus, Ohio: 45
Commingling (or Contamination): 29ff.
Commodities clause (of Hepburn Act): 50
Common carriers of oil: status of, 22–23; liability of, for loss, damage, or delay caused by act of God, *et al.,* 38, 111–17; voluntary devotion to public use, 114–15; public grants to, 115; eminent domain, 115–16; general business legislation of, 116; defined, 119ff.; different from private carriers, 127ff.; accounting systems of, 138ff.; *see also* transportation
Common-stream flow: 30, 37
Compensation: for pipe-line property, 115–16, 127
Competition: alleged inequalities of, engendered by major pipe line ownership, 20, 49–59; kinds of, 60–68, 69ff.; complaint concerning inequalities of, 163
Concentration: four reasons for, 9–12; 85ff.; *see also* integration
Condemnation proceedings (rights): 115–16
Conglomerate integration: 58, 92

175